When
Poverty Mattered

When Poverty Mattered

Then and Now

Paul Weinberg

FERNWOOD PUBLISHING
HALIFAX & WINNIPEG

Editing: Brenda Conroy
Cover design: John van der Woude
Printed and bound in Canada

Published by Fernwood Publishing
32 Oceanvista Lane, Black Point, Nova Scotia, B0J 1B0
and 748 Broadway Avenue, Winnipeg, Manitoba, R3G 0X3
www.fernwoodpublishing.ca

Fernwood Publishing Company Limited gratefully acknowledges the financial support of the Government of Canada, the Canada Council for the Arts, the Manitoba Department of Culture, Heritage and Tourism under the Manitoba Publishers Marketing Assistance Program and the Province of Manitoba, through the Book Publishing Tax Credit, for our publishing program. We are pleased to work in partnership with the Province of Nova Scotia to develop and promote our creative industries for the benefit of all Nova Scotians.

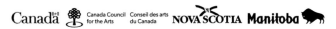

Library and Archives Canada Cataloguing in Publication

Title: When poverty mattered : then and now / Paul Weinberg.
Names: Weinberg, Paul, 1960- author.
Description: Includes bibliographical references and index.
Identifiers: Canadiana (print) 20190137312 | Canadiana (ebook) 20190137401 | ISBN 9781773631806 (softcover) | ISBN 9781773631813 (EPUB) | ISBN 9781773631820 (Kindle)
Subjects: LCSH: Poverty—Canada. | LCSH: Public welfare—Canada. | LCSH: Economic assistance, Domestic—Canada. | LCSH: Poor—Services for—Canada. | LCSH: Poverty—Political aspects—Canada. | LCSH: Equality—Canada.
Classification: LCC HC120.P6 W45 2019 | DDC 362.50971—dc23

Contents

Acknowledgements

When Poverty Mattered: Then and Now represents an expansion of a 2,500-word article that I wrote for the *Monitor* (Canadian Centre for Policy Alternatives) in March 2015. Here, I explored the RCMP surveillance of a short- lived anti-poverty research institute that was active in the late sixties and early seventies. The headline read as follows: "The Praxis Affair: There's a reason we put limits on spying within Canada." Seeing some parallels today, I decided to take my Praxis story into a broader context after speaking to historian David Tough, who has studied and written about how poverty figured prominently under Prime Ministers Lester Pearson and Pierre Trudeau almost fifty years ago.

Making this book possible is my publisher Fernwood — founder Errol Sharpe, Brenda Conroy, my copy editor, and Beverley Rach, managing editor. My appreciation also goes out to the staff at the Toronto Reference Library, Hamilton Public Library, McMaster University Mills Library, Queen's University Library and Library Archives Canada. Plus, this project would not have been possible without financial assistance from Ontario Arts Council and the Canada Council and the encouragement from my partner, Cathy McPherson.

Preface

An officer conducting, in his words, "discreet surveillance" for the RCMP's Security and Intelligence Branch (SIB) in the fall of 1969 was standing in front of a semi-detached house on leafy Huron Street, just north of the University of Toronto campus. We don't know if the students walking on their way to class took any notice of this person jotting down notes. Days earlier, the local newspaper had reported that the Just Society Movement, a high-profile poor people's group, was moving to this address to take up space with other activist organizations. The same SIB officer wrote the following about the other attached house: "Several U/M [unidentified males] wearing beards etc. were observed entering #371 and it would seem it is a rooming house for university types of the hippie caliber" (RCMP SIB 1969a). But the main interest lay with the primary tenant at 373 Huron, the Praxis Corporation Research Institute for Social Change, which was leasing the house from the University of Toronto, the owner of many houses on the street. The same or a different investigator (it is not clear) recorded the following observation a month later: "It is increasingly evident that organizations of this nature and stature are deserving of our attention. Failure to do will leave us sadly lacking in being able to comment upon the impetus behind social unrest at the grassroots level" (RCMP SIB 1969b.)

So rather inauspiciously begins the forgotten story of Praxis, an independent research institute focused on social issues, community organizing and education. The story is dealt with briefly in historical accounts of the RCMP Security Service in the early 1970s but never fully explored. Suffice it to say that unidentified members of the Security and Intelligence Branch, or the RCMP Security Service as it was known starting in 1970, were already monitoring Praxis's activities in the fall of 1969, as shown by these reports. University professors Stephen Clarkson and Abraham Rotstein, who founded Praxis in late 1968, had ambitious plans for their new organization, but they probably never anticipated this kind of attention, when poverty was high on the political agenda. The close working relationship between Praxis and poor people's groups, of which there were many in Canada in this period, led to a three-year investigation, surveillance and ultimately undermining of the activities of the research institute.

An estimated 800,000 Canadians in social movements, from women's rights and Indigenous groups to peace organizations, were similarly watched closely in the late sixties and seventies by RCMP security and intelligence services, which appear to have had difficulty distinguishing between legitimate dissent and what was perceived at the time to be subversion. Considering that files were kept on a host of other high-profile Canadians at the time, including Northrop Frye, Farley Mowat, Adrienne Clarkson and Tommy Douglas, this small research institute was in good company.

This book explores the intersection of two issues: the failure to tackle and reduce poverty in the 1960s and what happens when our security and intelligence services are allowed to spy on citizens who are attempting to tackle important issues. The decades of dismantling Canada's social safety net, which started in the 1970s and reached its crescendo in the mid-1990s, have been well documented. In this book I explore the less studied conversation about how poverty mattered between the mid-1960s and early 1970s and the manner in which the RCMP Security Service and its predecessor went after anti-poverty groups such as Praxis and played a part in putting this one organization out of business.

I start with an introduction to the radical politics of the sixties and the response of the government, followed by the rediscovery of the issue of poverty in Canada and the ebb and flow of policy under Prime Ministers Pearson and Trudeau. The bigger picture is viewed through the experiences of three organizations. To sum up, poverty went through various stages in Canada between 1965 and 1971: it started off as a surprising manifestation, and then became a national disgrace, followed by turning into an inconvenience and then a national security concern, before finally being put on the political shelf to gather dust.

At the centre of the book is the Praxis Corporation, an ambitious organization that sought to tackle the biggest issues of its time: poverty and democracy. Its close affiliation with the anti-poverty movement made it a target for the RCMP Security Service, which culminated in the so-called "dirty tricks" affair and the murky involvement of the extreme right organization, the Edmund Burke Society which has parallels in our time in the twenty-first century. The Just Society Movement started around the same time as Praxis under the leadership of feminist Doris Power. I look at the inner workings of one of most fascinating activist groups of the sixties in Canada. The book also examines the Hamilton Welfare Rights Organization, which was led by a dynamic young musician, Johnny Morris. He encountered considerable hostility from local Hamilton authorities and politicians in his efforts to address the failings in the welfare system.

I rely a great deal on the internal memos, reports and correspondence written by members of the RCMP Security Service, government officials, politicians, lawyers and the McDonald Commission on the activities of Praxis between 1969 and the 1980s. All of this came courtesy of Library and Archives Canada over a four-year period, following a thorough vetting process undertaken by CSIS (the successor agency to the Security Service starting in 1984 and separate from the RCMP) to determine what could be made accessible to the public. Documents formerly labelled secret are now available. However, there are also redactions or blank spaces on many of the pages where it was decided to keep some of the internal communications confidential for national security reasons. The result is that there is much we still don't know about the Security Service surveillance of Praxis. At the same time sufficient material exists to give us a good indication of the scope and nature of the monitoring and infiltration of the institute by the Security Service. I am careful not to quote scurrilous and inflammatory comments about individuals present in the files, especially from anonymous officers in their memos. I am calling this collective package "the RCMP Praxis files" (my label not the RCMP's), which arrived at my home in a series of mailed discs. Any researcher can make an application and look at the same material today at Library and Archives Canada. In addition, some background documents and correspondence were made available to me from two other sources — Praxis staffer and academic Howard Buchbinder, at York University's Clara Thomas Archives, and Paul Copeland, the lawyer for Praxis.

Introduction

This is a book about lost opportunities. Much of what we experience today in terms of social inequality, stagnant wages, the climate change emergency and disillusionment with democracy and politicians is the result of the unfinished business of the sixties and early seventies, before the building blocks of the neoliberal state — austerity and deregulation, among others — were starting to be put in place.

We have to remember that the sixties was the "radical decade," explained Praxis co-founder Abraham Rotstein, whom I interviewed in 2010 in the dining room at Massey College at the University of Toronto before he passed away. "Various interest and causes organizations came alive at that time. The name of the game was liberation movements. And there was a shared, strong, intuitive feeling, number one that the world was changing and, number two, one could have an effect on shaping that change. And number three, there were a lot of things that needed attention that were not just or adequate and that could be improved, often for moral reasons or for social reasons," he explained.

The reference to "radical" is important. In the sixties it was a term that was the exclusive property of the progressives, especially on the new left, who sought to get to the socio-economic root of political problems and achieve fundamental change, such as the reduction of poverty, ending the oppressive living conditions of Indigenous Peoples and putting a stop to US militarism. It was about the left returning to its original idealist form. This was a significant break with the old left, whether in the form of social democracy that had compromised with market capitalism and US foreign policy (as in the case of the UK Labour Party) or the reduction of people to automatons in authoritarian and brutal Soviet-style communism. The most receptive audience to this new radical politics happened to be on campus, with a mega-sized generation of students challenging the expanded university institutions, or "multi-versities," which were viewed primarily as factories pumping out obedient workers for the hierarchy of the workplace and the consumerism of the marketplace. In this scenario, radicals believed that learning and scholarship for their intrinsic value were getting lost in the shuffle. University students, in their revolts against campus and political authorities in 1968 across the globe from Paris to Tokyo to New York, were the canaries in the coal mine in terms of reflecting "a restlessness and an impatience" with entrenched power structures in all existing organizations in society, not just the campus institutions, according to Rotstein. He says that Praxis was established in the 1968–69 period when the "political mood" was powerful, intense and brief — the latter was not anticipated.

As early as 1966 there was an understanding in Ottawa that this new energy and enthusiasm among young people of the baby boom generation represented both a valuable opportunity and something to be harnessed and controlled. That is one common explanation for why the federal Liberal government of Lester Pearson set up the Company of Young Canadians in 1966 to assist and help organize poor people, or the disadvantaged, as part of its new welfare state policy. But it was Pearson's successor, Pierre Trudeau, who sought to go further. Trudeau successfully used slogans like "just society" and "participatory democracy" in the 1968 federal election to capitalize on the mood for social change that Rotstein described. The anti-poverty movement in Canada experienced an upsurge inspired both by Trudeau's election and the temper of the times, which stressed new forms of political commitment.

In this book we discover how security officials in Ottawa, watching campus unrest manifest in the US and Europe, became nervous about a similar radicalism emerging in Canada. Pierre Trudeau and the Liberals sought in his first term to encourage members of constituencies of grievance and discontent, such as the poor and the young, to apply for grants from federal programs whose names included phrases like community development, local initiatives and opportunities for youth. It was a strategy that worked and succeeded. Activist-minded civil servants were hired to work with like-minded people in communities to fund a variety of projects that employed people, filled social needs like childcare, set up legal clinics and nurtured grassroots citizens and cultural activity. The critics say this was a clever means to co-opt and contain anybody who might upset the status quo. Others argue that this is what government should be all about, which is to give young people the scope and means to do creative things while on a salary.

One thing the Trudeau government did was to help people in marginalized communities — the poor, women and Indigenous Peoples — to hire staff, rent offices and set up their own organizations in order to have their voices heard. This represented the fulfillment of the new prime minister's promise of a participatory democracy. Up to now, only the members of powerful and financially well-endowed business lobby groups had the capability of being heard by the politicians.

Two out of the three organizations profiled in this book, Praxis and the Hamilton Welfare Rights Organization (HWRO), accepted government financial aid to give them a firmer footing to advocate and lobby for change without the constant worry of looking for money to sustain their operations. In the end this made them both effective and ultimately vulnerable. On the other hand, the Just Society Movement (JSM), which ironically took its name from Pierre Trudeau's 1968 election campaign, refused government money but had no alternative sources of stable funding. The JSM also fell apart after three years because it functioned in the typical sixties activist new left mode — leaderless, spontaneous and outside any established circle beyond a little assistance in terms of resources from Praxis and the United Church.

It is likely that the government officials handing over the money and the activists at Praxis and the HWRO accepting the funds each saw advantages from their own point of view. The politicians approving the programs may have perceived that they were helping to create a base of young people more willing to work within the system and possibly support the Liberal Party electorally. At the same, the activists saw this as an opportunity to do organizing, reach a broad audience and achieve radical social change.

What was dubbed "the Ottawa grant boom" was explored by historian Leslie Pal in a somewhat theoretical 1993 book, *Interests of State: The Politics of Language, Multiculturalism and Feminism in Canada*. As the title indicates, the author decided to concentrate on specific non-profit groups and their relationship with the federal Department of Secretary of State – whose mandate was to promote a national unity agenda and new, more inclusive definitions of Canadian citizenship. Pal wrote that he decided to focus exclusively on this single department since to tackle the complete infrastructure of financial support for outside non-profit and advocacy groups by all federal departments and agencies in Ottawa would have been a gargantuan task and monopolized his entire academic career. The book was published before the reduction of the scale and size of the federal government undertaken by Liberal finance minister Paul Martin and his successors in the mid-1990s.

The RCMP was candid about the intention to dampen down the radicalism of the sixties. In 1973, a senior Security Service officer, Ron Yaworski, typed up some brief background notes for an upcoming meeting with his boss, the director general of the Security Service. "We have grown to appreciate the functional and social benefits derived from governmental subsidization of activists. This became particularly evident in respect to other government departments such as Opportunities for Youth and the Local Initiatives Program where they had a noticeable moderating effect upon the activities of dissident youth," he wrote. This is another sample of comments gleaned from previously secret memos and internal reports on Praxis by the RCMP Security Services that were made available by its successor agency, CSIS, under federal access to information legislation.

Chapter One

Poverty Is Rediscovered

Establishing an objective measure of poverty in Canada is difficult. There are two distinct and opposing methods used to illustrate the basic level of income that defines poverty — absolute and relative.

The absolute approach is based on the belief that poor people only require the absolute necessities of life that can be objectively established, such as substandard housing and the bare essentials of food and clothing. This view stems from the belief that poverty is an individual's own doing and should not be rewarded or encouraged by the provision of adequate levels of social assistance … The relative approach rejects the absolute notion that poverty can be objectively defined without reference to prevailing community standards. Rather, a poor Canadian household exists in the context of a highly interrelated, prosperous Canadian community; therefore the economic, social and political functioning of that household is relevant.

A well-known national measure based on the relative approach is the one developed by the Canadian Council on Social Development (CCSD), a non-profit organization, and the special Senate committee on poverty. The CCSD poverty line is based on average Canadian family income. If a family income is less than half of average family income, it is defined as poor. Adjustments are then made for family size but not for place of residence. (Ross 2015)

Poverty was a huge news story in Canada starting in the mid-1960s, when people found out they had gotten it wrong in assuming that all of the social problems of the twentieth-century, such as hunger and income inequality, had been eliminated with the economic boom that followed World War II. Michael Harrington's 1962 book *The Other America: Poverty in the United States* created a sensation when it put the spotlight on the existence of poverty and thus social class differences in the United States. This book described both white rural Appalachia and segregated African American urban neighbourhoods. This new awareness of poverty had an impact on Tom Kent, principal advisor to Prime Minister Lester Pearson from 1963 to 1966 and the man credited as the architect of the modern Canadian welfare state. Kent understood that Canada had its own pockets of poverty, both in the major cities and in specific regions, such as the East Coast and the North.

"What was shocking was the realization that there were people living in Toronto who didn't have electricity, who didn't have heating in their homes, and grew their own food, which in most neighbourhoods of Toronto at that time was illegal," says David Tough, historian and post-doctoral fellow at Peterborough-based Trent University who has written extensively on poverty and taxes (Tough 2017).

James Struthers, historian, professor emeritus at Trent University and author of *The Limits of Affluence: Welfare in Ontario, 1920–1970* (1994), suggests that Canada did not simply march lockstep with the US in redis-covering poverty in the mid-1960s. He points out that social scientists in Canada — in particular Leonard Marsh and Sylvia Ostry — had been working on developing statistical models and techniques to measure poverty since the end of World War II and ultimately contributed to a deeper understanding of the issue (Struthers 2018). In addition, John Porter's 1965 Canadian sociological classic, *The Vertical Mosaic*, also made a valuable contribution to understanding social class and the formation of elites in Canada.

The difference between poverty in the US and poverty in Canada in the late 1960s and early 1970s was that the Canadian poor included fewer racialized peoples. (Immigration from lower-income counties was just beginning following the loosening of federal restrictions). People of British, Irish and French origins made up the majority of those living in economic destitution. The most notable exceptions were Indigenous Peoples who lived on and off reserve across Canada and a small but not insignificant Black population in Nova Scotia and New Brunswick, descendants of forced and voluntary immigrants during the eighteen and early nineteenth centuries who suffered historical and ongoing economic and social discrimination.

It was probably Tom Kent's own experience of growing up in poverty in Britain during the 1930s Depression that shaped his understanding of social class. Kent worked as a journalist at the Manchester *Guardian* and the *Economist* in the UK and, when he immigrated to Canada, held the editor's job at the *Winnipeg Free Press* from 1954 to 1959. In 1960 he made a political splash in the Liberal Party by pushing for strong welfare state programs and policies in our country. David Tough believes Walter Gordon, then a powerful figure in the Liberal Party, encouraged Kent's engagement within the party fold, particularly its influential reformist or left wing, which supported these new social measures.

Kent became Lester Pearson's principal advisor after the 1963 federal election. In his adopted country, Kent was largely responsible for getting the ball rolling on social welfare, pensions and health care. During the sixties Pearson led two separate minority governments, from 1963 to 1968. His party and government were facing serious competition from the recently established New Democratic Party — the latter having for the first time a closer relationship with the labour movement than its predecessor, the Co-operative Commonwealth Federation (CCF), which had kick-started public health insurance in Saskatchewan.

The War on Poverty in Canada

Tom Kent convinced Pearson to borrow Johnson's 1964 War on Poverty slogan for the Liberal Party's 1965 re-election campaign to make a case for a series of new measures. The most significant was the government's new social welfare legislation — the Canada Assistance Plan (CAP) — which had been on the drawing board since 1962, well before the issue of poverty had heated up. The Liberals ended up with their second minority government but momentum for a new Canadian welfare state continued. The Pearson government was intent on establishing a shared-cost federal/provincial plan to replace a host of fragmented shared-cost services for the non-working poor. Designed by officials in the federal Department of Health and Welfare who had social work backgrounds, CAP reflected an understanding of the reality of economic needs rather than traditional assumptions about the poor. Through CAP the federal government would be pumping new money into what were separate welfare programs in the provinces (which had constitutional jurisdiction in the area of social services). Ottawa was to pay 50 percent of the cost, while 30 percent would come from the province and 20 percent would come from municipalities.

In exchange for this outlay under CAP, the provinces agreed to meet specific legal stipulations: assistance was to be paid on the basis of economic need. Furthermore, both residency requirements and workfare schemes (where one must work to receive welfare) were banned. In addition, an appeal process was to be made available for those denied assistance. As we learn later, there was insufficient federal enforcement to ensure that appeals were possible, and it was left up to the provinces to determine the level of social assistance for the poor. "A national minimum level of adequacy was never defined. Provinces didn't want one. And moralizing judgements continued to be embedded within the delivery of social assistance through CAP, although much less so than before its creation in 1966," says James Struthers (2018).

Age-old prejudices and judgemental attitudes about the deserving and undeserving poor dating back to the nineteenth century and the early Industrial Revolution still governed how welfare was administered through the municipal offices, where people in economic distress applied for help. CAP did not set out an adequate level of welfare for the basic necessities of living, such as food, shelter and fuel. It left this up to local authorities, and municipal welfare offices had a great deal of discretion in how much assistance recipients received. I interviewed lawyer Herman Turkstra, then a city controller in Hamilton, Ontario, who described Lloyd Priest, the man running the local welfare office, as an "a tough customer," who was like a character out of the Dickens novel *Bleak House*. Applicants would be confronted by a row of welfare workers who sat like tellers behind metal bars and made unflinching decisions on how much applicants could get. The policy was to "only give if they absolutely had to," Turkstra said. Priest called those who protested these conditions "habitual gripers" (Winsor 1971a).

Following the introduction of CAP, Ontario established two streams of welfare for the non-working poor. One was family benefits, which replaced the mother's allowance and was aimed at those who were out of the workforce for a long time or permanently. The. second was general welfare assistance, which provided temporary assistance for potentially employable people.

Women were drawn to anti-poverty groups like the Just Society Movement because such groups challenged traditional gender norms in the welfare system. The "man in the house" rule, for example, reinforced the notion of men as the principal breadwinners and mothers and their children as dependent on men. "For a man to go in and ask for the help for his family was demeaning, and their attitude would be well, 'why are you not working, get out there and work,'" remembers Doris Power, the co-founder of JSM. Housing was also a challenge in the late sixties early seventies for women who were single parents. Single mothers and their children on assistance faced discrimination from landlords of rooming houses, which were in larger supply and were one of their only alternatives (Power 2018).

Welfare authorities did not approve of women on assistance sharing an apartment with others to share living expenses and child-rearing tasks and to provide emotional support. The only option for the isolated mother on welfare was public housing in the provincially managed Ontario Housing Corporation. In Ontario, a point system governed which of the single parents were higher on an internal list or desperate enough to be considered for an apartment in buildings run by the provincial government. Points were given for deleterious conditions of one's current private accommodation, such as mould on the wall or bad wiring. The highest number was given to mothers living in cramped conditions who did not have enough space to house their children. This was what was facing Doris Power who gave up one of her children temporarily to the local branch of the Children's Aid Society (CAS) and in turn a foster family (that Power knew and trusted) to demonstrate to the Ontario Housing Corporation that her accommodation was so inadequate that it was forcing a family breakup. The OHC responded favourably to Power's application for a more suitable unit in one of its public housing projects in Toronto. After the approval she then arranged for CAS to return her child for the move to the new place. Power says she was not the only single mother living on welfare who resorted to such desperate measures to obtain housing.

This strategy did not work if a mother only had a single child and proceeded to hand him or her to CAS and a foster family. The OHC could possibly turn around and refuse to provide housing because the mother had theoretically been relieved of the economic burden of raising this child and so the size of her living accommodation was now irrelevant.

Children's Aid in turn could refuse to return this same child because it did not like where the mother was living. Such were the complex circumstances facing poor single mothers in the late sixties. Notwithstanding that, says Power, it was generally safe for mothers of multiple children to put at least one of their offspring into the care of Children's Aid on a temporary basis without fear they would never be returned. "Mothers often voluntarily placed their children in the CAS to get them clothes, to get a rest, or to get more points on the point system used to obtain social housing" (Power 2018).

The Culture of Poverty Thesis

In the fall of 1969 a striking photo of a man from New York City, wearing horn-rimmed glasses, a goatee and a moustache, peered above his op-ed article in the *Toronto Daily Star* entitled, "Welfare Council Can't Cure Poverty, Critic Claims" (Buchbinder 1969: 7). Howard Buchbinder was like an unwanted guest gate-crashing a polite social gathering. He had just arrived in Canada the previous June to take on the job of poverty research director at Praxis. He was determined to shake up public dialogue around these issues. Just a few months in a new country, he was already disputing a seventy-eight-page booklet entitled *Social Policies for Canada, Part 1*, which had been submitted by the Canadian Welfare Council (CWC) to Senator David Croll's Special Senate Committee on Poverty. What upset Buchbinder was the emphasis the CWC placed on the thesis that poverty was rooted in culture, lifestyle or long-term dependency rather than having origins in social class and income inequality. This culture of poverty view was an unfortunate byproduct of Michael Harrington's influential 1962 book *The Other America*, which used this reasoning to explain the phenomenon of generations of families with children living in certain regions and urban areas on social assistance.

A professor of social work, Buchbinder questioned this orthodox view of his profession, held by the social agencies and voluntary charities that made up the CWC membership: "The directions proposed for Canadian social policies by the Canadian Welfare Council have little to do with resolving the sources of the social and economic disparities and contradictions which affect close to one third of the population most directly." The Praxis spokesperson said that the culture of poverty thesis reinforced stereotypes held by those in richer areas of the country about more economically depressed regions, such as the Maritimes (which remains economically marginalized even today). Buchbinder drew parallels with his experience in the US, where he felt there was a similar misreading of destitution. He argued that the CWC failed to make any recommendations that covered the activities of corporations that employed local people and exploited the resources of regions or considered the unequal distribution of wealth in Canada as a whole. "When the large companies have done with the land and the workers, the social welfare program steps in to salvage what is left of the pieces … in the area."

Beside Buchbinder's opinion piece, the *Star* published a rebuttal from Reuben Baetz, the executive director of the Canadian Welfare Council, in a much shorter piece headlined, "We must work within our system." Baetz told readers that neither capitalism nor socialism had solved the poverty problem, but he remained optimistic that the "free enterprise system" (a phrase now out of favour in our more corporate concentrated reality of the twenty-first century) still had the potential for repair without the social and political disruption, labelled "Marxist social doctrine," that Buchbinder was recommending. However, in his rebuttal the CWC director did not address the question related to the culture of poverty (Baetz 1969: 7).

The phrase "culture of poverty" had become common vernacular in the discussion of poverty through the work of Oscar Lewis. His 1959 book *Five Families: Mexican Case Studies in the Culture of Poverty* took up the concept long before Michael Harrington made it central to his profiles in *The Other America*. Social commentator Barbara Ehrenreich (2012) argued in *The Nation* on the fiftieth anniversary of the publication of *The Other America,* which followed the election of US President Ronald Reagan, that conservative elements had twisted Harrington's thesis in a reactionary and racist direction. Their thesis, she explained, was the following: "Poverty was caused not by low wages or a lack of jobs but by bad attitudes and faulty lifestyles. The poor were dissolute, promiscuous, prone to addiction and crime, unable to 'defer gratification' or possibly even set an alarm clock. The last thing they could be trusted with was money." Ehrenreich wrote that these stereotypes did not fit how she remembered members of her own extended family and forbearers who happened to be poor but also valued work and sometimes demonstrated "fierce" ambitions. The behaviour of single-mother-led African American families in poor, segregated neighbourhoods in the US were cast as dysfunctional rather than in need, in this way avoiding the deeply rooted consequences of white supremacy and segregation in their country. The end result was a campaign to "end welfare as we know it" by President Bill Clinton.

Ehrenreich knew Harrington personally as both were active in the Democratic Socialists of America, which he helped found. She says her colleague never expressed any animus towards the marginalized communities that he described in *The Other America*. It is possible, she argued, that Harrington wanted to avoid the sociological and left-wing lingo of social class so he adopted Oscar Lewis's anthropological language of a "culture of poverty" to ensure he would be heard and read widely in the political atmosphere of early sixties America, still reeling from the anti-communist purges in the 1950s. Ehrenreich says that the socio-economic origin of poverty was a sensitive subject in the Cold War period within the social services field.

The culture of poverty and other concepts, such as addressing the underclass, never sunk as deep roots in Canada among policy-makers and social work professionals, however, as they have in the US and Britain, says Jonathan Greene, a professor in political studies at Trent University who studies contemporary anti-poverty protest movements and teaches a course on the subject (2018).

During the sixties young middle-class people almost counter-intuitively began to view those living on the margins and in poverty in North America, such as African Americans, the rural poor in Appalachia and people from Hispanic and Indigenous communities, as demonstrating greater authenticity in terms of music and other cultural forms than what existed in the mass consumer mainstream. In addition, a number of new left thinkers took the position that the potential for revolutionary and political change came from those who had not benefited from the prosperity and economic boom in the 1950s and 1960s. The argument was made that the working class had abdicated the traditional catalytic role as prescribed by Karl Marx by becoming complacent and middle class. The irony was that this view resulted from the struggles by the labour movement during the twentieth century to win a seat at the bargaining table with management and corporations in the post–World War II economic boom. Those who had been left out of the mainstream were resisting the shallow values of traditional jobs and work culture. The notion of the nobility of poverty has its roots in early Christianity. The reality, wrote Senator David Croll in his 1971 Special Senate Committee report *Poverty in Canada,* is that many of the working poor and the welfare poor held traditional middle-class values, which made their inability to have insufficient income to raise a family much more excruciating (23–36).

The idea that the poor had different and more positive values was what led local Toronto writer Norman Browne pen an article in the *Toronto Star* carrying the following headline, "I'm poor by choice — It's more fun," which resonated with some readers and appalled others. He revealed that he lived on a maximum of $25 a week to ensure his freedom and independence. (The cost of living was different then.) "Nowadays, everybody feels sorry for poor people. Even the government has gotten into the act and wants to upgrade poor people with job retraining programs, guaranteed annual wages or negative incomes taxes. Well, when it comes to my turn to be upgraded, I'll pass thank you. I'd rather stay poor — it's more fun. And please don't pity me, you should envy me. Hell, I pity you" (Browne 1969: 7).

At thirty-six Browne was too old to be a long-haired counter-culture hippie and too young to have experienced the adventures of hobos who rode the trains across North America during the dirty thirties. Yes, his low income meant there was budgeting on things like meals. But his article hinted he lived alone and had no dependants. Browne emphasized a preference for casual or seasonal labour jobs that paid little but held promise in terms of meeting people doing useful things. This was more exciting than taking drugs, he wrote. He had no hesitation leaving behind onerous jobs, including the one where he spent nine hours doing something for pay in a rat-infested windowless factory. Menial jobs were better because they lacked serious commitment beyond getting a day's work, he told readers. Readers were not to worry. Browne was not a "scrounger" (the right-wing stereotype of the welfare recipient). He had no interest in living off the proposed guaranteed annual income. "The adventures of the rich are contrived and artificial whereas by being poor I find that life is itself an adventure."

Brown was employed for a couple of years at small town newspapers. In between there were different labour jobs and lengthy periods on either welfare or unemployment insurance benefits. He did manage to get a paying editor job at *7 News* (a highly political community paper in the Ward 7 in the downtown east side of Toronto), where he edited pieces by voluntary contributors. There was a photo of him in the *Star* with others on the paper intently going over the copy.

After reading a *Star* article about Browne, Rev. Barry Morris, a United Church minister at the local Christian Resource Centre, was so taken by the writer that he got in touch with him. "I tracked him down and more or less recruited him to the Just Society Movement, especially *7 News*, Don Vale Community Centre and even CRC involvements. He had worked with the mainstream press in some capacity and brought that into his work with *7 News*, rather well at that," said Morris in a 2018 interview. However, the women on welfare at the Just Society Movement, for whom poverty was not a choice, would not have related well to the writer. Doris Power today has no memory of Browne, who called the welfare rights organization a failure and urged more structure and a workable constitution — but could not get any buy-in and then apparently left (Morris 1971: 24). Rev. Morris echoed these concerns throughout his own report on the challenges that the JSM faced in building a movement that could attract new members and sustain their interest.

The Special Planning Secretariat

Despite the disappointment of the 1965 federal election, with the Liberals facing a second minority government after running on the War on Poverty platform, Tom Kent refused to give up the issue of poverty. A Dalhousie University–based historian and post-doc fellow, William Langford, captures the essence of Kent's political philosophy in his PhD thesis and other writing on the welfare state. Lester Pearson's adviser, he says, fitted well into the Liberal party of the sixties. A pure Keynesian, Kent was heavily influenced by Canadian-born American economist John Kenneth Galbraith in accepting the necessity of public investment in services, infrastructure and social programs (Langford 2018/19). Here are Kent's own comments:

> The poor are in many cases poor because things once went wrong for them — they were ill, or in the wrong place, or got little school-ing — and they have never had a good second chance; they have been trapped on the outside, unable to push open a door into the affluent society. The purpose of the Canada Opportunity Plan is to create second chances, to open doors, to ensure that people are

not needlessly shut out of the affluent society. Such a program is not, however, a program for the poor alone. It is a program for all Canadians, because there is no more effective way to encourage economic expansion than to turn an unemployed slum-dweller or a sub-marginal farmer into a normal worker, a normal spender; to open up opportunities for people is to put new driving forces into the engines of economic expansion." (Kent 1965)

After the 1965 election Kent left the Prime Minister's Office for a stint as the deputy minister of Citizenship and Immigration while his former assistant, Bob Philips, was hired to head up the new Special Planning Secretariat within the federal government. This bureaucratic body coordinated and promoted the government's initiatives on poverty. It was a much smaller body than one similarly established in Washington under President Lyndon Johnson's War on Poverty program. Nevertheless, there was much common ground between the solutions being offered in Canada and the US in their respective wars on poverty, says James Struthers (2018). In both countries, emphasis was placed on increasing opportunity for those who had fallen through the cracks economically via jobs and skills training rather than on poverty reduction through systemic change.

The Special Planning Secretariat published material on poverty and backed the making of a documentary film, *The Things I Cannot Change*, by the National Film Board about a Montreal family in difficult economic circumstances. The film was a profile of poor people living isolated lives and focused on their own day-to-day routine to make ends meet and was watched by three million Canadians during a single showing on CBC TV on May 3, 1967 (Tough 2014).

The government body became the instrument for policy stock-taking within the federal bureaucracy and among social scientists operating in the universities about the effectiveness in solving poverty of the new social programs in Canada's welfare state. There was a preponderance of "smart and ambitious" people expected to generate new ideas about social policy even with no expertise in the area, says David Tough, the author of a 2014 paper on the Special Planning Secretariat. The problem was it only served to antagonize already existing experts inside departments such as Health and Welfare and morphed into a talk shop "that went into a corner and didn't do much [except] produce a lot of material" (Tough 2017).

Some of the ambivalence among the Liberals in the late 1960s towards their own expanded social programs originated before Trudeau came to power. It was reflected in what was coming out of the Special Planning Secretariat, which expressed the concern that the new welfare state bureaucracy was becoming too expensive and creating a culture of dependency (another manifestation of the culture of poverty thesis).

William Langford makes an interesting point in his PhD thesis (2017) that the Canadian welfare state of the sixties under Tom Kent was unique and different from the more limited social programs that came earlier in Canada. Langford argues that there was a direct connection between a domestic drive in Canada under Pearson to ensure social stability and the international strategy led by Washington to manage global poverty without allowing matters to get out of hand (and thereby jeopardize US corporate interests overseas). That explains the appearance of national aid and development agencies in the major capitals of the NATO countries. One example is the formation of the Canadian International Development Agency in Ottawa in 1968. The gross inequality both in the new states emerging from colonialism and in the Latin America countries, which had won their independence from Spain and Portugal in the nineteenth century, became a subject of concern in Washington during a Cold War period of rivalry between the US-led Western alliance and the Soviet bloc of countries.

Influential US theorist and policy advisor Walt Rostow promoted a "modernization model" that involved the grafting of the American model of large-scale industrial development and mass consumer markets onto largely rural societies in the Global South. This strategy was pursued under President John Kennedy as an anti-communist initiative against movements in the Global South that originated under local conditions of inequality and were pushing hard for land reform and social equality. Similarly says Langford, Tom Kent was seeking to improve the lives of the poor within a specific framework of liberal Keynesian capitalism, which meant an expanded and positive role for the state in Canada as shown by the dramatic increase in government spending — from 19 percent in 1951 to 47 percent by 1982. In addition, there was the encouragement of nation-building projects, such as the construction of the Trans Canada Highway and labour mobility programs to help people move from high unemployment regions to places where the jobs were located (Langford 2017).

Chapter Two

Pierre Trudeau's Ambivalence about Poverty

The Just Society Movement was one of approximately two hundred groups representing people in poor and marginalized communities in the late sixties, reported Mario Carota in a major study for the Canadian Association of Neighbourhood Services and financially supported by the Department of Health and Welfare (Carota 1969). The author was one of many American expatriates moving north to avoid the turmoil surrounding the Vietnam War in their home country. He reported that citizens groups in Canada were organized almost spontaneously by a few people who were generally young with similar needs, but often with little contact with each other across the country. A common theme in the report, *The Citizen Group Movement Among the Low-Income Citizens of Urban Canada*, was that people were not willing to wait for either government or a private agency to solve a problem. They were also tired of the studies done on the poor during the sixties with no resulting action.

The new anti-poverty groups typically had no professional and political assistance at their disposal, lacked staff and an office, and there was no money to help to pay for basic resources to spread the word. It was the lack of slickness or amateurish aspects of the organizing that made these new citizens groups attractive for local people. Their preferred activities were to deliver briefs to government, hold public meetings and support fellow citizens in their communities on various issues. "If there is one outstanding common trait to be found in the movement it is the feeling of hope. The citizens are angry and impatient but they are not depressed. And every little success and victory over the problems and authorities reinforces their feelings that they can do things, accomplish results and solve problems," Carota said (28). The consultant discovered that Canadians who had experienced a great deal of injustice and indignity did not react with violence and hate. Instead they turned to peaceful marches and gatherings. Militant groups espousing violence "are difficult to uncover and are to be found more in the files of the RCMP," he stated (16).

David Tough says the interest in poverty in Canada was probably at its most intense in the mid-1960s, after US President Lyndon Johnson launched his 1964 War on Poverty legislation as part of a series of bills to improve civil and voting rights for the African American population (Tough 2017). One of the features of Johnson's program was the concept of "maximum feasible participation" of the poor in community action programs (Rubin 1969).

The gold standard for organizing came from the techniques developed by Chicago-based organizer Saul Alinsky. He sought to build strong local organizations in low-income communities around specific issues that would challenge the decision-makers in local power structures. What was unique about the sixties was that keen young people were available to pursue this style of community organizing both in the US, with the Students for Democratic Society, and in Canada, with the Student Union for Peace Action, founded in 1964 in Regina.

Tough argues that the poverty issue lost steam in the late sixties both in government and among the population in Canada (Tough 2017). But one could also say that it evolved into a different phase beyond the federal bureaucracy as Pierre Trudeau and his new Liberal government in its first term (1968–1972) began funding anti-poverty groups across Canada at the same time. Was this a calculated move on the part of the Prime Minister knowing he would be ditching these groups eventually? The explanation from historian and University of Toronto post doc fellow Christo Aivalis is that these programs for anti-poverty groups represented the legacy of the reformist social democratic wing of the Liberals from the Pearson era. It would take more than one term in office before Trudeau's neoliberal policies would begin to take shape (Aivalis 2018a).

Concerns about the Consequences of Inaction

Poverty was enough of a hot issue in the late sixties and early seventies that the major media outlets had reporters in the field covering welfare recipients demonstrating in the streets. Experts and organizations such as the National Council of Welfare were warning about the consequences of inaction. David McQueen, vice chair of the Economic Council of Canada

(ECC), spoke on April 25, 1969, before the Special Senate Committee on Poverty about US-style troubles coming to Canada. He was worried about complacency, pointing to the riots in Regina in the 1930s, which arose out of the frustration of the rising numbers of unemployed at the height of the Depression. He warned that the Canadian record in avoiding violence was threatened by the example of what was happening south of the border. "This situation in Canada is a signal to get busy. We can't sit back; dissatisfaction is going to grow" (quoted in Goldblatt 1969b: 29). The ECC had just in the previous fall produced a comprehensive study on inequality which showed that one out of five Canadians was living in destitution and that the country's Indigenous population was at the top of the list. It was a conservative estimate, says James Struthers (2018), putting the numbers somewhere between one in four and one five, based on other research at the time.

A few months earlier, in November 1968, newly elected Prime Minister Trudeau had echoed concerns of potential violence among Canada's alienated poor. He was speaking before a large number of students during a question-and-answer session at Queen's University (Trudeau 1968). One audience member wondered about the Trudeau government's plan for a foreign and defence policy review. It came on the heels of racial turmoil south of the border. Months before the prime minister's election there had been an uprising by impoverished African Americans in the large segregated communities in cities across the US following the assassination of Reverend Martin Luther King in Memphis. Trudeau agreed that Canada, as the smaller country population-wise, was not immune to all of this: "I believe that if in the half a dozen years or so, there were to be great riots and beginnings of civil war in the United States of America, I am quite certain they would overflow the borders and they would perhaps link up with the underprivileged Mexican and the underprivileged Canadian. It might be the peon south of the American border but in Canada it might be the Indian, it might be the natives, it might be … lots of underprivileged in Canada. I don't think it would be the separatists, but that is another argument."

We know in retrospect that Trudeau's predictions turned out to be skewed, especially with regards to the country's Indigenous Peoples, who he probably did not understand. Those designated as Status Indians living on reserves only received Canadian citizenship in 1960, and their leaders were focused on redressing the injustices of colonialism through the legal and political system. One example was the successful lobby against the new federal Liberal government's initial proposal to abolish the historic treaties with the Crown. Furthermore, the Prime Minister made his remarks about Quebec two years before the October Crisis and the kidnappings by the underground Front de libération du Québec (FLQ). He appeared equally out of touch with the social and political unrest in his province, which was rooted in the social and economic imbalance between an Anglophone business elite and a Francophone majority, wrote both reporter David Allen and economist Dian Cohen in separate *Toronto Daily Star* articles (Allen 1970c: 11; Cohen 1970: 11).

Historians have noted an ambiguous attitude towards the poverty issue by Pierre Trudeau. Was it from his point of view a social tragedy, an opportunity, an inconvenience or a national security concern? It seems it was any of the above at different times. His most famous slogan, "the just society," was coined by historian Ramsay Cook, who had switched from the New Democratic Party to work for the Liberals, and the phrase was given prominence in Trudeau's acceptance speech after winning the Liberal leadership race on April 8, 1968: "The Government has to orient the country to progress, economic and social progress and make the Canadian society a just society" (quoted in Seale 1968a).

In late November the "just society" slogan was described in a *New York Times* article as little more than a "philosophical concept" that was meant "to give every man his due." The newspaper quoted Trudeau admitting to no grand plan in the works and that Canadians themselves were now responsible for directing the concept past the slogan stage: "I especially want people to understand ... there is no great authority called the Prime Minister who gets messages from God — who makes great laws. If we come up with more ideas, it will only be accepted if the people are prepared for them, which means involving them, discussing with them, convincing them" (quoted in Walz 1968: 1).

Here we see roughly outlined the basis for Trudeau's other slogan from the 1968 campaign — "participatory democracy." In hindsight, we now know that Trudeau's interests from the beginning of his political career lay primarily in expanded opportunities for Francophones in the federal civil service, legislated multiculturalism, the Canadianization of the Constitution, a future charter of rights and the initial modernization of the Criminal Code in areas like abortion, birth control and homosexuality — (paraphrasing his comments) to keep the state out of the nation's bedrooms.

One political announcement which did get made in the days leading up to his successful June 25, 1968, election was Trudeau's three-pronged program to deal with regional poverty, which arose out of his substantial interest in national unity: "No less a real threat to our country's unity is the presence of economic inequalities between the people who live in various regions of this country. People in the less favoured regions of Canada are often alienated from our national life because they are denied the opportunity to fully participate in it" (quoted in Westell 1968a: 10). Trudeau continued, venturing into the area of the culture of poverty with his description of conditions in the east and the north of Canada: "These conditions create a cycle of poverty perpetuated from generation to generation because the people cannot break out from poor education, poor training and poor health services. These people cannot meet the demand for skilled labour, industry won't move in because there is no skilled manpower in the areas and the result is despair and lack of incentive."

A good way to understand Pierre Trudeau comes from a new book by a scholar who was not alive when this prime minister was in power. There was lot of image-making around the charismatic Trudeau before and after his first election, especially with regards to his alleged progressive orientation, argues Christo Aivalis, author of *The Constant Liberal: Pierre Trudeau, Organized Labour and the Canadian Social Democratic Left* (Aivalis 2018b). Trudeau had worked with unions and engaged in past dalliances with the CCF in joint alliances to oppose the authoritarian Union Nationale government of Quebec premier Maurice Duplessis, but in reality, he never became a card-carrying member of the CCF or NDP.

Aivalis makes a compelling case that poverty eradication, taxes on the wealthy and redistribution of income were not priorities for Trudeau. Furthermore, his policies were a significant departure from the direction of Tom Kent and Lester Pearson. Trudeau was primarily an economic conservative wanting to make a break from his predecessor's investments in expanded universal social programs. This was the sentiment of the growing business wing of the ruling Liberal Party. "There is a sense that by the mid-sixties, the cost of these programs had grown faster than expected," stated the author in an interview in 2018.

One has only to step back to the 1968 election, where Trudeau made it very clear to large crowds in towns across south western Ontario that he shared their fiscal conservatism. "You know that no government is a Santa Claus and I thought as I came down the street and saw all the waves and handshakes that I'd remind you that Ottawa is not a Santa Claus. We don't intend raising taxes any more than we have to and therefore we aren't making many promises in this election," he said in Listowel on a bright May afternoon (quoted in Stevens 1968b: 8).

A major theme in the 1970s in the Liberal government was placing the task of fighting inflation mostly on the shoulders on workers and what were viewed as their excessive wages. On the June election trail Trudeau spoke about the "danger" to Canada of the "revolution of rising expectations" before nearly four thousand people in Brantford: "People expect more from the country. They expect more from the government. Well, we're not going around telling the people that the government will give them more and give great public works here and build a tunnel there and increase all benefits in the next place … because this is the surest way of undermining our dollar. It's by inflation. It's by promising more to the people than the government can afford" (quoted in Seale 1968b: 8).

This tactic of lowering expectations from the new Liberal leader just he was about to sweep the country through the full force of his engaging personality alarmed the more traditional-looking Tommy Douglas, who must have understood that the NDP's social democratic message was not making sufficient inroads. In an interview with the *Globe and Mail,* the federal NDP leader observed that Trudeau's rhetoric about the merits of a means test for future social benefit reminded him of the earlier 1930s Depression-era prime minister, R.B. Bennett, who had a reputation for being less than sympathetic to the plight of the unemployed (*Globe and Mail* 1968: 8). Two days later, Douglas went further and called Trudeau a "1930s Tory" and "far right" of Pearson. "[Trudeau]'s come out against the capital gains tax. He is against building homes because he wants to balance the budget" (quoted in MacFarlane 1968: 10).

The winning of a majority government in June 1968 meant that Pierre Trudeau, as leader of the Liberal Party, was no longer beholden to the NDP to stay in power, and he did not feel any pressure to go further left. At the same time the reformist wing of the Liberal Party, which had held sway in the Pearson era and supported the new welfare state, now went into decline. Trudeau was keen on "subduing" the left wing within the

Liberal Party because they were jeopardizing his objectives, says Aivalis. The new prime minister tended to talk about equality of opportunity (a business catch phrase) rather than social equality or reducing poverty. It was probably not obvious at the time but Trudeau was setting Canada on the path of austerity, deregulation and a passive reliance on economic growth to improve the lives of Canadians (going against the advice of John Kenneth Galbraith). "Trudeau was Canada's first neo-liberal prime minister," Aivalis notes (2018a).

The move toward centre-right in the Liberal Party was a gradual process and somewhat contradictory. John Munro, the minister of health and welfare, was implementing his party's promise of a just society and participatory democracy by providing monetary assistance to emerging anti-poverty groups. Yet, there were signs that the Trudeau government was backing away from a poverty agenda, warned David McQueen at the Economic Council of Canada before the hearings of the Special Senate Committee on Poverty in April 1969. "This is no time to speak quietly about poverty — to mute our concern … Poverty is among other things a massive and avoidable waste of human capabilities, a reflection of past failings to develop those capabilities" (quoted in Goldblatt 1969a: 4). McQueen also lamented the 1968 folding of the Special Planning Secretariat into the Privy Council; he wanted it revived to serve as an information exchange for people engaged in various types of anti-poverty activity (*Globe and Mail* 1969: 4).

Furthermore, the Prime Minister stuck to his guns in opposing the guaranteed annual income (GAI) on three separate occasions. The first time the proposal for a GAI came from Liberal Party members themselves, who endorsed the concept in a 1970 policy convention. This was the same gathering that also voted in favour of the legalization of cannabis. The Trudeau government simply ignored both votes and carried on. Then, in 1971, his government rejected the recommendation for a guaranteed annual income by Senator David Croll, who had been mandated by Trudeau in the fall of 1968 to hold cross-Canada hearings on poverty following the dire report from the Economic Council of Canada about the number of people living in destitution (ECC 1968).

James Struthers (2018) suggests that Trudeau reluctantly supported a three-year (1973 to 1976) exploration of the feasibility of a guaranteed annual income, undertaken by his former advisor Marc Lalonde, who succeeded Munro as the Minister of Health and Welfare. In the end it did not fly because of opposition from John Turner and his deputy minister Simon Reisman at the powerful Department of Finance. This was the epicentre of the animus against government spending and obsession with debts and deficits in the Liberal government and represented a precursor to the dismantling of government social programs down the road. Social reform was impossible under those circumstances, stated a former advisor to John Munro, Leonard Shifrin: "The central agency bureaucrats had enormous control and in particular this business of the budgets being the unilateral product of the Finance Department. It meant that they were able to deliberately undermine a Cabinet process that had been underway for three years [such as Lalonde's proposed GAI]. And they could do it unilaterally and there was nothing that could be done about it" (2011).

Trudeau did endorse the 1971 liberalized unemployment insurance program that had been pushed by his labour minister, Bryce Mackasey. It was popular with the labour movement and the left. But this same prime minister also oversaw the first stages of its eventual dismantling under successive Liberal governments in face of the demonization in the media and among some politicians of the victims of growing unemployment. Christo Aivalis says that the confusion over the Liberal messaging of Trudeau's just society ultimately resulted in the disappearance of the slogan from the government's lexicon after 1970. The Trudeau government faced pressures to spend less on the poor from various quarters, including the business community, he argues. An internal Liberal Party poll found that the public was less enamoured with new expenditures for the poor (Aivalis 2018a), but it could be argued that the political and media elite had laid the groundwork for this view with a relentless drumbeat of not living beyond one's means.

On the other side of the political aisle there were mixed signals coming out of the NDP and the labour movement despite their official support for a guaranteed annual income. It was something that author Bill Freeman spotted in Hamilton, the country's larger industrial centre and hub of union activity. In 1971 he helped to organize a local welfare rights group. "Remember, welfare recipients at that time were not very popular. Welfare was a polarizing issue. I was active in the NDP at that time and many party members did not support our work. In fact, it strikes me that today [in the second decade of the twenty-first century] there is much more sympathy for welfare recipients than at that time. The change in name from 'welfare' to 'social assistance' reflects that" (Freeman 2018). Another signal that poverty and social inequality were never a priority for Trudeau was his failure to include social and economic rights (such as the right to housing) in the Charter of Rights and Freedoms, a decision that still haunts us in the twenty-first century. Historian David Tough argues that the history of Canada might have turned out differently if, in the early 1970s, the reform or left wing of the Liberal Party had had the strength to push forward a tax on the wealthy, based on the recommendations of the Carter Commission, after Pierre Trudeau arrived on the scene. His finance minister, Edgar Benson, was forced to withdraw a proposed hike in taxes on the wealthy in his 1970 budget following an outcry from a lobby of tax lawyers, chartered accountants and bankers (Tough 2017).

Tough is the author of *The Terrific Engine: Income Taxation and the Modernization of the Canadian Political Imaginary,* which explores democratic possibility in the early twentieth-century introduction of the income tax (Tough 2018). The historian says that the Canadian welfare state which Lester Pearson had built was really a work in progress since it had not significantly reduced poverty and inequality in the country during the 1960s. Indeed, the financing of new and expensive universal social programs involving welfare, pensions and health care, student loans, etc. had been entirely reliant on revenue from the majority of Canadian taxpayers and that source was all maxed out. Echoing the journalist work of Linda McQuaig, Tough says an opportunity was missed in the decision by Trudeau not to target the privileged position of the rich and powerful in Canada, who had managed to avoid paying their share of tax (Tough 2017).

By the early 1970s poverty was slowly but surely slipping into yesterday's issues. The GAI model did survive over the long term in both the Guaranteed Income Supplement (GIS), which was set up 1965 and targeted seniors, and the child tax credit. The GIS made a substantial reduction in the poverty experienced by older people and still exists today. "It was much easier to move seniors out of poverty from the 1960s to the 1980s," says James Struthers. "First, they were seen as deserving because of the historical events they had lived through during their working lives: settling the prairies, World War I, the Depression and World War II, without the benefits of a welfare state, by the way, that their children and grandchildren would enjoy. Secondly, the Canada Pension Plan created in 1963–1965 came too late for so many of them" (Struthers 2018).

Yet, Trudeau's conservatism was not entirely obvious or even apparent in the first term of office of the Liberals after the 1968 election. For many young people graduating and looking for salaried government jobs this seemingly sophisticated and intellectual prime minister represented a breath of fresh air compared to the staid and boring spectacle of Lester Pearson battling his rival, Progressive Conservative Party leader John Diefenbaker. Also, not to be ruled out was that Canada was experiencing English-French tensions and this made having a prime minister from Quebec very appealing to Anglophone Canadians concerned about their country's future.

A New Generation of Civil Servants

In revisiting Trudeau's November 1968 question-and-answer session at Queen's University it is wise to note that his remarks about the possibility of upheaval similar to what was happening in the United States coming to Canada was really part of a call for a rethinking of the binary Cold War conflict of the West versus the Soviet Union that dominated planning in NATO (North Atlantic Treaty Organization). "We are not so much threatened by the ideologies of communism or fascism or even I would say, we are not so much threatened by atomic bombs and ICBMS [intercontinental ballistic missiles], as we are by the very large sectors of the world, two-thirds of the world's population, that goes to bed hungry, every night, and large fractions of our own society, which do not find fulfillment, in the society."

In the same address at Queen's University Trudeau showed his conservative side in talking about the controversial Company of Young Canadians, which had adopted the community organizing philosophy of the student new left across Canada and the United States. Former members of the Student Union for Peace Action were working inside the CYC because they thought this would be a more effective use of their energy and idealism. The Ottawa head office was apparently under watch by the Security Service, says Kevin Brushett, a professor of history at the Royal Military College in Kingston and the author of a forthcoming book on the CYC. And there was an accusation that the CYC in Montreal had been infiltrated by the FLQ. "We have our hands full with the Company of Young Canadians. The Secretary of State will announce the appointment of a new director," Trudeau told his audience. "We hope to install new vigour, and perhaps control at least in the financial sense, in the Company of Young Canadians. I still think it is a very valid idea. Our government does hope that it will permit the young people of Canada to get involved in our society, in a creative way. We are extremely hopeful that the company of young Canadians will be a vehicle for change within the structures of the society."

At Queen's Trudeau sought to influence young people, who tended to be cynical and sceptical about the motives of the elites. He warned against a thinking that presumed that politicians are "stooges of some foreign power" or that they take their directions from Wall Street or Bay Street. "I think that more and more young people if they want to change the society from within should consider entering the civil service. I think they [should] consider working for the provincial or federal government [or] school boards or municipal councils," he told the gathering.

Indeed, the decision was made by the new government to clamp down on all of the grassroots activity of the CYC after it had been given a surprising amount of autonomy to set up programming between 1966 and 1969, notes Kelly Pineault, author of a master of arts thesis, *Shifting the Balance: Indigenous and Non-Indigenous Activism in the Company of Young Canadians, 1966–1970*. Never "before or since" had a government-funded body enjoyed so much independence from either the bureaucrats or their political masters in Ottawa, she says (Pineault 2011: 3). CYC volunteers were given complete freedom to make the primary decisions about their organizing in the field.

Going to work on projects in isolated Indigenous communities was especially popular among the idealistic non-Indigenous youth joining the CYC. Not all of the projects were successful, and there were sometimes cultural differences between local Indigenous communities and CYC people, or there were differences of opinions within the communities about their dealings with this Ottawa-based organization.

The fact that the largely conservative provincial premiers in western Canada opposed the presence of the CYC in their jurisdictions meant it was probably doing something worthwhile in challenging racism by the white Canadian settler society. CYC personnel set up mechanisms for young Indigenous activists across Canada to meet and engage in campaigns to improve the education of other young Indigenous people, produce film, video and music and set up newspapers. For example, the *Kenomadiwin*

News/Lightbulb in north-western Ontario offered fresh perspectives on racism and the Trudeau government's controversial proposals for the Indian Act, which could not be found in the mainstream media. In one instance, it published excerpts from historical letters from local Indigenous leaders beseeching the Crown to respect hunting and fishing rights negotiated in the 1850 Robinson-Superior Treaty. This Indigenous publication made the rather paternalistic federal Department of Indian Affairs very uncomfortable (Pineault 2011: 107–83). In retrospect historians tend to be dismissive of the CYC as being largely an eruption of excessive sixties idealism among middle-class white youth. What they miss is that Indigenous youth had the opportunity for the first time to engage and mobilize their communities on a more pan-Indigenous basis (193–97).

This is a natural segue into another group of young Canadians who accepted Trudeau's argument that the way to change the world was to join the federal civil service and work with his government. One good source on this subject is Kevin Brushett's 2014 unpublished paper "Guerrilla Bureaucrats." What he observed was that individuals and groups with a new left perspective, including Praxis, found a receptive ear and were in demand in Ottawa as part of the rush to raise the government's intellectual capacity. Gone were the grey men who ruled Ottawa and loyally served Prime Ministers Mackenzie King and Louis St. Laurent during and after World War II. Ottawa journalist Sandra Gwyn wrote that "guerrilla bureaucrats" were now the dominant force in key departments in the Trudeau government (quoted in Brushett 2014). Brushett notes that they were typically well-educated and confident people who were steeped in new ideas and influenced by the thinkers of the time, such as Marshall McLuhan, Alvin Toffler and Herbert Marcuse.

Reflecting this trend, Gerard Pelletier, the Minister for Secretary of State, was keen on having leading-edge managers in charge of new programs. Among the by-products were the establishment of Local Initiatives and Opportunities for Youth, which funded innovative projects by young people — like legal clinics and live theatre — and created jobs for them. John Munro, who headed up the Department of Health and Welfare, was doing something similar in funding low-income groups in community development. Guerrilla bureaucrats at the Department of Health and Welfare and Central Mortgage and Housing Corporation hired Praxis on separate research projects because of its expertise and contacts among poor peoples' groups.

During the three years of Praxis's existence (1968–72) this research institute engaged in a wide range of research assignments in Ottawa. It evaluated and advised the Department of Health and Welfare on which anti-poverty groups should receive funding to set up offices and hire staff. It conducted evaluations on both the Company of Young Canadians and Digger House — a facility for lost youth in Yorkville in Toronto. It was also hired to organize a national poor people's conference in Toronto, in conjunction with Leonard Shifrin, president of the revived National Council of Welfare, for early 1971 (Shifrin 2011–13).

Shifrin was a former provincial Liberal candidate in Ontario who worked briefly after the 1968 federal election advising John Munro, the minister of health and welfare, before leaving government to head the National Council of Welfare (NCW). At that point Shifrin became the go-to guy (in addition to Doris Power) to provide background information and observations for quote-hungry reporters who wanted an expert opinion on poverty. Throughout his professional career in Ottawa and later as a social policy commentator it is apparent that Shifrin had dual loyalties — one to the poor of Canada and the other to John Munro. Balancing and reconciling the two was not easy.

Shifrin explains it was his idea to revive the NCW, which had been a "toothless" body in its inception in the 1960s. He also found common cause with John Munro and senior officials at Health and Welfare in the focus on the participation of poor people in the political process in Canada, along the lines of what was happening in the US with community organizing in the War on Poverty and new grassroots organizations like the National Welfare Rights Organization.

Ken Battle is the co-founder of the independent social policy think-tank, the Ottawa-based Caledon Institute. A former assistant to Shifrin, Battle discussed his boss's role in the late sixties and early seventies at a February 2017 memorial in Ottawa following Shifrin's passing: "The notion that poor people could actually provide relevant perspectives on what needed to be done on poverty was 'thinking outside the box.'" Battle also noted that Shifrin, as an activist policy-maker, opened up during the late 1960s public discussion on poor children, single parents, legal aid, feminization of poverty, pension reform and unemployment. But Battle also acknowledged the later setbacks, such as the disbanding of the NCW under the government of Stephen Harper (2006–15).

In practice, the NCW was an independent arms-length operation governed by a board containing poor people and social work professionals rather than bureaucrats. There was for instance no hesitation in taking on the policies and programs of John Munro and Prime Minister Trudeau from the start, reported one *Globe and Mail* article in the spring of 1971, several months before the release of Senator Croll's report on poverty in Canada. A thirty-three-page NCW report took dead aim at the federal Liberal government for lacking any long-term strategy to reduce poverty. Furthermore, a sudden massive increase in unemployment in Canada was blamed on the fiscal and monetary policies coming out of Ottawa (Goldblatt 1971: 11).

Shifrin told me in an interview decades later that he had a premonition of the political process turning against the poor following a conversation with Marc Lalonde after the Liberal victory in 1968. As a young man and loyal Liberal, Shifrin expressed a great deal of excitement about new social policies in a fresh new government. "I told Lalonde, we are going to do all those things that we talked about in the policy conferences, and he said, 'yeah, we would be able to if there was only the money'" (Shifrin 2011–13). It was a major reality check from the powerful Lalonde, who was an advisor to Pierre Trudeau on political priorities. In the end, though, Christo Aivalis (2018a) argues that Lalonde turned out to be a stronger advocate for the guaranteed annual income concept than Shifrin's longtime friend John Munro, who was, like Trudeau, lukewarm to the idea.

Leonard Shifrin expressed disappointment over the general failure by Canada's politicians to pursue a guaranteed annual income, making Shakespearean allusions to "the tides in men's affairs." Instead of criticizing Munro or Pierre Trudeau, he primarily blamed the more radical members of the anti-poverty movement, including Praxis, for failing to take a strong stand in favour of it. This was an admission that Liberals like himself relied on the left to push issues from outside on centrist governments. But the left in the sixties and seventies, like today, was split on the merits of the guaranteed annual income.

The National Council of Welfare was profiled in the *Globe and Mail* just as Shifrin was leaving his post on May 22, 1975. The organization was described as the generator of "sober" reports on the state of Canada's poor, with titles like *Prices and the Poor* and *One Child One Chance*. It billed itself as non-partisan in giving hell to all governments, federal and provincial, whatever their political stripe, for their meagre social policies. John Munro told the *Globe and Mail* in the same article that he did not mind the sharp criticism from his former assistant. He relished the valuable feedback from the NCW to explore and take stands on poverty that he and the Department of Health and Welfare were averse to taking because they were not "politically acceptable" (Cooper 1975: F10).

Shifrin remained wedded to poverty eradication even if his beloved Liberals had left the station on the matter. In another interview with the *Globe and Mail* at the time, he drew parallels in what poor people were trying to achieve with other oppressed groups. "The powerless poor are banding together and asserting poor power. The powerless students are banding to assert Student Power. The powerless Indians are asserting Red Power and the powerless Blacks, Black Power." The NCW head also saw comparisons to the powerless workers who had banded together to form unions and assert labour power decades earlier in the twentieth century. "It was a long and bloody struggle before we accepted labour power and adjusted our power structures accordingly" (Russell 1969a: 5).

"Poverty is the great social issue of our time. Unless we act now, nationally in a new and purposeful way, five million Canadians will continue to find life a bleak, bitter and never-ending struggle for survival." This statement is the first paragraph of the 1971 report *Poverty in Canada*, issued by the Special Senate Committee on Poverty (Croll 1971). Its chief recommendation, a guaranteed annual income, was greeted with "the usual mutterings" that it was too expensive from both Pierre Trudeau and John Munro, commented a *Globe and Mail* editorial (1971b: 6). Munro had himself ruled out the GAI months before, even as the Senate hearings were underway. Poverty was now slipping as an issue and was soon to be crowded out by new anxieties surrounding inflation.

Meanwhile, outside of a group of journalists writing lengthy magazine profiles of Canadian businessmen (virtually all men at the time) and their companies, there was less serious discussion about the behaviour of the rich and wealthy in Canada and their desire to contribute less to the country through lower taxes. Their activities were considered normal and productive for the country. Poverty, on the other hand, was abnormal, a crisis and potentially threatening for Pierre Trudeau and his government.

Chapter Three

The Media and Poverty

A general- assignment reporter for the *Vancouver Province* in 1969, Kathy Tait, observed that the poor in Canada were organizing at a "tremendous speed." It had reached a saturation point in BC, with television reporters going to news conferences, demonstrations, sit-ins and confrontations: "For the first time poor people were willing to speak publicly. They did not refuse to have their names attached to their words and actions" (quoted in NCW 1973: 14–18). Picking up on this trend was the *Globe and Mail* in the first paragraph of Lou Lee's reportage on July 10, 1969: "The majority of poor may still be silently long suffering, but a new breed is emerging. Articulate and activist, their frustration gives them the motivation and drive to fight a system they feel smothers and degrades them and their children" (Lee 1969: W1).

The New Poor

In her early thirties, feminist Doris Power fitted the description of those who became known as the "new poor." The Just Society Movement, which she and another single mother on welfare, Suzanne Polgar, founded together was a novelty in Toronto. It was started almost exclusively by young women, with a little bit of help from local churches, who engaged in a variety of high-profile events to attract media attention. That is why Lynn Lang, a university student coming from a low-income background and a future leader in the women's movement, was drawn to them. (More on her later.) Men who had their lost their jobs through injuries in the workplace also joined the JSM. Power, a single mother, was celebrated as one of the newsmakers of 1970 for her articulate explanations about poverty (*Toronto Daily Star* 1970: 45). "I feel completely alienated and outside the community. I'm different than other people because I can't afford to take part in the community," she told the press (*Toronto Daily Star* 1969: 25).

Margaret Little, a Queen's University professor and anti-poverty activist, chronicled the Just Society Movement in a 2007 article in the journal *Labour/Le Travail*, "Militant Mothers Fight Poverty: The Just Society Movement, 1968–1971." She wrote that local consumers of news in 1969 Toronto were given a steady diet of everything you needed to know about Doris Power, including her opinions, actions and even the impending the birth of her latest child. She quotes the *Toronto Daily Star*, which described Power as "the small, hard pretty woman with an old-fashioned pony tail … and a blow horn," which appeared to be a dig at the advocate and her seriousness (Little 2007: 191).

From Power's perspective, the transformation from a single mother struggling privately with economic deprivation to a celebrity poor person was becoming a full-time job. There were the telephone calls, public speaking engagements and invitations to sit on panels. The overwhelming attention led to her wearing dark glasses and an Afro wig as a disguise in order to not get recognized while taking streetcars or walking around in the city. "If you're the only game in town, everyone wants a piece of you. People today cannot imagine the media we attracted. The minute a government paper would be released in Ottawa, my phone would start ringing with reporters wanting my reaction to it … and I'd be home just trying to look after my kids and deal with my neighbours," she explained when I interviewed her in 2018 (her quotes below are from our telephone and email conversations).

Power accepted an appointment on the board of the Ontario Welfare Council, which was financed by wealthy philanthropists focused on social policy: "They were all very nice, polite, upper middle-class people." The Just Society Movement co-founder also expanded her scope by participating in the Abortion Caravan, which organized a nation-wide campaign of women to push Pierre Trudeau's government to reduce the bureaucratic barriers to lawful abortions. (These procedures were especially difficult economically and socially for women living on low incomes or dependent on their partners or families.) But she feared that the government was trying to contain and manipulate the poor. Power gave a firm "no" to a job offer from Ottawa which would have involved travelling the country and evaluating which poor peoples' groups should get grants to set up offices and hire people full-time. This was a job that the Praxis research institute ended up taking.

Rather than provide a typical well-researched policy brief, Power issued what the *Globe and Mail* headline described as a "shocking" retort for Senator David Croll's committee hearings on poverty. She seemed to signal that this public interest in poverty was starting to wane. News cycles were a little longer in the pre-digital age but it was bound to end. "We have a new fashion in the land of Canada. We have discovered the poor. Our thought, research and action are more and more focused on the poor and poverty ... We talk about them, study them, get angry at them and even send around Senate committees to search for answers. And answers seem so hard to come by. Let's stop kidding one another. Let's not play games with each other and let's end the ritual. We of the Just Society decry this cynical game." What concerned Power was the lack of a similar investigation of the power of corporations and wealth in Canada (*Globe and Mail* 1970a: 27).

This intuitive ability of Power's to grab attention and become a public figure came about as major urban newspapers were assigning reporters to cover poverty in its broadest aspect during the late sixties and early seventies. The *Toronto Daily Star,* for instance, sent David Allen to cover the cross-Canada hearings of Senator David Croll's committee on poverty. Outfitted with a budget to fulfill his task, he was given assurance by his editors at the *Toronto Daily Star* that his copy would not be edited without his consultation (NCW 1973: 13). But by 1973, like most news subjects, the topic eventually started to fade away. Allen was reassigned to cover Ontario politics in 1972. He subsequently quit journalism and became a press aide for Roy McMurtry, the province's attorney general.

This information about David Allen is recorded in a 1973 National Council of Welfare (NCW) report, *The Press and the Poor: A Report by the National Council of Welfare on How Canada's Newspapers Cover Poverty.* Another person who appears in the NCW document is Ron Haggart, a lively newspaper columnist in his day and future executive director for CBC TV's award-winning investigative show *The Fifth Estate.* In a commentary that seems fresh today, he told the NCW that TV was primarily a vehicle for official pronouncements from leading figures such as cabinet ministers or city politicians. "But public attitudes are also conditioned by the steady day-in and day-out reporting of current events and situations. For this, television is superb for reporting a man on the moon but (so far at least) unequal to the task of reporting the poor at home." Haggart added that subjects like poverty require more subtle coverage that are beyond the capacity of television news, which consists of "quick and physical acts suitable for the camera," (2–9). It is noteworthy that little has changed since he made these remarks.

Reporter Kathy Tait was also interviewed for the 1973 NCW report. She indicated that her newspaper, the *Vancouver Province*, cut back its coverage of poverty and welfare issues in 1971. The explanation was straightforward: "Not because the media were no longer interested but the poor were making news to a lesser and lesser extent. In a sense everything had been said" (14–18). She claimed that the Senate hearings on poverty, the subsequent 1971 report, *Poverty in Canada* by Senator David Croll and the publication of Ian Adams' best-selling 1970 book, *The Poverty Wall*, had told people in Canada all they needed to know on the subject. Putting Tait's remarks in context, the National Council on Welfare came out with its report on the media at a time when newspapers had clout, generated enormous profits, were generally part of chains and had an impact on a broad readership. Poverty was an issue in Canada as long as the federal government sought to make it one and offered services and programs in that area. But once the government policy-makers lost interest, so did the reporters, whose bread-and-butter assignments tend to be press conferences and announcements, reflecting the general weakness of mainstream journalism.

The third journalist interviewed by the NCW was former Canadian Press reporter Ken Kelly, who maintained that the overwhelming number of media outlets missed the biggest story on the poverty beat (9–12). Essentially, it involved how provinces were failing to create effective appeal procedures for people whose applications for social assistance were rejected by their province's welfare plan. He noted that the provinces were receiving millions of federal dollars even as they were failing to meet this important legal obligation under the Canada Assistance Plan. The Ontario government, for instance, had delayed for three years the establishment of an appeal process before appointing James Band, a veteran of less-than-compassionate relief programs going back to the 1930s, when he was a hard-nosed relief inspector (Struthers 2018–19). After this discrepancy was finally exposed by a single reporter, Ottawa was forced to put pressure on the provinces to set up appeal panels for social assistance. Kelly complained that perhaps hundreds of people in need had been victimized by arbitrary welfare administrators and "robbed" of their right to make an appeal for denial of benefits (NCW 1973: 9–12).

What Made *The Poverty Wall* Different?

The Poverty Wall, written by Ian Adams and published in 1970, is one of those books that had a long-term impact beyond its immediate publication. The author says it sold 100,000 copies, went through four printings and appeared on the syllabus of social work courses in universities. "His book was my bible for a long time. I used to get people to read it," says Bill Freeman, organizer for the Hamilton Welfare Rights Organization (Freeman 2018).

I managed to catch up with its author, the now retired Adams at one of his favourite watering holes on Bloor Street in Toronto (Adams 2018). He has fond memories of working as a magazine journalist for *Maclean's* in the sixties. What made *The Poverty Wall* different from everything else written on poverty in Canada was that it was a readable and compelling account of Adams' personal experience with desperate economic circumstances after abandonment by his Irish-born parents in Africa — first in an orphanage and later dumped unceremoniously in his teens in Canada to fend for himself. Adams wrote about the isolated "small worlds of poverty" in the following excerpts from Chapter 1 of his book:

> I have slept on those twenty-five cents a night mattresses in Montreal flophouses and lived for weeks on end in dollar a day Vancouver rooming houses where the transoms were made of chicken wire. I remember a landlord telling me that the chicken wire made it easier to check on any destitute roomer who might have attempted suicide … I started working for a living before I turned sixteen and since then, I have left behind countless hours of my life in heavy menial labour and various mind-numbing industrial jobs. I mention all these things because I believe they are in a way, my credentials for writing about poverty in this country. To find out how the poor live and work was not a "project" for me: by my early twenties, the bitterest years of my own poverty, I understood only too well where I stood in society. By that time, my experiences had seeped like dye into my consciousness, indelibly colouring my thoughts …

Later, as I slowly acquired the skills of a journalist, I came to understand something else: that in this country journalism is for the most part in the hands of the middle class, that much of the reporting that is done is based on the prejudices of that class. (Adams 1970: 11)

Some parts of the book came out of material he had written for *Maclean's* in the mid-1960s, when the magazine took a deep interest in the subject of poverty. It was Adams' hankering for photography that pulled him out of the mindless menial jobs; he went to art school and then got a job developing film at the *Winnipeg Tribune*. That led him to covering police courts and getting a firsthand look at how the law treated homeless people and sex workers.

The Poverty Wall only devotes so much space to the author's own story. One chapter stands out for many of us in Canada today because of its depiction of the tragic story of Charlie (Chanie) Wenjack, which Adams first wrote about for *Maclean's* in the February 1967 edition. Adams attended a coroner's inquest into the death of Wenjack in Kenora, which in 2016 was the subject of a poignant album, *Secret Path*, by the Tragically Hip and lead singer Gord Downie, close to his death from cancer, as well as a graphic novel and an animated film. The Indigenous boy died from exposure and starvation in the cold emptiness of winter in north-western Ontario near the CNR train tracks. He was trying to make it home to his family, four hundred miles from a residential school which he had been forced to attend. Adams himself had a chance to view Wenjack's body, when it was lying in the morgue. The journalist later walked along the same isolated stretch of track in the woods to try and imagine the thoughts in the twelve-year-old's mind in those final moments of an abbreviated life.

Adams recalls from previous reporting the sheer racism facing destitute and hungry Indigenous people moving to Kenora from the surrounding reserves. It was like something straight out of the US South, except this involved Canada's original inhabitants. Local white citizens were so offended by something he had written previously in another magazine that an ugly mob gathered at city hall to vent their anger. Indeed, a local lawyer managed to calm the crowd down with the suggestion that a defamation suit be launched — which in the end did not go anywhere. Later, when Adams returned to Kenora the tension over the negative publicity about the town had not subsided. Strangers telephoned the hotel knowing he was staying there and left behind death threats. The magazine journalist found that the local cops resented the pressure from whites to clear the streets of down-and-out Indigenous People as if the cops were working for the city's garbage department.

Adams' original magazine article about Wenjack had failed to make a dent in the issue of the government forcing Indigenous children into church-run residential schools for the purpose of robbing them of their culture, language and identity. Instead of any soul-searching, the federal Indian Affairs department responded by issuing a new effective search mechanism for runaway children from these institutions, according to historian John Milloy, author of *A National Crime: The Canadian Government and the Residential School System, 1879 to 1986* (2017: 286–87).

Prejudices against Indigenous Peoples were openly expressed. Adams says the editors at *Maclean's* were happy with the Wenjack story but then he received a disturbing letter from the publisher: "I got this note from Robert Chalmers saying he didn't think my writing belonged in his magazine. It was just about three lines [the note]. It was sent to me by the internal mail." Adams raised the matter with his immediate editors, Borden Spears and Alexander (Sandy) Ross, thinking this meant he was being fired from the magazine. "Borden didn't say anything and Sandy said 'don't worry about it, we will take care of it.'"

The idea for a book came about when Adams was working late one evening in the late sixties at *Maclean's*. The high-profile publisher Jack McClelland telephoned out of the blue. Adams apologized that the name was not familiar to him. But McClelland persisted, stating he had been following with interest Adams' magazine work, which included coverage of the Vietnam War, Expo 1967 in Montreal and the plight of Canadian soldiers who had been interned in a Japanese prisoner of war camp during World War II while their senior officers had managed to escape this fate.

Adams and McClelland met at a local bar on Dundas Street in Toronto, and Adams was asked if he had ever considered doing an entire book. The journalist replied in the affirmative and indicated having sufficient material on poverty. "What do you need for an advance for the project?" McClelland asked. Adams replied that $3,000 (a large figure back then) would help. The publisher filled out a cheque for that amount and handed it across the table. After that the question was how much time did the journalist need to complete the project. He replied that a manuscript would be ready in two months. Adams met the deadline.

Discovered in the McClelland & Stewart papers at McMaster University Archives are some of the author's proposed titles for the book before the decision was made to stick with *The Poverty Wall*. The original choice, *Roar of the Silence*, failed to explain what the book was all about. The files show how the publishers struggled to come up with an appropriate and winning title. Adams himself issued more possibilities, all of which were rejected: *Bad News from the Other Canada, The Hated Poor, A Reality Trip for the Just Society, Poverty without Pity, Bitter Bread, Bad News for Pierre, Mr. and Mrs. Bad News, World of Want, Poor Against the Wall, Pawns of Poverty and Armies of the Poor*. There is a small note from an unnamed editor warning that Adams did not want a title that was insulting or stereotypical. "He is extremely anxious that *Stench* not be used" (Poverty Wall file).

Adams remembers that the editing, marketing and publishing process was seamless. "McClelland never bugged me. I delivered my manuscript; he really liked it. He got behind it, promoted it. And it sold a lot of books; he made a lot of money." But the failure to hire an agent resulted in Adams not receiving much in terms of royalties from the sales of *The Poverty Wall*. "I was amazed because I didn't see the money that I had expected would be coming." (I tried several times but was unable to reach writer and publisher Anna Porter, who was an editor at McClelland & Stewart in the early 1970s, for a response to this accusation from the past.)

It was McClelland's idea to pitch the book to libraries and schools, which seemed to work. The book ended up on reading lists for university social work courses dealing with poverty and social issues in Canada. The publisher also made an arrangement for Adams to go on a cross-Canada tour.

> I did a book tour across Canada. I did all kinds of interviews with all kinds of media. There seemed to be a surprise that poverty existed in Canada, and it was sort of like a new news story ... There was a general positive acceptance of it but a lot of hostility from television interviewers. It was a very strange thing ... I remember being interviewed on CBC, in Alberta, in Calgary, and this woman, this right-wing interviewer [was] accusing me

of making money out of poverty. I mean her questions were so ridiculous, and at the time I said, "the book costs $2.95. I was just in your cafeteria to get a sandwich and there was nothing below four bucks." (Adams 2018)

Book reviewer Kenneth Bagnell in his *Globe and Mail* profile asserted that Adams had established his writing craft from scratching out a harsh living day to day. The newspaper writer also reflected on the changing attitudes towards social issues just as *The Poverty Wall* was coming off the presses in Toronto in March 1970. Down the street at the St. Lawrence Hall, a large crowd had gathered to listen to a denunciation of proposed taxes on the wealthy in the budget set out by federal minister Edgar Benson. These measures were depicted as an attack on hard work and the middle class by small business lobbyist John Bulloch. Eventually, Pierre Trudeau's government was obliged to back down (Bagnell 1970: A17).

Meanwhile, it is noteworthy that Adams was writing about poverty in northern Ontario Indigenous communities in the 1960s, when federal and provincial politicians paid scant attention to the issue in the negotiations to establish the new programs of the Canadian welfare state. Some shocking statistics came out of the 1971 report *Poverty in Canada,* produced by Senator David Croll's Special Committee on Poverty. The report noted that the average Canadian lived to the age of 62 years (people did not live as long then as now), compared to 36 years for Indians or First Nations and 20 for Inuit. At the same time the population of Indigenous Peoples was close to half million in 1971, and it was the fastest growing part of the Canadian population, expected to double in the following fifteen years.

James Struthers, in his book *The Limits of Affluence: Welfare in Ontario, 1920–1970* (1994), observed that the Ontario government had been expanding its social services reach into Indigenous communities. Band councils on reserves were allowed to provide relief to those needing it. Starting in the early sixties in northern Ontario there was a growing migration of destitute Indigenous People from their reserves, and they ended up in shanty communities outside of towns such as Kenora, Red Lake, Moosonee and Sault Ste Marie. Even though Indigenous Peoples were a federal responsibility under the British North America Act because of their relationship with the Crown, one Ontario government official complained in a note that the civil servants in the federal Department of Indian Affairs were almost studiously indifferent to their plight.

Meanwhile negotiations in the later 1960s with Ottawa were breaking down as the feds were refusing to provide sufficient financial assistance to help Ontario cope with this new crisis. In turn Ontario Premier John Robarts balked at his government investing money in the newly set up Indian Development Branch inside the provincial Department of Social and Family Services. Finally, in 1969, frustrated with this stalemate, the director of Indian Development Joseph Dufour staged his own protest, threatening a mass resignation of his field staff if the province did not fork out a promised allocation of about $1.5 million so they could do their job. However, the premier refused to budge and so Dufour and most of his staff left. Ontario stood firm at the end of the decade that the crisis in northern Ontario was too big, and it had to be tackled by Ottawa since Indigenous Peoples were its responsibility (Struthers 1994: 226–30).

One of the members of the Just Society Movement, Susan Abela, came into frequent contact with Indigenous women arriving in Toronto who were fleeing domestic abuse but then coming into contact with unsympathetic welfare officials. "The one woman I was working with was told that she should go back to the reserve or she should lose custody of her child because she wasn't a good enough mother. But it was really racist. It wasn't any reason," Abela says (2018). Abela was volunteering at the Just Society Movement office in the West End YWCA at Dovercourt and College in west Toronto where she encountered these Indigenous women and eventually shared a house with some of them to protect each other from these men looking for them. "If one of the abusers showed up at the front door there were enough of us to do something." Domestic violence shelters had not opened yet in Toronto and so the women of the Just Society Movement were left to devise their own solution. "It was just women figuring it out on our own, doing it for ourselves," Abela says.

Chapter Four

Praxis and Its Contribution

"Very briefly the idea is to create an Institute of Social Studies whose *raison d'être* would be to encourage research and long-range imaginative thinking on the various aspects of the future development of our society," political scientist Stephen Clarkson wrote to one of his colleagues on October 23, 1968. The young academic, just in his early thirties, complained that it was appalling that his academic colleagues were doing so little research into the Canadian social problems of the day — such as poverty in the midst of plenty. "There is a lot of research done of varying degrees of scholarly sterility on past or present social aims," he lamented (Clarkson 1969).

Getting Off the Ground

Clarkson was a political scientist of considerable reputation especially in the area of foreign relations and later in free trade between Canada and the US, but social policy was not something he had written or studied closely. One might say he was completely disregarding the advances in statistical measurement in post–World War II Canada that gave a number of academic social scientists a sophisticated handle on who constituted the poor. It was their work that made the Economic Council of Canada's landmark 1968 report on income possible. Yet, David McQueen, the vice chair of the ECC, echoed Clarkson's complaint while appearing before Senate David Croll's Senate Committee on Poverty. McQueen publicly lamented that no Canadian university in this time period when poverty was on the agenda had set up a multi-disciplinary institute on the subject, to pool the expertise from various academic fields (Goldblatt 1969a: 4). This was furthermore a time when there was serious concern about the lack of Canadian course material, as well as Canadian instructors, in the academic setting. Clarkson, an economic and cultural nationalist, would have been acutely aware and sensitive about this festering issue in the late sixties.

York University–based professor Howard Adelman, who was on the Praxis board back in those days, said in an interview that the name of the new research institute originated from a Marxist and Hegelian philosophical concept — "the combination of theory and political practice." An academic journal called *Praxis* already existed in Canada, Adelman recalled. "We were familiar with the term [as] as our main emphasis was on democracy in the workplace [and] democracy in the community" (Adelman 2011).

Praxis was set up in the same spirit of serious learning that underpinned the movements for alternatives in education in the public school system. The new institute was not formally affiliated with any post-secondary institution. Indeed, no formal courses were going to be taught nor any degrees granted, although it had accredited academics on staff. What was being offered instead was a comfortable environment for scholars. Graduate students, working scholars and serious-minded people off campus in the community would have the opportunity to work individually on research projects of their choice and engage with others intellectually (Praxis 1969).

Praxis at the end of 1968 was clear about its intention to work with like-minded professors, graduate students and non-academic thinkers and writers on multi-disciplinary research that mattered. The new research institute was conceived "as a laboratory for bringing people and ideas together from the wider community on both a short- and longer-term basis." Furthermore, its prospectus revealed plans to publish books and pamphlets, sponsor seminars and participate in television and radio programs on current social issues.

A precursor to political think-tanks that would later mushroom in Canada, Praxis began with an ambitious agenda to engage with the wider Toronto community. Among the immediate local issues that galvanized the organization's attention were contentious urban renewal projects that threatened to make mincemeat of older homes and buildings in downtown neighbourhoods — where working and poor people still lived. The way local decisions were being made at City Council became a prime issue. A catalyst for this debate was the proposed Spadina expressway, which threatened to carve through downtown residential areas like the Annex. The project was part of a series of expressways developed for the city and the surrounding suburban boroughs under a separate layer of municipal government, Metropolitan Toronto, by its transportation planners. The matter brought to the fore the reconciling of cars and people in the city. Stephen Clarkson envisioned Praxis offering research assistance to "some of the town planners and architects [who] are worried about the problems of [the] long-term evolution of the city environment" (1969).

Right from the start Praxis sought to be independent of the University of Toronto and at the same time not have an antagonist relationship with an institution where the core leadership of the new research institute still kept their day jobs. The other Praxis co-founder, Abraham Rotstein, put it this way in a 2010 interview: "It had a Canadian twist. We were regarded not as a militant protest movement but as a learning experience on a massive scale. So, the university came [on board] ... we assured them we wouldn't start breaking windows and marching on Queen's Park but that we were going to raise important issues among the public at large."

An older and greyer Clarkson informed me later that he was inspired as a young professor by a widely held belief in the late sixties that despite being next door to an America stuck in racism and militarism, Canada was still relatively untouched by all of this and had the potential to maintain itself as a liveable place. But it also appeared that Praxis was not sufficient to contain his ambitions in the late 1960s. In a typed note dated December 1968 and written on U of T Political Economy Department letterhead, he enthused about the Liberal Party's formal entry into Toronto municipal politics, where he expected to play a major role: "I left the Toronto Lawn and Tennis Club two weeks ago with a great hope. Not only did it seem possible for us in Toronto to work out what the future shape of our city should be. There also seemed to be a real chance that the embryonic municipal Liberal Party might become the right kind of political organization able to turn such a vision into reality."

One year later, after Praxis was already in operation, Clarkson ran and lost as the official Liberal candidate in a mayoralty bid in the city against sitting mayor William Dennison, a crusty and conservative New Democrat. Another high-profile city councillor, Margaret Campbell and a fellow Liberal, was in the race but not running on the party label. The problem was that Clarkson was the lesser known of the three, and this was his first time running for office, wrote *Toronto Daily Star* reporter Andrew Szende (whose name appears at one point on the Praxis board). It seems that local Liberals were not solidly behind their new bright light, following a divided leadership convention: "One of his worst headaches is the fact that he is being ignored by senior personnel in his party. So far, the federal organizers, canvassers and money raisers have been staying away in droves. Former finance minister Walter Gordon [a stalwart of the Liberals' left wing] is the only big-name person on Bay Street trying to raise money for the campaign" (Szende 1969: 26).

Clarkson, as a public intellectual, saw the mayoralty bid as a vehicle for discussing the serious urban issues of the day, but he found himself tripped up by his university pedigree. He told me that incumbent mayor Dennison kept referring to him as the "perfessor." Michael Enright, then a reporter for the *Globe and Mail*, provided a picture of a smartly attired Clarkson as the candidate for swinging or hip Toronto, which may have alienated more conservative (and less with-it) older Torontonians. "[Clarkson] manages to look younger than his 31 years. He likes three-inch sideburns and yesterday appeared in an expensive corduroy jacket" (Enright 1969a: 5).

Clarkson tried and failed to rework the political magic that had put his fellow Liberal and another intellectual, Pierre Trudeau, into power in the June 1968 federal contest. Dennison was decidedly old school in backing the proposed north-south Spadina expressway, which would stretch from the top of Toronto to the lake. The mayor was also nervous about the rhetoric surrounding citizen participation coming from the new urban reform movement and epitomized by the new politicians coming on stream — like John Sewell, a young lawyer and community organizer, who dressed in long hair and jeans and won in Ward 7 in the downtown east side in the 1969 election.

Clarkson was ahead of his time — he sided with the opponents of the Spadina expressway and endorsed citizen participation, which put him on the same wavelength as his colleagues at Praxis. His brand of progressive municipal reform bore fruit three years later in the 1972 election of David Crombie to the mayor's job, accompanied by a band of urban reformers, including Sewell, elected to Toronto City Council. (Dennison had decided to retire and not offer again.) Running on the partisan label had been a mistake for Clarkson. Hardly anybody, including Dennison himself, ran on their individual political affiliation locally, although the incumbent mayor did have the endorsement of the Labour Council as well as developers. The preferred practice for a person running in municipal elections was to offer themselves as independents.

Not all Liberals were enamoured with Clarkson's stand on the Spadina expressway, which hurt his candidacy. The Conservatives were also split on the matter. One of them was Crombie, who represented a downtown ward. He sided with the urban reformers in their opposition to the proposed road and stayed away from any party label when he ran in and won the 1972 mayoral race in a three-way contest. By then the expressway project had been effectively killed by Ontario's Red Tory premier, Bill Davis, who decided it was not worthwhile to alienate potential voters in the older Toronto neighbourhoods.

Praxis's Brown Bag Lunches

A variety of high-powered and fascinating people dropped by the early brown bag lunches at the U of T, which Clarkson sponsored in early 1969 to seek out advice on the direction Praxis should take. At the top of the list was urban writer and theorist Jane Jacobs. She had just arrived with family in tow from the US to avoid having her two young sons drafted into the American military, which had been sent to fight what many viewed as a futile and lengthy war against a communist and nationalist insurgency in what was then South Vietnam. Her intellectual guns were already ablaze, having established an international reputation with *The Death and Life of Great American Cities* (1961), which tore apart the conventional wisdom of the planning profession. "I hope you had a pleasant last 48 hours on the beach and [are] all vitaminized for the New Year. Things are moving quickly with Praxis Corp," Clarkson wrote in a short note to a friend that also appears in the Praxis minutes. "Jane Jacobs has joined our weekly meetings which have been a great inspiration and guarantee that theory does not stray too far from practice" (Clarkson 1969).

Jacobs would have been the most important find for the new research institute if she had stuck around. She was a woman intellectual working outside the university system in an organization entirely dominated by male academics. The urban thinker did participate in a few meetings and offered some tantalizing suggestions about the direction for Praxis. In a Praxis meeting on January 7, 1969, the minutes note that Jacobs proposed a study of a block or street in the city to build a deeper understanding of poverty from a human, social and economic perspective. It was described as a granular approach in profiling low-income residents' dealings with public services such as health, welfare and the law, which purportedly serve them but end up perpetuating their disadvantaged and unequal situation.

By the spring of 1969 Jacobs was slated to be one of three Praxis fellows in residence working on their respective projects. She had a book on "the city state" in the works. The other two hired experts had their separate research topics — Howard Buchbinder (poverty) and Gerry Hunnius (community and workplace participation). But Jacobs' involvement turned out to be short-lived. Eventually, she gravitated to the anti-Spadina expressway campaign, where Clarkson was also engaged. The urban thinker saw echoes in Toronto to what she had faced in New York City, opposing Robert Moses's nightmarish four-lane highway through Washington Square Park in Greenwich Village, where she and her family had lived.

Jacobs discovered that she and the people at Praxis held similar opinions on the Vietnam War. Clarkson and Jack Ludwig, a writer in residence at the U of T, took advantage of their contacts within the Liberal government to lobby for a more humane approach to helping Americans fleeing military service to come to Canada. Canadian border officials were deliberately turning back young men who had deserted from the US military because of their refusal to serve in the war. The Immigration Department in Ottawa had circulated an internal and secret memorandum that urged refusal, even though nothing existed in Canadian immigration law that justified barring people fleeing service in another country's army (Squires 2013: 84). Canada had said yes to Hungarians who were in a similar dilemma while escaping the invasion and crackdown by the Soviet Union in 1956. Arguments were made that this approach should also apply to Americans, especially since no contrary law was on the books.

Naomi Wall, a spokesperson for the Toronto Anti-Draft Program, told a spring Praxis lunch in 1969 that US deserters were having difficulty at the border getting secure landed immigrant status, a necessary ingredient to getting a job and supporting oneself in Canada. She noted that the issue was not receiving any kind of traction in the media, especially through the CBC, which seemed "wary" in covering the deserter issue. As a result, the Committee for a Fair Immigration Policy was formed. Ludwig represented the group when he travelled to speak to politicians in Ottawa. "Jack learned from these encounters that there was not Cabinet solidarity with the Minister's stand [on keeping out US army deserters] and that continued pressure might produce results," the Praxis minutes state.

Ludwig, a prolific Canadian fiction writer, was born and grew up in Winnipeg's Jewish north end but had lived most of his life in the US. During his year as writer in residence at Massey College (1968/69), he participated in early Praxis discussions. At the end of term, he returned to teach at the State University of New York at Stony Brook, but he kept his ties to Canada through sports journalism in *Saturday Night* magazine. Plus, there was the notoriety of a character in Saul Bellow's remarkable novel *Hertzog,* supposedly modelled on Ludwig (Levin 2018). Before his passing, Ludwig declined to discuss Praxis and his short time there with me. One insight into how he felt about his stay at the U of T comes from an entry in Clarkson's minutes where Ludwig complained of the short-comings of his campus residence: "Jack Ludwig reported that Massey College's unisexual academic life was 'depressing.'"

Another legacy of Praxis was the establishment of the Transitional Year Program (TYP) at the University of Toronto, which was designed to bypass the systemic economic and racial barriers facing specific groups, in the entry to post-secondary education. Among the first students in what had already been modelled in New York for high school dropouts were young people of African Canadian origin, says U of T political scientist Peter Russell and a former Praxis board member (2019).

One of six African Canadians taking full advantage of a summer pilot for the TYP was Elaine Maxwell, a divorced 33-year-old single mother living in Toronto's Regent Park housing project. She had taken one year in teachers' college back home in Nova Scotia but that was fourteen years previously. "The thought that I couldn't make it, that I would have to stay here frightens me," she told *Toronto Daily Star* reporter David Allen (1969b). Maxwell was receiving $249 a month from Ontario welfare but a $100 was taken back by the provincial housing branch. That left her with $149 a month for utilities, food and clothing for her and four growing children. Under the headline, "Project gives poor a hope of escape," Allen wrote that the TYP had been inspired by a determination that Toronto not venture down the US path by having a marginalized and racialized population living west of Bathurst and north of St. Clair, where many Caribbean immigrants were putting down new stakes.

One of the catalysts for this project was 23-year-old Jamaican-born York University political science student Horace Campbell. He had discussed the necessity for this kind of program with Jack Ludwig, philosopher and

Praxis board member Charles Hanly and Halifax-based activist Rocky Jones, according to the *Star* reporter. Campbell then met on June 1969 with the Praxis board members, including Hanly, all of whom were sitting on orange plastic chairs in a circle at their regular meeting on Huron Street. Classes for the pilot were underway a month later, according to the newspaper. What motivated Campbell was the reality of an insufficient number of Black professionals in Toronto offering inspiration and hope for younger members of his African Canadian community, who were stuck in a social and economic rut because of racism. Maxwell herself was admitted as a full-time student at the U of T, taking a variety of humanities courses and considering a career in social work "The project is only a small beginning," Charles Hanly told the *Star*.

The TYP went through some initial difficulties during the 1970s, which included accusations that it was dominated by Marxists (there was an activist focus initially in the instruction) but over the long haul it managed to weather all of the political storms that came its way. Today, the program functions with much less profile or fanfare. "The TYP was the most important initiative that was started by Praxis and continues until today," recalled Abraham Rotstein (2010). But the problems the TYP was aiming to solve were too big to be handled by a single university program, a point that the originators had conceded. Racial discrimination, segregation and bias in terms of schooling and employment opportunities in Toronto have actually deepened and gone suburban since then.

Also showing up in some of the early Praxis meetings was James Lorimer, a leading figure in Toronto's urban reform movement, a regular contributor to the *Globe and Mail* and an advocate of citizen participation. He pushed for a workshop for community workers to support the Toronto Community Union Project (TCUP), which was operating in the Trefann Court area in the downtown near Parliament. But while sympathetic with Lorimer's goals, Praxis had other irons in the fire (Clarkson 1969).

At some point a realistic appraisal was conducted to figure out what Praxis could accomplish with limited resources and finances. The original vision of a scholarly haven was simply too ambitious and had to be amended. Clarkson was clear in the minutes about what the research institute was all about. "In my view there is a great need for Praxis to develop into an institute where the most urgent social and political problems can be not just discussed but acted upon in an intellectual community that has roots both in the academic, professional, media and business worlds." Albeit a nice sentiment it was perhaps not sufficiently radical for the new hires at Praxis. After his appointment in June as the director of poverty research, Howard Buchbinder nailed down a tougher and clearer vision for Praxis: "The overall aim of Praxis was to promote ways of organizing more democratic control by communities and individuals. It was this view which led to a focus on anti-poverty organizations, specifically the Just Society Movement and the trade union movement in the area of industrial democracy." (2000). Buchbinder had just left a position as an assistant professor of social work at the Jesuit University in St. Louis. But it was his experience in community organizing as a veteran of the War on Poverty program in the US that had made him an attractive candidate for Praxis. Also onboard was a second academic, Gerry Hunnius, who had developed a reputation from his writing and research in workers' self-management experimentation in Yugoslavia and others forms of industrial democracy (Hunnius, Garson and Case 1973). Placements were still to be accepted from graduate students in social work at the U of T who would work under either of these two staff directors. (It would have been three if Jane Jacobs had stayed.) The kicker was that Buchbinder and Hunnius had to individually raise funds to pay themselves and their own staff and to support their various projects at Praxis. Every person in the new institute, from the two experts to the office workers each earned about $10,000 a year, said David Buchbinder, the son of Howard Buchbinder and Judith Weisman, when I interviewed him in 2011. He said the low salary created a lot of economic hardship for his parents in an already tense marriage; they eventually split up.

Stephen Clarkson was rueful about the long-term ramifications of this decision to be a more a more ambitious operation: "There were lots going on; we were going to change the world. In some respects [hiring Buchbinder and Hunnius] brought Praxis to an end because we insti-tutionalized [our activities] with two employees and when you have employees, then there are big financial demands. We had to have some substantial funding to make that possible, but then it wasn't permanent. Neither [man] bought money to Toronto. They had to start from scratch" (Clarkson 2011–12).

Once Buchbinder and Hunnius came onboard, Clarkson stepped back from the day-to day administration, giving free rein to the two new hires in setting direction for the institute. "Howard Buchbinder may have been the most ideological of the whole group. Now it's not clear what that term might mean. But he seemed to have the deepest convictions against the operations of the [political] establishment. Those were the ones that carried him through; he was really the one who was seemingly the most committed," Abraham Rotstein explained (2010).

Meet Howard Buchbinder

The New York City–born director of poverty at Praxis passed away in 2004 before I had a chance to interview him. So, all of the personal information about him comes from his first wife, Judith Weisman, and their sons David and Amnon Buchbinder. Howard Buchbinder served in the US army in Japan just as the conflict in World War II was ending, so he did not face serious combat. He also spent time living on *kibbutzim* in Israel with his wife, also born in the New York. (In later years he and Weisman broke with their earlier Zionist allegiances and developed a more pro-Palestinian stance.) The couple moved to St. Louis, where he spent five years at Washington University as the chief psychiatric social worker at its Child Guidance Centre and an instructor in psychiatric social work in the Division of Child Psychiatry. His involvement with President Johnson's War on Poverty came about in 1965, when he was hired as the neighbourhood coordinator and staff training specialist in the St. Louis Human Development Corporation (Weisman and Swift 2011; D. Buchbinder 2011). The latter turned out to be a disillusioning experience as Buchbinder was taken out of community organizing, which he loved, and moved into administration, which he disliked.

Following that, he spent three years (1966–69) as an assistance professor of social work at St. Louis University. There he developed and taught a course with a colleague, Jack Kirkland, on the then-controversial subject of the social causes of poverty. This was popular among the students but not with the conservative social work department. "We were the two most progressive professors in the faculty of social work," says Kirkland. "We wanted [students] to be involved with the community. Class was an issue. There were people in that department who said what we were doing was too avant-garde for [the university administrators]. We left St Louis at the same time. Howard was prominent at the university, highly visible. We were colleagues; he was a good person to work with" (2011). Both academics were denied tenure for their efforts. Kirkland managed to land his feet at another university; Buchbinder left for Canada.

Leaving America was not easy. Their son David recalls that Buchbinder and Weisman had shared active and fulfilling lives in St. Louis, both in their opposition to the US military intervention in Vietnam and their support for a local African American political organization, the Black Liberators. Similar to the Black Panthers in terms of a macho posture and the wearing of fatigues, they were in practice non-violent. The Liberators found themselves in a nasty confrontation with local police officers, who invaded their office and roughed up both their work space and the people inside. "It was not long before we left [the United States] when their office was broken into. The cops had smashed up everything in their office and beat the crap out of a couple of guys," says David Buchbinder. His parents held a press conference in the Buchbinder family home about what had transpired in the Liberators' office. "There was a literally a doctor showing what had been done to them."

It was not just the political social work course that put Buchbinder in the doghouse at St. Louis University. The administration also did not appreciate his off-campus public profile, which included speaking out against the Vietnam War, says Judith Weisman. "He was told in no uncertain terms if he did not stop speaking so publicly he would never get tenure." That threat was carried out. After his university contract ended in 1969, Buchbinder was hired at Praxis and he and his wife moved to Toronto (Weisman n.d.).

Gerry Hunnius and the Workers Control Project

Gerry Hunnius was a fellow at the Institute for Policy Studies in Washington and planning to return to Canada in 1969 when Praxis contacted him about his writing and research into workers' control. Before his involvement in this issue, Hunnius had devoted much of his time in the early sixties to the peace movement in Canada and the UK. In the early 1960s, for instance, he was the part-time executive director of the Canadian Committee for the Control of Radiation Hazards, which worked with various scientists and academics to lobby for an end to nuclear weapons testing by both the US and the Soviet Union (Hunnius 2011).

Hunnius was the polar opposite to what David Buchbinder describes as his father's reserved personality. "Gerry was really laid back in a lot of ways — displayed none of the mannerisms or styles of the sixties," says his wife Valerie Hunnius (2018–19). "He was a little older than some of the others in the movement with him. He dressed casually in slacks and open necked shirts and sweaters and scruffy shoes. When he was at York [University] a few years later, he was approached by students in the hallway asking him if he could replace a light bulb … I guess because his appearance suggested he might be on the janitorial staff. He kept his hair a comfortable length — a short style but not too short. No side burns. He definitely wasn't 'stylish.'"

One of Hunnius's workers' control sessions took place at the Westbury Hotel in downtown Toronto. Union activists and some prominent NDP politicians happened to be in the audience. Ed Broadbent, the future NDP leader, was there because of his strong interest in the subject but he preferred to use the term "industrial democracy." John Lang, now a veteran union activist and leader, was there and remembers challenging this reluctance to say "workers' control" out loud: "I said to Ed in no uncertain terms, look we're not politicians. You call a spade a spade. We wanted change. We are looking for a change in the workplace" (2018).

Hunnius was diplomatic during the proceedings, not tipping his hand in either direction during this exchange, says Lang, who later headed the Confederation of Canadian Unions. "It was always hard to read Gerry. He didn't react negatively to that [exchange]. To be fair … Gerry wasn't the type of guy who walked into the room and sort of becomes the centre of attention … he was kind of a low-key academic guy."

Providing an interesting perspective on Ed Broadbent and industrial democracy is pollster Marc Zwelling, who back in the sixties worked as a reporter covering labour for the *Toronto Telegram*. Broadbent made a strong pitch for industrial democracy in his first failed stab at federal NDP leadership in 1971. During that time, the politician wrote a book on industrial democracy. But Broadbent left the issue behind in the accession to the federal NDP leadership in 1974, says Zwelling, "because no one was interested" in the labour movement. Simply put, union leaders opposed industrial democracy because they thought it would put them out of business and business people only wanted to consult their workers when they were in financial trouble and needed a bailout" (2018/19).

"Broadly accurate," is how the long retired former politician responds to the account provided by Marc Zewelling. "I was in part an idealistic and naive new politician and new to the labour movement. I discovered that what was of interest to me, and made sense conceptually from the point of view of social democracy, was really going against the grain of the tradition of the Canadian labour movement," explained Ed Broadbent in an interview. He argues that unions in countries with a stronger social democratic tradition, such as Sweden and Germany, have been willing to experiment with the notion of greater democracy in the workplace, including representation on company boards. But he adds that the concept is probably more relevant today and might be a way to help revive and rebuild the labour movement (Broadbent 2019).

Hunnius had the unfortunate fate of bad timing. The period of militancy among younger, largely male, factory workers was extensive in the middle 1960s, but it had petered out by the time he arrived on the scene and began organizing conferences and smaller sessions with invited guests in his home on workers' control. In the mid-1960s these young workers, like their generational counterparts in the university, were caught up in a desire for greater personal freedom and autonomy and also were affected by the youth counter-culture, says University of Waterloo historian Ian Milligan, the author of the 2014 book *Rebel Youth: 1960's Labour Unrest, Young Workers and New Leftists in English Canada.* This was expressed in the number of wildcat strikes that took place in Canadian factories between 1964 and 1966 in defiance of both management and labour leadership, neither of which wanted to upset what had already been negotiated between the two sides in collective agreements. Strikes were illegal if they were staged outside the allowable times set out in provincial industrial legislation, but that did not matter for rebellious young men working long hours in what Milligan describes as tedious and dangerous working conditions, while raising families on low budgets and coping with intrusive management and company town policies.

The historian found that it was a challenge to find much information about these wildcats from the labour archives because of the legal ramifications. These illegal actions were staged almost spontaneously over long-standing grievances but with no spokesperson around to speak to the media. Unions, with some notable exceptions, had become bureaucratic and conservative following the labour struggles for recognition from politicians and employers after World War II, which resulted in the Rand formula, which required a trade-off where unions derived their revenues from automatic dues deducted from workers' wages. This created a distance between union locals and the people they were elected to serve on the shop floor.

So, while these young workers did not call for industrial democracy per se they might have been receptive to someone like Gerry Hunnius if he had been around, says Milligan, who had not heard of this Praxis director before I contacted him (2018). Milligan estimates that between 1965 and 1966 there were 575 strikes, and somewhere between 20 and 50 percent were wildcats. Not all can be traced to young workers, primarily male at the time. At the Chrysler plant in Windsor, for instance, there were 55 wildcats in 1966 stemming from unrest among low seniority workers on the engine line. The author quotes the director of the United Auto Workers, George Burt, denouncing these illegal actions as "denial of our democratic procedures" undertaken by "hotheads" (Milligan 2014: 45–46).

Similar wildcats in the mid-1960s occurred within union locals represented by the United Steelworkers at the Hilton Works steel plant in Hamilton, the Inco nickel mine in Sudbury and among railway workers who were members of the Canadian Brotherhood of Railway, Transport and General Workers Union. The *Globe and Mail* editorialized that union leaders had to exercise greater control over these undisciplined young workers (44). If Hunnius had been around during these wildcats strikes an effort on his part to communicate directly with these alienated younger workers would have been strongly opposed by the same union leadership from whom he was seeking to raise funds for the Praxis operation and research.

There was some scepticism within Praxis about what Hunnius was trying to achieve. Laurel Ritchie, who worked at the institute near the end of its operation and later became a veteran unionist and women's movement activist, commented that Hunnius took an approach that was perhaps too theoretical for workers (2012). Where Hunnius had the most receptive audience was in Saskatchewan, under the 1971–82 NDP government of Allan Blakeney. The former Praxis co-director was in regular contact as an advisor during this period, with Robert Sass, then associate deputy minister in charge of industrial relations inside the provincial department of labour. This encounter turned into a rich and fruitful intellectual relationship for Sass, who says he was probably more radical than the social democratic government — comprising an unwieldy alliance of farmers and city industrial workers — that he was trying to serve. The former government bureaucrat remembers sitting in an office with Premier Allan Blakeney, who cautioned that he was not presiding over a purely "labour government" (2018).

At the same time Hunnius was smarting from an inability to secure a firm footing for his ideas of worker participation in the Canadian trade union movement. So, the two mavericks, Sass and Hunnius, found common ground. Sass had a background in militant New York City–based unionism and in his eighties still speaks in an accent thick as molasses and bears a reputation for innovation in the field of industrial relations. Sass was responsible for the setting up of a regulatory regime during the 1970s in Saskatchewan that emphasized the right of workers or employees to be informed about dangers in their work environment, the right to participate in the daily detection, evaluation and reduction of workplace hazards and the right to refuse to work in dangerous conditions.

Joint occupational health and safety committees became the by-product in provincial workplaces, but Sass and others in the NDP government sought to travel down a more radical path by introducing the concept of industrial democracy into the Potash Corporation of Saskatchewan, then a Crown corporation. This was accomplished through setting up the Work Environment Board (WEB), where six workers and six management representatives met outside the collective bargaining process. There was also a smaller executive committee comprising three union representatives, the president of the Crown corporation's mining division, an engineer and a mine manager. Behind this effort was the assumption that industrial relations should be different in the new Crown corporation, which was engaged in the mining of the potash resource in the province in four separate locations and experienced what was called an unacceptable level of industrial accidents.

In the beginning the atmosphere in the WEB was harmonious, with mutually agreed decisions to investigate the occupational health and safety concerns of the workers. Management in the Crown corporation was not averse to the WEB, but this changed as broader issues, such as technology, production methods, types of supervision, the organization of work and increased worker participation, were put on agenda — thus challenging traditional management prerogatives and the corporate model. These new ideas would have meant a withdrawal from an authoritarian relationship in the workplace (Sass 1997).

Hunnius, by then at York University teaching in the social sciences, was brought in to solve the fractious divisions at the WEB inside Potash Corporation and deepen the worker role by interviewing managers, workers and union officials. A September 20, 1982, report was submitted to the WEB after the NDP government had been defeated in a provincial election and a less sympathetic Conservative premier and majority government came to power in Saskatchewan — and so it was ignored. The Crown corporation had also then decided to stop participating in the WEB (Sass 1997).

One of the innovative aspects of the WEB was the introduction of a fund to support research into industrial hazards and working conditions at the Potash Corporation by experts with a more worker-friendly perspective than what might be available from the major academic contributors to this field. The experiment had sufficient buy-in for union members at the Potash Corporation that they considered taking legal action against the Crown corporation for the termination of the WEB agreement. But this did not come to pass after the change in the provincial government, the appointment of a new president at the Potash Corporation by the Conservatives and a downturn in the potash market. The WEB concept was never revived in subsequent NDP provincial governments.

Workers' control, or industrial democracy, was a serious political response to the still existing inequalities and limitations of the postwar work environment, despite the greater presence of unions and full-time jobs. The concept was a phenomenon of a time before employers had access to technology to fully automate job functions in manufacturing and in white collar office jobs and thereby further downgrade the scope of worker involvement in an operation.

Chapter Five

Other Poverty Initiatives

The Poverty Project

The *Toronto Daily Star* indicated a willingness to provide financial assistance for poverty research, support that was especially gratifying for Praxis. The newspaper has been governed since its inception by a social justice mandate, established by its founder, Joseph Atkinson. It helped that Rotstein, Clarkson and *Star* publisher Beland Honderich shared similar views on the importance of Canadian economic and cultural independence in the face of US domination. Rotstein was also at the time providing training sessions in basic economics for some of the *Star* reporters: "My job was to make them more conversant with economic issues. And what the economics was behind current issues. [We] had some debates; [I] tried to explain how the balance of payments works and some other things. I taught courses only for two or possibly three years" (Rotstein 2010).

In a memo to Praxis board members, Clarkson described a February18, 1969, meeting that he and another board member, University of Toronto professor Meyer Brownstone, had with the *Star* publisher. "Mr. Honderich agreed in principle to the poverty project proposal we presented to him … Today, Meyer and I worked out the details of a working agreement between the *Star* and Praxis for the project publication rights: independence; consultation, mutual veto. We will have this in writing by the end of the week. So [we] should spend next Tuesday lunch going over the individual items in the agreement for our approval. As this is our first contract it will be important to think through possible implications. Please come if at all feasible. For competitive reasons the *Star* wants to keep this project kept as confidential as possible" (Clarkson 1969).

The *Star* donation totalled $35,000, which was a considerable sum in those days, but Clarkson somewhat optimistically was already envisioning further fundraising to make Praxis a sustainable operation. The Praxis minutes note: "With untied revenue of $100,000 per year we would be free to engage in radical and innovative projects not requiring prior approval from the traditional funding bodies. In my view it is crucial that we generate commitments for such continuing funds this spring so that our first year will be significant."

In the end Praxis's relationship with the newspaper lasted a mere six months. Honderich quickly became frustrated that Praxis was not able to produce a steady supply of solid news stories about poverty. One note handwritten by Clarkson at the time illustrates a breakdown in communications between the newspaper and research institute: "Left in a fog by the *Star*."

Gerry Hunnius suggests that it all came down to different approaches to poverty. "What the *Toronto Daily Star* wanted was not stuff about policy but the sort of stuff that is good for publishing in a newspaper, personal stories of people in poverty, that sort of thing. We were looking at it politically — what are the causes of poverty?" (Hunnius 2011).

The publisher alone made the final determination to quit the deal with Praxis in what Howard Buchbinder described as a "brief and one-sided meeting," observing that neither the editor, Marty Goodman, nor poverty-beat reporter, David Allen, had been informed ahead of time of their boss's intentions. "Honderich did all of the talking as Goodman sat silently. The publisher announced that the arrangement was not working. Honderich did not wish to have the original $35,000 grant returned but he did want to terminate the relationship with Praxis. No discussion was invited and Honderich quietly left the room after his announcement" (Buchbinder 2000).

As all of the major people in this story (Goodman, Allen, Honderich and Buchbinder) have passed away, it is difficult to learn any new insights on the *Star*'s internal decision-making at the time. Honderich's son John, now on the board of the *Toronto Daily Star*, had no comments about his father's actions. And before passing away, Buchbinder suggested that Praxis's political profile might have made the publisher uncomfortable. "Later, it became apparent that these media and government connections would create too much conflict for the *Star*." Beland Honderich was described at the time as a domineering and controlling publisher at the *Star*. However, the Praxis affair did not end the *Star*'s interest in poverty.

David Allen continued to write about the subject for the newspaper, at least until Senator David Croll came out with his report in 1971.

Changing the Social Planning Council

Wilson Head, a transplanted American with a PhD in sociology, was on track to becoming the new executive director of the Social Planning Council (SPC) of Metropolitan Toronto, as well as the first person of colour in that job. It was 1968 and the 54-year-old man went on a summer vacation to Europe, where he witnessed the unfolding of student idealism and protest on campuses and in the streets. Unrest flowed across the continent and put France off balance after an alliance with unions almost succeeded in overthrowing the government of Charles De Gaulle while the president was out of the country (McGrath 1998: 89–90).

Upon returning home Head was sufficiently inspired by the events overseas to compose a detailed seven-page memo, dated September 23. He argued that the Metro Toronto Social Planning Council had to stop "propping up a destructive welfare system," and instead perform more of an advocacy role focused on the social and economic conditions leading to inequality. Labelled "For staff discussion only" this treatise was presented at a Saturday workshop for the council. The memo read: "There is evidence that the welfare system has frequently contributed to the demoralization, disillusionment and alienation of the welfare recipients by the manner it often subjects clients to — a denial of civil rights, humiliation and invasion of privacy" (Head 1968).

But on Monday morning his pointed comments were met with hostility, and Head was labelled a "communist" by the Social Planning Council board, a pejorative typically directed at any advocate for social change in the Cold War atmosphere of the time. He did not get the top job at the council and instead eventually landed at Ryerson University, where he taught in the School of Social Work and headed up the department (McGrath 1998: 89–90).

All of this came about as a result of conflict with the business executives who ran both the Social Planning Council and its parent body, the United Community Fund (UCF, precursor of the United Way), the latter responsible for the annual fundraising to support the voluntary charitable social agency sector. This was a small, powerful crowd that had a stake in maintaining the charity model of assisting the poor where a large amount of the assistance came from donors in the community. They were not comfortable with the new model emerging in the sixties of generous government programs funded by the taxpayers.

Both the Social Planning Council and its preceding organization, the Toronto Welfare Council, were opposed to studying the socio-economic origins of poverty, says Susan McGrath, a York University social work professor who did her 1998 PhD thesis on the history of the Social Planning Council. Apparently, Wilson Head was not the first person to face this kind of backlash. In 1943 Bessie Touzell, the executive secretary of the Toronto Welfare Council, quit her position after the Board of Trade criticized as extravagant a proposed increase in food allowances to meet the requirements of nutritious diet of recipients for assistance. She and others around her were also accused of communist sympathies (52–55).

At its founding in 1957 the board of the Social Planning Council was dominated by senior business executives from the insurance and the financial sectors, including the president, Wallace McCutcheon, who viewed himself as more enlightened on the subject of social policy than his colleagues on Bay Street. There were strong interlocking ties between the corporate establishment and the non-profit social agencies. What they shared was opposition to a state-run health insurance plan even as it was getting off the ground in Saskatchewan. These business owners made their reputations as self-proclaimed good corporate citizens by their engagement in the social services, says McGrath (65–66).

Cate Pritchard, the author of an unpublished paper, "Private Fundraising, Expertise and Welfare Rights: Radical Social Workers Confront the United Community Fund of Greater Toronto" (2012), says the Social Planning Council between 1969 and 1971 received about 80 percent of its funding from the business-dominated United Community Fund — which consolidated all of the fundraising drives of the city's charitable agencies (Pritchard n.d.). The Social Planning Council assisted the United Community Fund in allocating funds to the member charitable agencies by conducting reviews of their annual programs. Council staff also did research on the social issues and maintained an index of social services in the city.

With the new developments in the statistical measurements of poverty, the business stranglehold on social planning would prove to be untenable. It looked like the Metro Toronto Social Planning Council was stuck in a time warp unwilling to change with the times. That made it an appealing target for Howard Buchbinder, who in an alliance with the Just Society Movement began recruiting activists to run for the council's board in the 1970 annual general meeting. But it was not enough for him to open up the Social Planning Council to progressive social workers. Although trained in social work and still teaching the subject part-time at McMaster University in Hamilton, he had little use for his own profession, which he saw as focusing too much on troubled clients' individual pathologies. He felt there was not enough emphasis on taking into account looming social factors, such as the stress of not having enough money to support one's family. In Toronto, Buchbinder hoped that a new campaign could break down the economic, political and social barriers that perpetuate poverty and social injustice.

In an article he wrote about the Just Society Movement after this was all over, Buchbinder explained that his short-term demands included 50 percent representation of people living in poverty on the Ontario Welfare Council, the Social Planning Council and other boards in the public and private welfare sector, a $3 minimum wage (which would have been significant at this time), immediate higher welfare benefits and a comprehensive daycare system. "The political, economic and social structures within which we live are not responsive to people. Rather, these structures perpetuate poverty and injustice at all levels," he noted (1979).

The potential for change at the council board of directors was already apparent before Buchbinder's arrival in Toronto. In February 1969 during its annual general meeting, one of the veteran board members and a U of T professor in industrial relations, John Crispo, gave up his seat in order that Just Society Movement member Suzanne Polgar could take his place. It was viewed as a first step to expanding the council's engagement with poor people directly. "The 32 men and 13 women who sit on the Social Planning Council of Metro Toronto represent the cream of Toronto's voluntary welfare establishment. Yet, they have built their council reputations on a system that Wilson Head says has failed to make a significant impact on the most glaring social ills of society," wrote *Globe and Mail* reporter Loren Lind in the spring of 1969, in one of a series of articles on the council. He also quoted Head as saying that board membership should not be based on an individual's business ability, their philanthropic prowess and their status in the voluntary welfare establishment. The former acting executive director also wanted the Social Planning Council staff to have a greater say and voting power on key board committees (Lind 1969b: 5). In response in the same article, comments by one of the board members, Stephen Berger, an executive with Amcan Holdings Ltd., demonstrated a long-standing suspicion of social workers and social researchers in the voluntary social establishment. The council staff members, he argued, were too close to their jobs and suffered from what he called "professional deformation," which could only be corrected by "a non-professional board," dominated by people like himself.

Lind provided a picture of a council board impervious to change or reform in 1969. But Howard Buchbinder was not deterred. His organizing had recruited nearly 700 people, some with connections to the Just Society Movement, to show up for the annual general meeting of the council to elect directors to its board. Among the new breed of activists seeking positions on the board were Bruce Kidd, a well-known professional track and field athlete and a professor at the University of Toronto; and City of Toronto reform alderman Karl Jaffrey. Their appearance shocked one long-time board member, East York mayor True Davidson, famous for wearing large hats at Metro Toronto Council meetings. She, like William Dennison, had CCF-NDP roots and was similarly uncomfortable with the social transformation of the 1960s. The politician refused to put up her name for re-election, describing the arrival of the activists as "the slaughter of the innocents," writes Kevin Brushett, in his unpublished paper "Reaching Out and Biting Back: Grassroots Activism and Toronto's Social Service Community, 1960–1975," which is an early history of the Metro Toronto Social Planning Council (2003). Davidson was also quoted in the *Globe and Mail* as warning about an orchestrated takeover by "extreme left-wingers" (Enright 1970b: 15).

The initial public meeting in March 1970 had to be adjourned and rescheduled after a revelation that the ballots had been numbered and the names of the nominees favoured by the nomination committee marked by asterisks, continues Brushett in his account. Thirteen of the activists managed to get elected when the council reconvened for a second general meeting in May 1970. But the conservative side representing the United Community Fund still managed in a complex process to strengthen its presence on both the board and the executive committee. On the latter, only two reformers were able to get a foothold, Bruce Kidd and David Cowley.

A University of Toronto social work professor, Cowley had an expertise in community-based social work, and so he and the reformers, with the support of the staff, attempted to convince the Social Planning Council to abandon its professed elitism and turn itself into something more grassroots in order to regain its legitimacy. In response, the United Community Fund threatened to stop financing the council if this proposal was passed. The business-backed funders also commissioned a report indicating that it would be business as usual in social planning, taking a direct aim at the Just Society Movement. "It is of course not appropriate for the Social Planning Council to engage in any action which is illegal or politically partisan or which may seriously or permanently alienate large segments of the community as a whole or those bodies which are responsible for and empowered to bring about effective and necessary charge." So, the status quo of the consultative role of the Social Planning Council with the regards to the UCF would remain (Brushett 2003).

Buchbinder's reputed organizing prowess was called into question by Leonard Shifrin at the National Council of Welfare. In an interview many decades later, Shifrin indicated that Buchbinder had botched the 1970 annual general meeting for the Social Planning Council board. In his view Buchbinder naïvely relied on the intense media coverage of the proceedings, especially by the *Globe and Mail,* to attract a horde of sympathetic pro-activist supporters out to the meeting and make a significant stab at reducing United Community Fund influence. The Praxis director had underestimated the widespread conservatism in Toronto. The negative publicity surrounding the tactics and statements of the pro–United Community Fund side in the first vote should have in theory benefitted the activists. But that is not what happened.

Indeed, Shifrin discovered to his amazement that Buchbinder was not following the lessons of other professional organizers in using car pooling for instance to ensure that those on the activist side actually made it to the meeting. The conservative side, backing the United Community Fund, saw an existential challenge in the making and managed to organize a larger turnout of its supporters, which sped its side to victory. "Oh, lots of people showed up, overwhelmingly on the side of the institutionalists. They sold new memberships; they did all of the things, the old boys' network, as far as they were concerned, this was a great challenge, to their God knows what" (Shifrin 2011–13).

One might speculate that Buchbinder was simply overconfident that there were enough people in Toronto who cared enough about the Social Planning Council that they were willing to spend the evening at a raucous and lively general members meeting. Following the mixed success of the 1970 AGM, Buchbinder and his activists ruminated in their meetings on their challenges in the weeks before the next annual meeting of the Social Planning Council, in April 1971. It is evident that the Security Service had infiltrated these strategy sessions. There is a conspiratorial tone in the observations by the unidentified Mountie. "[Buchbinder and his colleagues] reviewed what had happened [in 1970] and it soon became evident that they were very disappointed in what had been accomplished in the way of control of the SPC or in hindering its work. They made clear that their goal is to control the SPC and make it responsive to their plans for radical action to bring about structural changes in government which seemed to be a polite way of saying: overthrowing the existing government" (RCMP Security Service 1971a).

A second RCMP Security Service memo by an unnamed officer described Buchbinder as positive about the prospect for change despite the doom and gloom among the activists at the same or a separate gathering. "The mood of the meeting was far from confident. They seem to feel they might have been outsmarted but Buchbinder and a few of his friends were still very determined. They felt that their image of extremism had worked against them." Also, during the course of the meeting, "Buchbinder spoke with confidence of further funding by government for his organization, Praxis" (RCMP Security Service 1971b).

The United Community Fund's move to consolidate its hold on the Social Planning Council in the April 1971 annual general meeting confirmed what the activists had feared was a disturbing trend. A record ninety-six nominees showed up to fill forty-five positions on the Social Planning Council board. United Community Fund directors past and present as well as representatives of the social agencies in Toronto also made their appearance as candidates. This served to further undercut the activists. After the dustup the only activist reformers who ended up elected were Kidd, Jaffrey and Cowley — all three of whom were nominally supported by the United Community Fund (Brushett 2003). Polgar and other members of the Just Society Movement had declined to run again. One new element that would radically alter the orientation of the council was the appearance of labour union representation on the board, which in the long term would side with expanding the scope of social research on poverty.

Cate Pritchard writes that the purpose of the challenge to the Social Planning Council in the original 1970 board elections, which was to expand the presence of the poor and those reliant on the social agencies, had been hijacked by social work professionals, students and professors, who ended up dominating the nominees from the activist side. She argued that Buchbinder, who was seeking fundamental political change, had difficulty reconciling his beliefs with his professional social work orientation. The problem with Pritchard's thesis is that not everyone in the Just Society Movement shared the position that the Social Planning Council represented a priority for their poor people's organization or that there was much value in filling up its board with more of its members (Pritchard n.d.).

Suzanne Polgar quit the council board after one term and vowed not to serve again, stating that her experience as the resident expert on poverty had been an utter waste of her time. She indicated in a spring 1970 statement that the lives of poor people would not be improved by having one or ten people on the board of the SPC: "Those who are members of the Board are far removed from the social issues that are relevant today. For example, poverty is something they are able to see only in terms of statistics and reports — not a reality to live with daily." She had hoped to alter these perceptions with her involvement but that proved to be fruitless: "I soon realized that I not only had no power to influence decisions but that it would not matter." Finally, "real change implies real power and that means the corporate and professional elite must not retain a monopoly of power." Here, Polgar was talking about the more difficult issue of social inequality (Morris 1971: 28).

After the disappointing 1971 election results, the general membership of the Social Planning Council slipped from 2,500 in 1970 to 150 in 1972. There was also considerable staff turnover. "You just had to look at all the people who showed up at that annual meeting two years ago — the young, old hippies, the handicapped, the poor and ethnic groups to know that one time, people in the city were interested in what the council was doing. It was a rare opportunity to get these people around one table for the first time, but the council panicked," a staff member told the *Toronto Daily Star* (Wainman 1972: 8).

The results of the 1970 and 1971 Social Planning Council elections proved to be a pyrrhic victory for the United Community Fund. Wilson Head's successor in the executive director's job, John Frei, tried initially to please the UCF. But at the same time he quietly hired Marvyn Novick to negotiate new relationships with the same community groups that had just been rejected (Novick 2013).

Historian Kevin Brushett makes the argument in "Reaching Out and Biting Back" that the Social Planning Council would have liberalized its research regardless of what happening in the early seventies board elections. He points to the appearance of social and community workers in the social agency sector making their own stab at community organizing during the 1960s and early seventies. This was confirmed by Novick himself, who in later years served as the dean of Social Work at Ryerson University. A Montreal-born work social worker, he received his post-secondary education at the University of Ann Arbour, in Michigan, where there was heavy emphasis on social work and community organizing among the welfare poor. "My first exposure to the dynamics of poverty took place in Detroit. I was placed in the Grace Episcopal Church … to do community work [part of a placement]. I was to organize a community corporation to preserve a neighbourhood. They burned it down that summer, and the community corporation rebuilt the neighbourhood. So, I came from activism in the States, my activism started in Ann Arbor. I became active in what was called Social Welfare Worker Movement, [worked] with students, with unions, and academics, and supported the work of people on social assistance in organizing and sit-ins."

Novick was living and active in the US when he met up with Buchbinder before the latter moved to Toronto. "I knew Howard from work that we were doing, in '66, '67 and '68. We did a number of actions. Howard was part of that, and then I went off to Baltimore, and got a job in the inner city of Baltimore." Here he worked linking Black community workers with white community workers and forming teams to work on various local issues including housing. All this ended when the program's funding was cut after Richard Nixon was elected US president in 1968. So, Novick came to Toronto and got a job in 1970 with the Metro Toronto Social Planning Council.

So, it was all very awkward that Novick started working with a social planning board run by John Frei, who was opposed officially to activists like his old buddy Howard Buchbinder trying to alter the organization at the top. Yet it turned out that Frei had intended to make significant quiet changes in hiring Novick that complemented what Praxis was trying to achieve, but was not obvious at the time. Novick had worked for Frei previously in Montreal and the two hit it off.

In his new job Novick was essentially "parked" in community organizing work at the Central Neighbourhood House, where, under Wilson Head's direction, he was busy building coalitions among residents opposing the disruption caused by city-inspired urban renewal until Frei "had figured out a way to surface me and make me public" amidst the turmoil on the Social Planning Council board instigated by his friend Buchbinder. He says he quietly supported the challenge that Praxis was making to the board: "Their action was to really deal with corporate charity, to define the agencies in the United Way as social control agencies, engaging in deceptive benevolence, good works as a substitute for social justice."

He describes Praxis as a kind of interconnecting tissue for a host of movements in Toronto that pulled together urban reformers with poverty radicalism and the Social Planning Council. "It was a place where the people in urban reform could pursue the social side of the reform agenda." What was his interpretation of his boss John Frei? "He was one of these European progressives who had survived World War II ... probably had to work under fascism ... was a refugee in Paris, where he did work for Peugeot Motorcycles, so he was able to live in a world of polarized relationships, and find a way to create space to do what he thought was important."

What cemented the dynamic for change at the Social Planning Council was the growing involvement of the labour movement, which had linked up with urban reform. Also, the availability of alternative funding in federal government programs such as Opportunities for Youth (OFY) and Local Initiatives Program (LIP) made it hard for the United Community Fund to exercise the same kind of veto over the Social Planning Council as it had in the past. In January 1972, Novick relied on LIP funds to open up the council's storefront on the Danforth in Toronto's east end to build new partnerships with community groups, the very strategy that had been rejected by the UCF two years earlier. Activities included assisting local groups to apply for OFY and LIP money as well as offer expertise. "That allowed us to do a lot of work, organizing injured workers, support and development of grassroots organizations," Novick says.

Eventually, both Metro Toronto and the Ontario government started to support new agencies, which included childcare facilities and seniors and community health centres. That was how community-based services got established across Canada, followed by a buy-in from the public to maintain them, explained Novick. Afterward, Novick continued to be profoundly active on the anti-poverty front. In our conversation at a small Italian café on College Street in Toronto he expressed a discomfort with the politics of polarization that was redolent of sixties activists such as Jane Jacobs and John Sewell. He did not add Howard Buchbinder to the list, perhaps out of respect for his friend.

The now retired professor discussed the Canadian tradition of a strong civic culture that allowed for the building of broad alliances to achieve social goals across party lines. He cited the growth of public services under Premier Bill Davis in Ontario. Since Novick passed away in 2016, it is apparent that Red Toryism no longer exists in the face of the new right-wing and radical conservative politics in Canada of Doug Ford, Andrew Sheer and Jason Kenney. In retrospect, Novick lost sight of the resiliency of corporate inspired neoliberalism.

Here one must return what happened to the corporate executives who sought after World War II to influence social policy through bodies like the UCF, the Social Planning Council and the voluntary social agencies. Susan McGrath, in her PhD thesis detailing the history of the Social Planning Council, writes that the corporate sector had sought to influence Canadian welfare through its control of the voluntary social agencies, via bodies such as the UCF and the Social Planning Council. But this was starting to wane in the late sixties as decisions regarding new social spending were being made by elected politicians at the federal, provincial and municipal levels. At the same time there were successful pressures by the advocates of greater citizen participation in social services. This would prove to be a temporary development.

As the 1970s progressed, new business-backed organizations like the Business Council on National Issues, the C.D. Howe Institute and the Fraser Institute sought to regain their hold on social policy (which they viewed as out of control in Ottawa) through a new form of advocacy at the national and governmental levels that successfully lobbied for all of the ingredients of a neoliberal society, including reduced social programs etc., which also coincided with the federal Liberals' backtracking on Pearson's welfare state (McGrath 1998: 139).

The Just Society Movement

In the late sixties the women's rights and welfare rights movements started to converge. All of those barriers facing young women in terms of childcare, the job market, social expectations and discrimination on the basis of gender were starting to come to the fore. Eligibility rules in the arcane provincial Ontario welfare systems were for instance starting to loosen for women whose husbands had left them. By the second half of the 1960s the number of families led by women living on family benefits had doubled, from a little over 10,000 to slightly above 20,000, according to James Struthers, whose book *Limits to Affluence* provides a lot of interesting data from that time period. Single mothers with their kids on either family benefits or general welfare represented a third of the province's entire welfare caseload by 1973 and over half the total increase in the numbers collecting social assistance (Struthers 1994: 242).

And yet the provincial government in Ontario by 1964 was spending less on daycare than it had twenty years earlier, therefore forcing mothers to go on welfare as the only option. There were some increases in municipal daycare spaces over the next six years due to federal funding, but it was hard for Ontario's welfare system to keep up with the growing number of children in families on welfare, now exceeding 100,000 each month, as the sixties progressed, noted the author of *Limits of Affluence*. Furthermore, there were 95,000 single mothers working full-time and not on assistance (Struthers 1994: 243). (Welfare comes in various forms and under different program names, such as mother's allowance, family benefits and currently social assistance.)

The contradiction between the original intention of the CAP (which was to liberalize and standardize social assistance delivery across Canada) and the arbitrary implementation at the provincial and municipal levels of these programs set the stage for a rights-based anti-poverty movement discourse involving women, says Queens University professor Margaret Little. She wrote in a *Labour/Le Travail* article that the first recorded protest by single mothers in Ontario on public assistance happened in November 1966 (the same year that CAP was implemented). The protest came in the form of a letter-writing campaign by fifty Sarnia women in November 1966 to Prime Minister Lester Pearson. They complained about hardship living on mothers' allowance in the face of the high cost of living in their city. It is not clear what Pearson's response was, but the complaints about welfare and their low rates continued (Little 2007: 183).

The Just Society Movement got started following a conversation between Doris Power and another mother on social assistance, Suzanne Polgar. The two women ruminated over their lives, their lack of money, their immediate needs and what could and should be done. They met for the first time during the summer of 1968 at a church camp for welfare families just outside Toronto. Power had a deep devotion to God as a Pentecostal and so the church camp attitudes were a bit of a shock: "They did not even consider [our] adult souls worth redeeming. Charity was meted out to us for prayers by people who appeared to have a bad smell up their noses if they had actually spoken to us" (Power 2018).

Polgar was described by reporter Lou Lee in the *Globe and Mail* as a "dark, gaunt intense young woman who vacillates between bitterness against a system and fervour to change it." She grew up moderately well off with four brothers and sisters on an Alberta farm. After graduating from high school Polgar married a man of a "higher social status" from Europe who had difficulty finding a job in Canada due to a lack of English and demonstrable skills. Polger worked a series of low paying clerical jobs while trying to support her children. She told the reporter of the grinding minutiae of her everyday life, spending all day with her small children, shopping for supermarket specials and not having enough money to buy clothes for herself and her family. There was also an understanding of what we call today the social determinants of health. "That's why the poor get mentally ill; there is a crisis every day." She expressed a desire for something more from life, puncturing another stereotype of the welfare recipients as having no personal ambition. At the same time, this woman was able to stand back and examine her situation in political terms: "People are not poor because of a defect in themselves but because of a defect in society. People who are in power are not going to give up that power. There has to be a redistribution of both income and power" (Lee 1969: W1).

Doris Power initially had to be convinced by Polgar that there was something of value in setting up a new poor people's organization in Toronto. But once Power climbed aboard, she became a major figure in the anti-poverty movement in Canada. The Just Society Movement co-founder made much of the fact that the organization had been started initially by women, with men joining later, without the assistance of a professional organizer or money from the federal government, unlike many other anti-poverty groups. Nevertheless, the founders had no previous experience in pulling together a new movement of poor people, and so they had to accept strategic advice and meeting space first from the United Church and then Praxis. There was no formal leadership, which was a common feature of some groups especially in the women's movement, and so to fill the vacuum decisions were made ad hoc by the most active. "A lot of decisions were made [informally] at my kitchen table in Ontario Housing around the corner," Doris Power stated (2018).

At some point Praxis staffers like Howard Buchbinder played a role to ensure that the Just Society Movement, after a burst of energy and activity, would not fall apart. Although its members appreciated Praxis's support, Susan Abela felt that the campaign at the Social Planning Council represented a major distraction for her group and took them away from other more useful activities, such as advising welfare applicants. Abela did participate in the joint Praxis-JSM campaign to put activists on the Social Planning Council board. And she did herself get elected. But looking back as an older woman she expressed her regret about all this activity in an interview with Margaret Little for the *Labour/Le Travail* article: "Praxis activities took us away from our agenda. We got pulled off track. The Just Society Movement was very grounded in the day-to-day. We helped people at welfare offices, we fought to allow women to go to university, we fought for day care, children services — that was our agenda and we were effective when we stuck to it" (Little 2007: 196).

Abela believes that the gender dynamics of the Just Society Movement changed with the involvement of Praxis members, who were mostly middle-class men "who didn't get poverty on a gut level." But Lynn Lang (her then married name; today, she goes by her original name, Lynn Kaye), who was a member of the Just Society Movement and later a staff person at Praxis, counters that this is a simplistic analysis. The Just Society Movement leadership was so caught up in the media attention that they failed to build an organization that could last and be sustainable. "Building such an enterprise takes a lot of work" (Kaye 2018).

The JSM held its first meeting on February 21, 1969, at the University

Settlement House with the help of neighbourhood agencies, the United Church and personal contacts. Their invitation read as follows: "Just Society has been organized by the poor, for the poor. Our purpose is to form a self-help group of people in the low-income bracket who are receiving assistance in the form of welfare, family benefits, pensions or unemployment insurance. We, the underprivileged, are meeting informally to discuss our problems and present our findings to those in a position to make the basic changes necessary to enable us to live with dignity" (Morris 1971: 1).

Its first welfare rights information and grievance office opened in the summer of 1969 at the Woodgreen United Church at 875 Queen Street East. In the beginning there was an emphasis on helping to steer applicants through the Toronto municipal bureaucracy to obtain a reasonable level of benefits. Publicity in the media helped the Just Society Movement attract hundreds of women and men to its ranks, leading to the opening of new offices across the city — including ones on George Street, Queen and Dovercourt, and Lawrence Heights. All were set up within the vicinity of official municipal welfare offices.

Just Society Movement members pored over provincial and federal welfare legislation after purchasing copies of the acts at a downtown government bookstore. Margaret Little spoke to two of them about how they set up booths or card tables in the waiting rooms of the welfare offices and informed applicants of their rights while also offering coffee or juice to put them at ease. But that was not the reaction of the welfare workers and administrators who tried without success to bar the Just Society Movement. The number of JSM volunteers participating was just too overwhelming and they would contact the media if there was any hassle from the welfare workers. This was the power of mass non-violent activism at its best, Susan Abela explained: "They couldn't arrest us. They looked foolish if they tried to stop us from helping people get welfare" (Little 2007: 187).

Doris Power stresses that the JSM also invited men to get involved because they had their own unique issues (Power 2018). In the area around George Street, known as the Don District because of its proximity to the Don River, the Just Society Movement set up an office to service out-of-work men, who were either unemployed through an economic downturn in their particular industry or had suffered a workplace injury and were having difficulty with their compensation claims.

All of this happened in the late sixties in the absence of legal clinics supported by province to deal with such issues. In one highly publicized case, Just Society Movement members staged a sit-in to prevent an eviction of a mother (Audrey Wilson) and her children from an Ontario Housing Corporation project. Audrey was banned unofficially because of her unruly son. "They were trying to evict a mother who had several children. But one of the children was disabled and in fact caused trouble. I guess you would call him ADD now, and she was on a [secret] list. But the housing authority wouldn't admit [to it]. So, the whole thing was about forcing them to admit to the list. And that they were going to throw this woman out and she would not get housing ever again" (Abela 2018). Wilson had wanted to stay in the neighbourhood, where services for special needs children existed. It was only after the eviction that the OHC admitted that it was excluding certain parents, continued Abela. A number of police officers arrested the protesting Just Society Movement members and took them away in paddy wagons.

Sometimes, anti-poverty advocates issued their own warnings about the consequences of inaction by government towards the plight of the economically disadvantaged. "If they don't want trouble in the streets, they not only have to let the poor participate, but make it possible for them to participate in the discussions affecting them … You can't just tease and give lip service, you have to give them real power," Susan Polgar warned (Lee 1969: W1). But members drew the line at violence. Both Power and Abela recalled discussing strategy at a particular Just Society Movement meeting. Abela had fortuitously obtained the architectural plans of the Toronto Stock Exchange. She had made the request as an arts student seeking to examine a building of significance. People at the meeting discussed how the centre of finance capital could be disrupted. A plan was hatched to interrupt trading activities to make a political statement. Power was even going to take off her top to distract officials. But when some men in the Just Society Movement pushed for planting bombs, that cast a pall on the discussion and the protest was effectively halted. "It was a really awful idea. A lot of us left at that point," says Abela. Apparently, the exchange got wind of the plot and had the building closed for a day, she added. (Power confirmed the basic elements of this account in a separate interview.)

Another favourite interviewee for the press was the highly opinionated John Mooney, who was the Just Society Movement's resident intellectual and thinker. He provided a lot of good copy for reporters that received the attention of the RCMP Security Service, judging from their internal files. The *Globe and Mail* caught up with him sitting in the George Street office of the Just Society Movement on October 16, 1969, which turned out to be a small attic room. There was a sign displayed stating: "Poverty is no disgrace; just ridiculously inconvenient." A second sign read: "Short-term goal — to obtain a single agency under one legislative act which would cover the entire field of the present welfare trap." Mooney was stationed in the office from 8:30 am to 7:30 pm. He had no family responsibilities, was separated from his wife, living with a friend and not receiving welfare. He was described in the *Globe* as "slim, blond, blue eyed and impatient" and a former newspaper reporter. It turned out that he had grown up in Montreal's tough St. Henri district and suffered from health problems that kept him hospitalized at times (Kirkwood 1969).

Mooney was often kicked out of the Just Society Movement because of his binge drinking and personal behaviour. He was accused at one point of stealing the organization's petty cash, leading to a discussion about how the Just Society Movement should respond. When he was fully sober Mooney could be articulate and thought-provoking, says Power. Since this was the sixties and still the Cold War, the obvious question was whether he was a communist. Mooney denied that he was but still expressed some radical ideas about capitalism. In a letter to the *Toronto Daily Star* on June 2, 1970, Mooney wrote that the poor were being "cautioned" against seeking change in a militant fashion. He called for the subsidization by the state of the Just Society Movement organizers but also expressed concerns that the organization would soon dance "to the music of the moderate professionals." He wanted the Just Society Movement to avoid "degenerating into a socially acceptable debating club ... Much more will be written about poverty in the future months and experts will continue to decry the terrible conditions of the poor. But unless the poor move together, in whatever way is necessary to eradicate the causes of poverty, nothing will happen." Doris Power knew John Mooney personally, defended him at Just Society Movement meetings and also participated in his expulsion from the group at one point. Today, she has no idea if he is still alive or where he can be found.

United Church minister Barry Morris, in a 1971 report on the Just Society Movement, called the George Street outlet the largest centre for dealing with welfare cases for single men in all of Canada at that time. He also thought it was a mistake for the organization to get bogged down in grievance processing and problem solving. Rev. Morris offered the example of the George Street office, which was shifting from a base of organizing to a "first aid station and direct complement" to the over-crowded lobby of the municipal welfare office across the street. He also wrote that the Just Society Movement might have lasted longer than its three years had it contained more structure and maintained a good set of records of cases, as it did at least in the George Street office (Morris 1971: 10–11). He incurred resentment from both Susan Abela and Doris Power for his reference to the largely male Just Society Movement members at George Street as the "doers" versus the more female-dominated "talkers" in other JSM offices. Both women expressed the concern to me that Barry Morris's report misconstrued the gender dynamics of the organization (Power 2018; Abela 2018).

This was a time before shelters for women fleeing violent partners and the ready availability of daycare. Birth control was finally legalized, but access was restricted to those who could afford the prescribed pills. The sixties was a different world. The new Liberal government had changed the Criminal Code to make abortion legal but it was not until the Morgentaler decision in the Supreme Court in the 1980s that bureaucratic barriers to obtaining a safe abortion in a hospital or clinic were removed. One Just Society Movement member dropped out early after a conviction for participating in an illegal abortion. She never contacted the Just Society Movement, and its members kept their distance, says Power, ruefully. "Everyone just backed off her and I never felt good about that" (2018).

Susan Abela had her own problems with finding housing in Toronto as a single mother on welfare. "Welfare didn't like us to live together because we would be saving money, thus they thought it would be 'cheating' welfare. Landlords could and did discriminate however they liked so it was hard to find a place that would take children at all. Women with children at that time would rent a place, houses usually, and declare to welfare they were living separately; that it was just a rooming house. This also made women safer as many were single because they were escaping abusive partners. They would keep the doors locked and everyone would know who to let in and what to tell them" (2018).

Today, in her seventies, Abela works as a psychotherapist focused on victims of sexual assault. She is happily married and has grandchildren. But in the late sixties, after leaving an abusive family at the age of 16, she had to make a second getaway with two small boys from a violent first husband while they were living in a small town in Ontario. By the time Abela and her kids were in Toronto her ex-husband had disappeared and with it the support payments of $30 a week. Decent and lasting employment for a young and uneducated person was hard to find and she ended up on welfare. Abela wanted more out of life and so she applied to go to the Ontario College of Art. That resulted in her being cut off of her social assistance benefits after she had applied for a provincial student loan. The attitude in welfare was that women with children seeking to improve their skills or education were "unfit mothers" whose children should be taken away, she recalls. "It was typical of the standard bullying tactics of the time to get us to go away ... They made it clear that the only reason I was cut off was because they didn't wish to support anyone in post-secondary education. And I was left penniless until I managed to get a student loan."

This created an economic hardship for Abela who found herself behind in the rent and resorting to food vouchers from the Red Cross to feed herself and her kids. There were no food banks then. Fortunately, she had made contact with the Just Society Movement and found other women with children and on assistance where welfare authorities had made objections about recipients furthering their education. Apparently, the news coverage generated by a public speech about her situation during a Social Planning Council election sufficiently embarrassed Toronto welfare officials to relent temporarily as long as she and her colleagues met one stringent condition: "Because people on OSAP [Ontario Student Assistance Program] lived at a higher standard than people on welfare, I had to sign a paper that said essentially I would not feed my children on OSAP money."

Another member, Laurell Ritchie, had her own unique experience. She was in her late teens living with her family in "the projects" in the Jane Finch corridor at the suburban edge of Toronto. She dutifully mailed what was "a pittance," i.e., what she could afford, to support the work of the Just Society Movement. At some point Ritchie moved downtown to live independently and took up residence in Rochdale, the hippie-run apartment building on Bloor. She began attending Just Society Movement meetings on George Street. By then she already knew Lynn Lang, who was a little older and of a similar socio-economic background. Eventually each gravitated to positions at Praxis and worked together on organizing the 1971 Poor People's Conference (Ritchie 2012).

Ritchie also got elected to the board of the Metro Toronto Social Planning Council as part of the campaign to reform this body. But for her it was an educational experience dealing with the so-called do-gooders and Lady Bountifuls, as she called the traditional types on the board who talked endlessly about poverty but steered clear of discussing the economics of capitalism as responsible for the continued existence and growth poverty.

After starting to come to meetings of the Just Society Movement, Ritchie remembers feeling it was her duty to explain to other members what it was like to grow up poor in suburban North York, which was then a separate suburban municipality from the older city of Toronto. "When I came downtown, I saw some things that were quite different. At the time I felt that in some respects there were even more challenges for people in the outer suburbs in terms of transportation and jobs and community. There was no real community centre of any kind in Jane Finch in that area. The [public housing] projects were very new. In fact, I think there was probably mud [on the ground] after the construction. And I saw some similarities with Regent Park [the housing project in the downtown east end]."

Ritchie sought to enlighten members of JSM, some of whom had originally moved from elsewhere in Ontario and only knew the older and denser part of Toronto and areas like the downtown core or the district west of Don River, for instance, where there was still housing for those of modest means despite the encroaching gentrification and proposed urban renewal. She spoke of the isolation and desperation while growing up in Jane Finch and how neighbours in the project kept to themselves, not coming out to do anything together as a community. She mentioned one of the unvarnished truths of the sixties — that not everybody had gotten the cultural memo coming from the music, books and commentators that this was the decade of political commitment.

What appealed to her about Doris Power and Suzanne Polgar and others in JSM is their passion and that they had not given up hope. Ritchie grew up in an environment where people were "embarrassed" about having fallen on hard times. Nobody had to spell it out: they had messed up and now did not measure up to the expectations of a middle-class-oriented society. It was something they felt inside as their own fault, explains Ritchie. There was a cascading series of events. She and her family had led typical middle-class Canadian lives which came to a halt when her father did not have his small sign business anymore, found it impossible to find other kinds of work and then suffered a mental breakdown. The family could no longer afford the house he had built or to stay in the area where they resided. Then he refused to go on welfare, which meant it was up to Ritchie's mother to keep the family financially afloat with a job at a laundromat, where Ritchie, the oldest of the children, did part-time work after school. Middle-class pretensions do not disappear even if you have dropped down quite a notch in income. Ritchie and her family wanted nothing to do with the rest of the residents in their public housing project. She still missed their previous neighbourhood. "Unlike my younger siblings I chose to keep going to the high school I had been going to. And I got up very early every morning to walk and take a bus and walk again in order to still be with my friends and the old school."

How did the Security Service regard the Just Society Movement? The grievances of Canada's poor were acknowledged by the police force in some internal memos but there was suspicion of the direction that Howard Buchbinder at Praxis was taking the JSM. "Controlled by the unseen hand of Praxis Corporation through Buchbinder and his associates the activities of the Just Society have taken on a decidedly militant form of expression reminiscent of the student confrontation tactics," wrote the authors of an internal thirty-one-page Security Service report, *The Changing Nature of the Threat from the New Left — Extra Parliamentary Opposition, Penetration of Government*, dated May 1971. The report continued: "The Just Society has been campaigning against the establishment through confrontation tactics such as the occupation of an Ontario Housing Corporation apartment in July1970 and the disruption of a Metro Toronto Social Services committee meeting" (High and Green 1971: 13–15). The latter was referring to a campaign against the chair Karl Mallette, an elected politician, after he advocated in the summer of 1970 the sterilization of parents on welfare heading large families.

Hamilton Welfare Rights Organization

The city of Hamilton has a rich history of labour struggles and unionization backed by community solidarity. There are parallels of this in countless other industrial communities across North America. This resulted in an unprecedented period of prosperity for the working class during the post–World War II period. As often happens, the legacy of the past, which was a major factor in this upward mobility, had become a distant memory for the generation of adults in the early 1970s. They or their parents had fled the poverty of the lower and older city for the suburban middle-class communities at the top of the Niagara Escarpment. There was little sympathy for those who had fallen through the cracks and could not make the climb.

On January 26, 1971, just a few weeks after the national Poor People's Conference in Toronto, the *Hamilton Spectator* reported that about sixty members of the Hamilton Welfare Rights Organization (HWRO) (some of whom had previously attended the conference) assembled in front of City Hall on a national day of protest. Mayor Vic Copps refused to meet them, a stance he would consistently maintain when it came to this new group of activists.

The welfare rights rally received pledges of support from local union leaders. During the event a federal government white paper on income security (which the NCW had criticized but in a less confrontational fashion) was symbolically set on fire to protest what the activists viewed as flawed document. "It is just another bandage covering up a sore," stated HWRO chair Johnny Morris. "A guaranteed annual income recommended in the white paper would just be another form of social assistance. I'd rather see the money used to open up new industry. People want jobs, not handouts," he told reporters (*Hamilton Spectator* 1971a). On the same day a sit-in by members of the HWRO followed at the Hamilton welfare office. In the evening a teach-in took place, featuring members of the Hamilton Social Planning Council and academics, who discussed poverty in the city.

The appearance of a new aggressive welfare rights organization in Hamilton was welcomed in some quarters and vilified in others, especially behind the portals of power among leading politicians. For three days the protesters maintained their presence at the municipal welfare office demanding to be allowed to set up a table inside and provide advice to applicants on eligibility rules and their right to receive social assistance.

The *Spectator* featured a photo showing a crowded waiting area, a card table and a large sign in front of it: "HWRO Hospitality Centre: Information and Assistance on Applications, Rates and Protection of Your Rights. Operated by Welfare Recipients. Hamilton Welfare Rights Organization. 448 York St. 529-2322" (*Hamilton Spectator* 1971b).

Hamilton city authorities refused to buckle, even though in Toronto the JSM was allowed to do the exact same thing. Both Hamilton City Council and the Board of Control turned down the request despite an approval given by the board governing Hamilton's welfare office. Also rejected was a proposal for a sign in the welfare office which would inform applicants that the HWRO was offering advice at its nearby office. City alderman Jim Campbell was the most vociferous opponent of the HWRO. For him it was a matter of who was in charge in the city. "Get that table out of there right away and keep it out. We are running this city, not the welfare rights organization," he told reporters (*Hamilton Spectator* 1971c). City politicians also nixed another demand of the HWRO — that welfare recipients be given seats on the welfare board in Hamilton. Campbell was one of a number of Hamilton politicians who believed that people receiving or applying for assistance had no right to be consulted on the welfare system, in contrast to the practice of citizen participation which was sweeping other cities in the country, such as Toronto. Indeed, Campbell resorted to name calling, dubbing the HWRO "militant scroungers" (*Hamilton Spectator* 1971d).

In Toronto, with its variety of media sources and three daily newspapers, the anti-poverty advocates in the JSM during the late sixties and early seventies were an intriguing news item and reporters competed to interview them. But in Hamilton, with one daily newspaper, the public debates about welfare went through a narrower filter of a single influential organ, the *Spectator,* which set a negative tone directed against the HWRO as soon as the new poor people's group got off the ground in early 1971. One published *Spectator* editorial disapproved of the presence of an information table inside the Hamilton welfare office because it "would only lead to nasty confrontation, perhaps violence and utterly defeat its purpose." The newspaper also questioned the purpose of the HWRO, arguing that citizens could simply contact their controller and alderman if they required help in applying for welfare. "If councillors do their job, and if needy folk cooperate, there will be no cause for a welfare crisis in Hamilton" (*Hamilton Spectator* 1971e).

Furthermore, this same newspaper raised the level of sensationalism by describing in another editorial "the harassing, street gang tactics of the Hamilton Welfare Rights Organization" (*Hamilton Spectator* 1971f). This editorial was focused on the attempt by the HWRO to block an official of the Hamilton Housing Authority from leaving his office after he would only speak to certain members of a large eleven-person delegation. The news coverage of the event was focused on a confrontation, "mild as it was," to the exclusion of the underlying context, stated Ron Haggart in an interview by the National Council of Welfare for its 1973 report on the media reporting of poverty (NCW 1973: 27–30). As in Toronto, the welfare rights activists in Hamilton were concerned about the rental policies of public officials at the Hamilton Housing Authority. In this highly charged atmosphere, three Hamilton MPs, including Progressive Conservative Lincoln Alexander argued that the militancy of the HWRO was endangering its federal funding (*Hamilton Spectator* 1971g).

City politician Herman Turkstra stood out for not following the automatic rejectionist stance towards the activists. He remembers a "dead silence" among his colleagues in the room at the Hamilton Board of Control in 1971 as a newbie elected politician when he picked the welfare department as his preferred area of speciality (Tursktra 2018). (This municipality was governed by two separate elected layers with different responsibilities — a board of control and city council — as well as an elected mayor.) By then, an economic downturn in Canada had led to rising unemployment in Hamilton. There were a growing number of young single men coming into the city from rural areas and the east coast who were frustrated by their inability to find work because of a downturn in the steel industry. They would find themselves on welfare and then get cut off from assistance. Turkstra agrees there was a concern at the time that these marginalized young men might resort to violence.

Although top labour leadership supported the HWRO, the new group did not receive any sympathy from the Canadian Union of Public Employees (CUPE), which represented the city's welfare workers, whose treatment of people coming into their office looking for assistance was being calling into question. But CUPE shot back that HWRO's tactics were a form of intimidation (*Hamilton Spectator* 1971h).

The HWRO's full-time community organizer, Bill Freeman, says the organization made an effort to channel the anger among the unemployed into non-violent political action (Freeman 2018). He was a graduate sociology student at McMaster in the early seventies and he later wrote about his experience in an article for the 1979 edited collection *Their Town: The Mafia, the Media and the Party Machine*, which he also helped to edit and assemble along with Marsha Hewitt.

HWRO's story began in 1970 with the Victoria Park Community Association seeking funding from the federal Department of Health and Welfare to pursue welfare rights advocacy in Hamilton. John Munro, the local MP for Hamilton East and the minister of Health and Welfare, was agreeable since it fitted his department's policy of nurturing new political voices in low-income communities. But he insisted that the requested money, totalling $35,000 a year for a three-year period, go to a separate group that was specifically focused on welfare rights. That is how the Hamilton Welfare Rights Organization got started — with Freeman hired by the Victoria Park Community Association to do the legwork to get it off the ground (Freeman 1979).

It was around this time that Freeman came into contact with Praxis, which gave the HWRO a favourable evaluation on behalf of its client, the Department of Health and Welfare. The positive evaluation was required in order to access federal funding. It was Howard Buchbinder, then teaching a part-time course at McMaster University, who wrote up the report. Freeman remembers a warning from the Praxis director about the dangers of relying on the government for funding. "There's a real danger in taking money from essentially the group you want to change. And what he meant was you've taken money from the federal government and if anybody is ever going to change this whole system [for poor people] it's got to be the federal government. And he was right" (Freeman 2018).

The loud and noisy start of the HWRO in January 1971 came straight out of the principles of community organizing that had been developed successfully by Saul Alinsky, the Chicago-based activist. Hamilton City Hall and its welfare department represented the test case for this strategy at the local level. John Munro from the start defended the practice of funding poor peoples' groups across Canada on the basis that marginalized communities had the right to have their voices heard in a democratic community. He was one of the most powerful politicians in the city, heading up a well-oiled political machine that was based in the largely industrial riding of Hamilton East. The only other figure with comparable clout was

Mayor Copps. They happened to both be members of the Liberal Party, which dominated the city's politics but failed to stem the rivalry between the two men (Jacek 1979).

With few exceptions the majority of Hamilton's local politicians questioned the federal grant to the HWRO. Mayor Copps lamented during an interview with the *Hamilton Spectator* about the failure of Munro to consult Hamilton City Hall about the decision: "I still think the federal government should have told us about this ... that the very people who are causing the difficulty which is bringing us close to a walkout at the welfare office are being financed by the federal government" (*Hamilton Spectator* 1971i).

Johnny Morris, the 25-year-old chair of the HWRO, stood front and centre for the cause of reform. A young Hamilton-born African Canadian, he was dubbed "the black knight" by Paul Mann in the *Spectator* (Mann 1970–71). Another reporter for the same newspaper, Don Stewart, introduced Morris and his white wife Frances as an attractive interracial couple living their life in the city at a time when such marriages were less common. In 2018 Morris spoke to me about the expectations of welfare authorities that poor people should grovel to get any kind of assistance and the stigmatization that came with that. "One of the things that really got into my bones was when they say that people on welfare, people on social assistance don't contribute to society or don't contribute to taxes. I said, well, if you are going to buy a loaf of bread or a carton of milk or a piece of clothing, you pay tax. You help to stimulate the economy. When you get the welfare cheque at the end of the month the city does very well. And they say, well we did not think of it that way."

Morris remembers other examples of the short-changing of the welfare poor in 1971 in Hamilton. "At one time if you were on welfare you couldn't have a car, you couldn't have a telephone. When you were buried you couldn't have a headstone. And [welfare workers] used to come [to your home] once or twice a month even without any notification to check your coverage, who you were living with."

Morris worked full-time in the HWRO office, above a variety store on Victoria Avenue North, just two hundred yards from the Hamilton municipal welfare office. Morris credits the combination of political activism and a stable marriage which influenced his change from an angry young man growing up with alcoholic parents. He was raised in area of Hamilton known as "the Bottom," a small Black neighbourhood that once existed between the boundaries of Stuart, Carolina, York Blvd. and Oxford and spawned local talent in rock and blues music, including its most celebrated performer Jackie Washington.

Morris told *Hamilton Spectator* reporter Malcolm Gray that he left home in Hamilton at 14 because his mother could not afford to care for him and his two brothers. He tried unsuccessfully to break into a shoe store because he needed the money to pay for food. As an adult he lost his job driving a city garbage truck after advising fellow workers in their conflicts with management. He also gave up a part-time bouncer job in a hotel after a warning that his welfare benefits would be reduced. Morris had no shame in stating he preferred welfare to support his family, including five children, in a sparsely furnished house on Pearl Street. The alternative was slaving away at low wage jobs, he explained to the reporter. His refusal to take jobs that paid less than welfare enraged the critics of the HWRO in Hamilton (Gray 1971).

Morris was frank with the *Spectator* about having a criminal record following assault charges, which made getting truck-driving jobs difficult since he would have to be bondable. Many of the fights he experienced, starting in his youth, stemmed from racist taunts from his employers and fellow workers (Gray 1971; Morris 2018). "When I was 16 I got myself in a bit of a jam, a lot of fights. You know I was called n–––– and black and even to this day I don't take that."

Later, he applied for and was granted a pardon by the National Parole Board in Ottawa, which resulted in the removal of the criminal record. He was seeking to avoid going down the self-destructive path of an angry young man striking out in all directions. "The thing is you learn. I said to myself, 'well John, punching or yelling at people is not the way to go. Use your brain. Use your brain. The way to get things done is through organizing. And with organizing you gain power. And when you gain power you gain respect.'"

The young man worked full-time at the HWRO, either sitting in the office advising people of their rights to welfare or handing out leaflets in front of the city's municipal office. "If I feel I'm right about something I'll talk for hours. I'm the mouthpiece of the group ... Maybe, I don't have much education [he had grade 10 through adult retraining] but I usually manage to get the point across" (Gray 1971).

Turkstra said he has a lot of respect for Morris's work at the HWRO. "What I know is this. Johnny Morris was abrasive; he did not back down. He was not ashamed of his position in life. He epitomized what I had been trying to say, which is that there are good people who are in situations where they need help just to find a place to live and to have something to eat. They may not be perfect, and John was not perfect. John was absolutely fabulous. If you add it all up together, he was a loudmouth, he was aggressive and he had some character defects [from society's perspective]. He was on government assistance; his family was on government assistance. He was the wrong colour, too many kids in the family and all that kind of shit [in white Hamilton]" (Turkstra 2018).

The other leader of the HWRO who garnered some ink in the press was a middle-aged woman by the name of Cora Davenport. "Cora was a very bright woman who wasn't going to take any shit from anybody I will tell you, which was great. In some ways, she was the real heart and soul of the organization," stated Bill Freeman (2018). A homemaker before becoming a welfare rights advocate, Davenport was described by the *Hamilton Spectator* this way: "With her stocky frame and thrusting chin it is difficult to imagine her ever being shy and retiring. This is especially after watching Davenport argue with welfare department officials and city hall politicians over welfare issues." She and her husband had eight children ranging from seven to sixteen years of age. They lived on $420 a month on assistance, which included both welfare and unemployment insurance and another $60 in family and youth allowance, in a small wooden house on Pearl Street. Cora's husband had a job driving a truck for the cemetery board but lost it after a dispute with a supervisor (*Hamilton Spectator* 1971j).

The *Spectator* reported on a "rough" four-hour meeting between Cora Davenport and other HWRO members and the city's welfare board. She had appeared a number of times complaining about an out-of-service emergency phone line, a time-consuming welfare applications process and the failure of welfare workers to identify themselves. Not liking what she heard from city officials Davenport shouted the following: "How is the staff always in the right and the recipient is always in the wrong?" Mayor Copps, who was in attendance, replied the following: "It is a question of whether we believe you or a member of the board or the staff. And I believe them" (*Hamilton Spectator* 1971k).

As early as August 5, 1971, John Munro was already hinting that the

HWRO's government grant might get cut. In December the minister finally announced in a letter to the HWRO that he was withdrawing the federal money to the organization following Morris's interaction with the callers on an open-line radio show hosted by the high-profile Tom Cherington. Morris told the callers that the HWRO was getting sick and tired of people, like one particular caller, "kicking us in the teeth and telling us to accept what you throw on the floor." Cherington asked rhetorically, what if "the people who are doing the paying say 'no more.'" Morris then replied, "I am sorry to say it but there will be armed revolution." The open-line show host then jumped in: "In other words the poor will steal at the end of a gun. If you hold a gun at me and say 'gimme,' you are stealing, aren't you?" That was the opportunity that allowed Munro to withdraw the federal grant from the HWRO, in lead up to the 1972 federal election (Winsor 1971b).

Much like a school teacher scolding young students for past behaviour, Munro complained to reporters about the militant tactics of the HWRO, specifically by Johnny Morris and Bill Freeman. The federal cabinet minister said he was influenced by the publicity generated by the organization which he called counterproductive. "The day of confrontation is past and excessive rhetoric is past" (*Hamilton Spectator* 1971m). Yet, what the HWRO did, which included sit-ins, formal appeals when welfare was denied to a needy person and picketing the Salvation Army, fitted the definition of non-violent political activity in a democratic society. The Sally Ann action was especially controversial at the time and may have nailed the fate of the welfare rights organization, says Morris. "We were the only, I think the only organization in the history of Canada that ever picketed the Salvation Army." The HWRO was accusing the agency of offering used and dirty bed sheets, laden sometimes with head lice, to desperate individuals seeking accommodation.

Yet, Munro must have known right from the beginning of its funding that the HWRO was following what had worked across North America in the tactics advocated by Saul Alinsky. The strident non-negotiating position of the city had simply raised tensions with the welfare rights advocates. It was the excessive comments coming from Hamilton City Hall and the exaggeration in the *Spectator*'s coverage that seemed to force the hand of the minister worried about re-election.

Bill Freeman observes that Munro, who represented the working-class riding of Hamilton East, relied on a political machine that was threatening to come apart if the support for the welfare rights group did not end. "He built up a political machine that was probably the best … that I've ever seen. That was basically run by lawyers and small business people. They could deliver votes. His riding was in working-class Hamilton. And that included the steel mills with a lot of industry and working people and they supported him. He had very strong immigrant support. Munro's own people were just going crazy. 'You've got this wild welfare rights organization; you've got to do something about it.' And ultimately he made the decision that despite the political flack he was going to have to kill our grant" (Freeman 2018).

After the cut in the federal grant, Johnny Morris kept the HWRO going for another couple of years but the lack of finances made it hard to continue indefinitely. He also worked for a time as a paralegal. Yet, the activism was not all in vain. Both Freeman and Turkstra emphasized that Morris and the HWRO forced the city of Hamilton to improve how its welfare office treated the poor. Also, the HWRO had trained welfare recipients to help other welfare recipients (Freeman 2018; Turkstra 2018).

Yet, the very nature of the power imbalance between the welfare bureaucracy and recipients in major centres like Hamilton and Toronto were not going away, stated Alan Borovoy, counsel for the Canadian Civil Liberties Association five years later. In a three-year study, which involved a thousand interviews (half in each city) with people on welfare, Borovoy reported on widespread interference by the social service systems into their democratic freedoms. He called for non-professional advocates to assist this vulnerable constituency of the poor to secure their legal rights (Bruner 1976: 5).

The experience of organizing also took an emotional toll on Bill Freeman, who eventually moved away from Hamilton. Currently, he lives on Toronto Island, working successfully as a professional writer. The early seventies "was the most intense period of my life. And I'm well into my seventies now. And what was so difficult for me. I'm a middle-class boy, okay. My father was a high school teacher. You don't get more middle class than a high school teacher. What was difficult for me was just spending most of my days with people in serious crisis. Emotional crisis. And it was tremendously draining on me as an individual. My marriage broke up. I retreated to McMaster actually to get some relief. Fortunately, I had some friends out there and I got a job in the Sociology Department. And it was a great relief." (Freeman 2018).

During the sixties the trade union movement was resting on the laurels of its militant accomplishments after World War II, Freeman notes. "I knew a lot of Steelworkers who were active in Local 1005; some were veterans of the '46 Stelco strike, but I couldn't get them interested in a campaign to help poor people." The exception was the United Electrical Workers, which had Communist Party links and rallied to support Johnny Morris and the HWRO. "They rallied to our support. They had two or three Westinghouse plants organized so they were a big, strong union in Hamilton. We had meetings, but that was about it. Mind you it was not obvious what they could have done."

Freeman knows of poor peoples' groups harassed by the Mounties in the early seventies but such was not the case with the HWRO as far as he can recall. However, Johnny Morris did have an encounter with two large young white men in suits barging into his HWRO office and demanding that he stop putting pressure on Munro. "Son, you are causing too much trouble for John Munro; we want you out of sight. We'll give you a job." Morris was nonplussed, stood his ground and said no to the job offer. "They started giving me shit, saying things like, we can lock you up and I said, 'okay, that is great, make a martyr.'" The intruders left grumbling, never coming back, he says. "They wanted me to slow my role — in other words get out — because I was causing too much heartache for Mr. Munro" (Morris 2018).

Chapter Six

Opposition and Surveillance

The RCMP Security Service took an interest in Praxis after Stephen Clarkson sent what he was thought was an innocent request in a February 1969 letter to External Affairs, which is part of the package of RCMP Praxis files. In an interview in 2010, Clarkson called the whole experience "depressing." Meyer Brownstone, a professor and his colleague on the Praxis board, was later frank about what he saw as sheer naïveté: "This was vintage Clarkson — utterly naïve at some levels. His image of an elite group of academics and participants from the community! This image was an honest reflection of Stephen's view of how to develop some progressive changes. I suppose you could call him a 'social liberal' intellectually" (Brownstone 2018).

In defence of Clarkson, the political scientist was simply trying to keep Praxis afloat with a staff and an office — and academic placements represented a reasonable source of revenue. That explains why he contacted External Affairs (today known as Global Affairs) to suggest that one of its diplomats take a sabbatical and have an intellectual re-fresh at his new research institute. This type of arrangement was not unusual for government departments seeking to develop a closer relationship with the Canadian academic community. The academic placement "would have to be conditional on our accepting the man and the project as sufficiently interesting. But there is a need to let top-grade diplomats return to academic reality and this might provide a useful experiment" (quoted in Williamson 1969).

What Clarkson did not appreciate at the time was that Cold War attitudes still pervaded the upper reaches External Affairs even with Pierre Trudeau at the helm of the government. With this request, the U of T professor inadvertently set off an alarm inside the department. Upon receiving the letter, E.R. Rettie, a top official in the security division of the department, contacted the commissioner of the RCMP, W.L. Higgitt. Rettie mentioned in the March 19, 1969, memo that three Praxis board members, including Clarkson and Rotstein, were members of the University League of Social Reform, which he described as "a group which promotes active participation of university facility in politics."

This was not the first time that Rettie had been in close touch with Higgitt about left-wing and student political activity on university campuses. They had frequently discussed the potential for "exploitation" by foreign states (i.e., the Soviet Union and its Eastern European bloc of countries). Rettie's memo continued: "It would, for example, be undesirable to associate the Department with individuals who are active in 'New Left' movements and who are connected in some definitive way with the more violent and politically oriented manifestations of the 'fascist' left evident in student/faculty dissent described in the briefs you have sent me recently. Early assistance in this regard would be much appreciated."

What Rettie and the RCMP Security Service shared was an aversion to all left-wing politics, including the left-Liberals, NDP social democrats and Marxists inside Praxis and the University League of Social Reform, tarring them with the same red-baiting brush and associating them wrongly with the authoritarian rule practised in the Soviet Union, which had nothing to do with the ideals of socialism. "In view of the composition of the Praxis Corporation and its apparent goals, we are of the opinion that it would be a considerable advantage for the government if the current and possible direction from the subversive elements within the corporation could be established," replied Higgitt, in early 1969 carrying the title of assistant commissioner and director in the RCMP's Security and Intelligence Branch, before it was renamed the Security Service (Higgitt 1969).

Higgitt urged Rettie to comply with Clarkson's placement request because the force was being prevented from gathering intelligence on Canadian university campuses. "Due to restrictions imposed regarding campus enquiries we have found it extremely difficult to penetrate groups of this nature in the past and therefore, are not in a position at this time to provide an in-depth assessment." (To fill this vacuum, military intelligence undertook its own surveillance of Canadian campuses.) The senior Mountie drew a connection between members of the Praxis board and other U of T organizations of a progressive bent, such as the University League of Social Reform, the Woodsworth Foundation (named after an early leader of the CCF, J.S. Wordsworth) and the International Forum

Foundation. They are "of continuing interest to us in view of the position taken on issues being exploited by the Communist Block." Higgitt also made specific reference to academics discussing the recognition of Communist China and withdrawal of Canada from its international alliances in NORAD and NATO.

The University League of Social Reform had been founded by two progressive U of T professors, Kenneth McNaught and Abraham Rotstein, and was following in the tradition of the now-defunct League for Social Reconstruction of the 1930s, which had laid the political groundwork for the CCF, the precursor to the NDP. It was essentially a nonpartisan but progressive forum and a publisher of titles about politics by a range of authors, including Clarkson.

"The Praxis Corporation would appear to have similar goals, i.e., a left-of-centre intellectual pressure group who feel they should play a greater role in the policy making process of the Government," stated Higgitt. Furthermore, he continued, "in our opinion organizations such as the Praxis Corporation will be of considerable interest to the government in future from the point of view of pressure that they will be able to exert in connection with the whole sphere of government policy ... For this reason, it would be expedient to take advantage of every opportunity to develop the information the government should have at its disposal to deal with the potential security threat and embarrassment to the government posed by groups of this nature."

What concerned the RCMP was the undue influence that academics on the left from a prestigious university might have on the government, as if this was somehow a new phenomenon. So, who was on the initial thirteen-member Praxis board in December 1968? They represented a diverse group of people: two active Liberal Party members; Stephen Clarkson and geography professor Ian Burton; unaffiliated but outspoken economic nationalist Abraham Rotstein; philosopher Howard Adelman (responsible for building student co-ops across Canada); George Montague, an investment banker; Peter Russell, constitutional scholar and university principal at certain times; and Mel Watkins. Rotstein and Watkins were high-profile economic nationalists concerned about American foreign ownership of the Canadian economy. Watkins had written a report on the topic for the Pearson government and later became one of the leaders of the Waffle movement within the NDP.

Not everybody at External Affairs shared Rettie's concerns. Ken Williamson, who served as a departmental liaison with the academic community, wrote in an August 1969 memo that he saw merit in Praxis's offer. "I said that there were of course some fields of policy or international affairs in which I could personally conceive some advantage to having an officer detached for a while from the department to do research in the appropriate environment and appropriate facilities available." It is likely that Williamson was the first official to have heard directly from Clarkson, says Greg Donaghy, co-author of a three-volume series on the department of External Affairs (2018). The novelist Jack Ludwig accompanied Clarkson on a trip to Ottawa to sell the fellowship idea and knew Williamson personally.

Williamson commented he considered Clarkson a bit condescending. "I suppose he thought that I was junior enough in the Service to be able to follow him," the civil servant noted in the memo. He observed that Clarkson "made some fairly harsh comments with his usual amiability on senior diplomats who were not likely to change their minds about anything even when subjected to new experiences of different intellectual approaches in Praxis" (Williamson 1969). The context here was that Clarkson had little use for External Affairs. "We need more open diplomats; we need more public participation in policy-making. But most of all we need to choose: to choose between the quiet, continental foreign policy we have followed in the main over the past decade and an independent foreign policy," he wrote earlier in the conclusion for *Independent Foreign Policy for Canada*, which he also edited (Clarkson 1968: 269). What finally made the Praxis offer untenable from Williamson's perspective was the $12,000 price of admittance to the fellowship. Because of Clarkson's death in 2016, we will never know why he wanted to charge this amount. Meyer Brownstone says the fee was news to him and he would have strongly opposed it (2018).

Williamson, in his lengthy and detailed memo, also portrayed Praxis as an embryonic organization living on a series of lunch meetings but with no building or office or appointed director to call its own. "There was a committee and $35,000 from the *Toronto Daily Star* to investigate poverty," he added. "They had made some start on that particular subject, bringing into play the concerned academic researcher, the poor people and the press" (Williamson 1969). The External Affairs official was right about all of the details about Praxis except for one thing. By the time he issued his memo the organization had an office in the form of a semi-detached house rented from the University of Toronto on Huron Street close to Bloor.

The Extra Parliamentary Opposition

Looming large at Praxis was the discussion of "extra parliamentary opposition" (EPO) and what it meant. In West Germany, this was what the peace movement originally called itself in the face of a pro-US foreign policy consensus among the major political parties on the right and left, wrote Gerry Hunnius in a short handbook about the German new left (1968). Here in Canada, federal politicians and security experts viewed this term with suspicion. It should be noted, however, that the EPO was the genesis for community organizing, housing cooperatives and participatory democracy in Montreal long after Praxis ended.

Several months after joining the research institute, Howard Buchbinder and Gerry Hunnius attended a November 1969 conference sponsored by the Montreal-based new left/anarchist journal *Our Generation*, where both men served as board members. Hunnius and the journal's editor, Dimitri Roussopoulos, had a long political association going back to when both were students at the St. George Williams University (since renamed Concordia University).

Around the time of the Ottawa conference *Our Generation* issued its EPO editorial, "Towards an Extra Parliamentary Opposition," which called for workers, the poor and members of discriminated-against minorities and other marginalized groups to join together in an alliance to spawn new institutions and forms of resistance to counter mainstream political structures not answering to their needs (*Our Generation* 1969: 3–19). "Extra Parliamentary is not a formal organization but rather a critical comment or a political term of reference ... the idea of extra parliamentary opposition is that a coalition of individuals and groups with a common critique of liberal democracy and a minimum programme choose to act together and separately within such a framework." The extra parliamentary opposition exists whether people doing the organizing and alienated by the parliamentary process are conscious of it or not, stated Howard Buchbinder in a separate article in *Our Generation* a year later. "The content of their everyday lives is one of exploitation and isolation from what the society potentially has to offer them" (1970). The unsigned EPO editorial in *Our Generation* in the previous year stressed there is more to democracy than electing representatives to Parliament every few years. Consultation with citizens between elections was one element but it had to be a deeper process. Canada is ruled by "managed politics," where people "passively consent to things being done in their name" (1969: 3–19).

From its inception, Praxis was interested in challenging top-down forms of parliamentary democracy in Canada and the inertia of traditional electoral politics by empowering marginalized groups, such as the poor, who had no voice in mainstream middle-class society. Democracy as it was constituted was out of touch with the average citizen, claimed Buchbinder, Hunnius and a third author, Grant Reid (then a social work graduate student), for the Praxis study *Citizen Action in Urban Canada* (1972), commissioned by Central Mortgage and Housing Corporation, a federal government agency. From the authors' perspective, what we come to understand as democracy had emerged in the nineteenth century in North America and Europe through a dynamic and radical process to expand the right to vote to members of the middle and lower classes, who were chafing under the authoritarian rule of an aristocratic minority in the industrial economies. But after the advent of universal suffrage and modern market capitalism in the twentieth century, the momentum had slowed down and was stalled. Academic theorists in the 1960s defended elitism and were opposed to increased consultation with citizens and citizen participation just as both were getting off the ground, especially at the local level, the Praxis paper emphasized. "We are told by contemporary political scientists and sociologists that an increase in political participation by present non-participants would upset the stability of the democratic system as we know it" (Buchbinder, Hunnius and Reid 1972: 8–30).

All this reflected what *Globe and Mail* journalist Michael Enright described in one article as the political "fad" of ordinary people having a direct say in decisions, such as at the municipal level. It was a direct challenge of an elected politician's authority. "But to Establishment politicians the participation movement has given rise to a new form of political disturber, the professional citizen. The Establishment fears this new breed of man and consequently will have very little to do with him" (Enright 1970a: 1). (As an aside, it is interesting to read the language of the sixties — the lack of gender neutrality and the reference to elites as the "Establishment.")

Some politicians in the sixties found this new style of politics downright disturbing. Raising the alarm about the emergence of Praxis and the EPO was Stanley Randall, an Ontario cabinet minister, in a December 1, 1970, letter to Robert Andras, the federal minister for Urban Affairs, which had hired Praxis for contract work. Copies were also sent to John Munro and W.L. Higgitt at the RCMP Security Service. Randall informed them that he checked to see if Praxis had received any grants from the Ontario government and was reassured that the answer was no. "We have advised all of our departments that under no circumstances are grants to be made to these groups without a thorough investigation." The provincial politician claimed that "prominent people" (not identified) were being "conned" into supporting a good cause and in the process were "sidetracked from the original good intentions" (Randall 1970). "Their reputations are being used by these radical groups to destroy our democratic form of government." Randall was complaining about the kind of tough questions raised by members of the public at open meetings. "Too often we in political life lend ourselves to these dissident groups and you will find that 90 per cent of the audience is made up of people whose political beliefs are not yours or mine and they are led by some very vociferous radical individuals who have nothing to lose and everything to gain by getting a platform at the expense of an invited municipal, provincial or federal official." Randall emphasized that he was refusing to participate in such gatherings.

Months later, in May 1971, the RCMP Security Service produced *The Changing Nature of the Threat from the New Left* by Col. B. High in a longer form and edited and condensed by K.D. Green in the force. The document gave voice to Randall's concerns about "counter" or "parallel" institutions" led by Praxis "to organize the poor and the dispossessed, the workers and the radical students." Their aim was "to boycott the normal socio-political structure, thus challenging and eroding the political legitimacy of duly elected government in the eyes of the 'oppressed'" (High and Green 1971: 2). All of this of course suggested a misrepresentation of what the *Our Generation* writers had contemplated.

A RCMP Security Service document dated October 19, 1971, which detailed federal Cabinet Directive 35, outlined why Praxis and the EPO were deemed "subversive." The Security Service was looking for examples of people "whose loyalty to Canada and our system of government is diluted by loyalty to any communist, fascist or other legal or illegal political organization whose purpose is inimical to the process of parliamentary democracy" (RCMP Security Service 1971c). (The word subversion was discarded from the mandate of CSIS, the successor organization for the Security Service that was set up in 1984.)

The major players identified in the force's documentation were all connected to *Our Generation*: Gerry Hunnius, Dimitri Roussopoulos, Peter Katadotis (founder of the Parallel Institute in Montreal) and Howard Buchbinder. In addition, the Security Service compiled a list of civil servants in the federal Departments of Health and Welfare, Central Mortgage and Housing and Secretary of State who hired Praxis to do contract research. The Ottawa Committee for Socialist Activities, made up of federal employees and identified as former university student activists before their graduation, were also added.

A separate internal RCMP Security Service document on Praxis (RCMP Security Service 1971d), entitled "Infiltration of Key Sectors," expressed concern that Praxis and the extra parliamentary opposition were securing federal funds to influence policy and unleash whistleblowers to disclose confidential data (presumably to the media). What were standard academic research contracts with various federal departments and agencies, such as Central Mortgage and Housing Corporation, the Ministry of State for Urban Affairs and Secretary of State, were turned into something more sinister by Mountie investigators. The same document noted that Praxis had infiltrated community activist organizations in Toronto such as the Metro Toronto Tenants Association: "The general tactic [by Praxis] involves finding fault with an existing social agency that is designed to help people in trouble and exploit the flaws of these agencies to encourage a hostile political climate."

There was also the intent "to organize and control militant social workers groups" and unleash "character assassination" against "selected individuals of the establishment and managerial class," according to another document entitled "Major Strategy and Tactics" (RCMP Security Service 1971e). No concrete evidence was provided for these charges. These memos reflected a fanatical and conspiratorial mindset at the Security Service, which wrestled with the non-violent image projected by Praxis. Everything that Howard Buchbinder and Gerry Hunnius did fitted the category of non-violent democratic debate and discussion, such as organizing conferences that featured speakers on workers' or community control. Unidentified Mounties in a separate March 18, 1971, memo speculated that these events "allowed Praxis to disseminate its radical program, to form activist groups and to make invaluable contacts." They also made the following observation, in a memo dated March 19, 1971: "The modus operandi of Praxis allows them to remain behind the scenes while controlling the activities of community groups which because they are thought to be bona fide endeavours, are morally and financially supported by the poor and unemployed, as well as the general public and the Government. It provides Praxis with a front to shield its real activities of creating a revolutionary force to destroy our political system while at the same time be funded by the very Government structure it intends to eradicate" (RCMP Security Service 1971f).

There was no formal membership in the extra parliamentary opposition, wrote L.K. Parent, an assistant commissioner and deputy director general in the RCMP Security Service, in an October 12, 1972, Security Service memo. That made nailing down the conspiracy of people suspected of sinking their roots into sensitive departments (the so-called "microbes") a challenge for the force. This memo was sent to Robin Bourne, head of the Security Planning and Research Group at the department of the Solicitor General (RCMP Security Service 1972a).

K.D. Green, the co-author of the RCMP's May 1971 *The Changing Nature of the Threat*, tried in a separate memo, "EPO Brief — Operational Comments," to connect the dots in a grand conspiracy between a major spokesperson of the Toronto urban reform movement with the extra parliamentary opposition: "Colin Vaughan's involvements in the Confederation of Residents and Ratepayers Association [CORRA] and Stop Spadina Expressway committee (both in Toronto) should be watched in view of the fact that he is a member of the Praxis Corp" (Green 1971).

In addition to his chairing of CORRA and working professionally as an architect, Vaughan had participated in early Praxis brown bag lunch meetings, was on its early board and continued to be in contact with the research institute. Vaughan's profile had been raised locally while serving as a spokesperson in the late sixties and early seventies for the Stop Spadina/Save Our City Coordinating Committee, which was based in the Praxis house on Huron Street until the fire and burglary in Dec

101

1970. "That Vaughan's own political objectives are synonymous with the radical EPO position of Praxis Corporation is indicated by the remark he made in connection with the Spadina Expressway," stated *The Changing Nature of the Threat* document (High and Green 1971: 19). What caught the Security Service's attention was Vaughan's comment that the Spadina battle represented a battle that was about more than just transportation in the political landscape of Toronto. This was not an unusual sentiment for an activist to express. Vaughan was seeking to enhance local democracy through greater citizen participation. He never made any bones about that.

None of these internal communications prevented Vaughan from getting elected to represent a ward on Toronto City Council, along with other urban reformers, in the 1972 municipal election. His mop of white hair and glasses was also a familiar sight in Toronto City Hall. After leaving politics he embarked upon a fruitful career as a municipal affairs commentator for a television station. His son, Adam, also a former journalist, is currently a member of the Liberal government in Ottawa.

Not all members of the Security Service were as suspicious of local citizen activism. This was revealed by one intelligence officer (not named) in an internal September 1971, four-page RCMP Security Service document, entitled "The Penetration of Canada" (a metaphor for subversion that was popular in the male police and security force). "We in the Security Service find ourselves caught in the midst of these forces of change. To condemn them all as subversive would be a grave injustice to so many well-meaning participants, and moreover would leave us out of step with a [federal] government which is itself encouraging activism" (RCMP Security Service 1971g). But then the author double-backed and stuck with the necessity of rooting out "New Left penetration into vital sectors of society," by quoting Pierre Trudeau, following the passage in Parliament of the War Measures Act to restrict Canadian civil liberties during the October Crisis in Quebec. "But to allow our frustrations to erode our conviction to continue the job would be tantamount to a victory for the 'weak-kneed, bleeding heart liberals,' as our Prime Minister so aptly described those individuals who rush to the defence of political extremists."

One former Praxis board member and long-retired from academic life, Meyer Brownstone (he passed away at the age of 96), ruefully wondered if Praxis might have survived if it had not so proudly worn the extra parliamentary opposition label, which the Security Service successfully demonized, on its collective lapel. Brownstone said that using this term, rightly or wrongly, implied a general dismissal of the existing parliamentary system, which was not what Praxis had intended (Brownstone 2018). The research institute was seeking to "empower" those marginalized groups, such as the poor, who were left out, he explained. Brownstone had had a distinguished career which included serving as the deputy minister of municipal affairs among other responsibilities in the Tommy Douglas–led CCF government of Saskatchewan, taking up the responsibility of supervisor of research at the Royal Commission on Bilingualism and Biculturalism and heading Oxfam Canada as its chair. He noted in one interview that the CCF government nurtured cooperatives in general, including social/cooperative housing, cooperative industries, various cultural activities and urban agriculture. Furthermore, it created the Department of Co-operatives and Co-operative Development, which supported an extensive civil movement for social change. It provided Crown land for groups that wanted to form cooperative farms. When oil giants left the "socialist" province, the state granted many leases to the cooperative movement, which included setting up a refinery. He remarked that Buchbinder, whom he helped to hire at Praxis in the spring of 1969, came from a country with no history of the social democratic left coming to power. "I liked Howard's social work background. I thought him a person with great strength and integrity and strongly committed to Praxis as a culture. His big weakness was his lack of exposure to the state mechanisms, not in the broad Marxist terms, but the working mechanisms."

Buchbinder was unrepentant in his own unpublished writings about his choice of words. "The resolution of social problems addressed by Praxis was, for the most part, not resolvable through the legislative processes but required broadly based citizen action which did not limit itself to lobbying and elections. There was nothing hidden about Praxis's approach. As the story unfolded it appeared that EPO was seen as a major threat by police agencies and the government. This was made explicit in government correspondence related to the activities of Praxis" (Buchbinder 2000).

Buchbinder was talking about mass protests and mobilized public opinion making an impression on unresponsive political representatives. There was a history going to the 1930s of groups of the unemployed doing exactly that. The picture that the Mounties painted of a rogue and potentially violent revolutionary body set to replace the existing democratic process in Canada was completely off, says Hamilton-based historian Peter Graham in a 2018 interview. He read through all of the writings produced by Howard Buchbinder and Gerry Hunnius and others in Praxis and found nothing approaching the conspiracy envisioned in Ottawa. "I don't recall either of them specifically using the term revolution, though they were essentially calling for one, i.e., radical social change via non-electoral means. So, I kind of see the use of that term as simultaneously hyperbolic and accurate. At least one organization they were affiliated to — *Our Generation* — would have been essentially calling for a revolution as well. But nothing as specific as mounting barricades, emulating the Russian Revolution, etc." Graham is the co-author of the 2019 book *Radical Ambition: A Portrait of the Toronto New Left*, which charts left-wing ideas and rhetoric in Canada and more specifically Toronto (where Praxis was based) from the late 1950s to the late 1980s (Graham and McKay 2019). Although the new left around the world was indeed heavily influenced by global liberation struggles, which had involved overthrowing entrenched elites, revolution was for many Canadian leftists more a metaphor for radical progressive change.

The relationship between Praxis and the Parallel Institute was also exaggerated in *The Changing Nature of the Threat from the New Left*; Col. High and K.D. Green wrote that the Montreal-based activist Peter Katadotis (years before the latter became a senior executive at Telefilm) was working with others to "use the Parallel Institute to implement the New Left's EPO program in much the same way as Praxis." Katadotis in an interview over the telephone laughs this off, insisting that he had nothing in common with the Praxis organizing strategy or Howard Buchbinder. "The thing about Buchbinder is he was so dismal all the time. We found him also a bit pompous, unfortunately you know. I just couldn't relate to him" (Katadotis 2011).

Personal assessments of people are always subjective and contextual. A different recollection of Buchbinder comes from former graduate student and Praxis staffer Peter Holland: "Howard didn't publish a lot [as an academic]. People who were students of his loved him; he was a terrific teacher. But he wasn't a warm guy. No hugs from Howard, but a force in the room. You felt the energy, you felt the intellectual and emotional kind of force. He wasn't interested in small talk. I respected him, liked him, and that was a common attitude" (Holland 2012).

A couple of years after Praxis's demise, the Parallel Institute was given a more positive commentary in some July 1973 background notes exchanged between senior officer Ron Yaworski and the director general of the Security Service: "Parallel is still functioning and our concern about its links with the EPO are constantly tempered by recognition of the very positive contributions which it makes in attempting to resolve social problems. The dilemma is that they are not simply working towards 'reforming the system,' but towards replacing it, however remote that goal may be and they are utilizing resources of the system itself to effect this transformation" (Yaworski 1973).

Parallel no longer exists today but its lasting legacy is the building of a community of co-op housing with federal government assistance in the Milton Park area in downtown Montreal, remarks Dimitri Roussopoulos in an interview. The project consists of 1,500 people living in 647 housing units on land that is collectively owned and legally protected in the form of a land trust. "We have abolished private property. You cannot buy and sell within that area. We have taken six city blocks in Montreal off the private capitalist market."

There is an assumption in the internal memos of the RCMP Security Service that the whole notion of an extra parliamentary opposition died with the demise of Praxis. But such is not the case, continues Roussopoulos: "The EPO did not die in the early seventies. It actually evolved into municipal democracy." He maintains that the concept became the germination for new forms of participatory democracy at the local urban level in the Montreal Citizens Movement, which at its height had a membership of close to twenty thousand people. "In the program of 1976, we had a whole series of meetings and conferences here in Montreal. We articulated at a very sophisticated level, neighbourhood governments and neighbourhood councils and how to decentralize power from the centre from City Hall to the neighbourhoods. And in fact, eventually that is what happened in Montreal several decades later where we adopted a structure that is the envy of Toronto" (Roussopoulos 2018).

The different directions that Parallel and *Our Generation* went on the one hand and where Praxis ended up on the other hand (more focused on organizing and research) demonstrates some of the sharp differences that continue to exist on the Canadian left between Quebec and English-speaking Canada. New forms of democracy on the local level beyond citizen participation never caught on in Toronto as it has in Montreal, which Roussopoulos calls "the most decentralized city in North America." He adds that much of the pertinent Canadian political material on enhanced democracy happens to be in French and out of reach for English-speaking activists in the country.

Finally, Roussopoulos confirms that the RCMP Security Service kept a close watch on his political activities. His knowledge comes courtesy of a provincial law in Quebec which requires the Ministry of Justice to inform a citizen that their telephone has been tapped. "I know that of course I was spied upon."

RCMP Surveillance

The RCMP Security Service invested considerable resources in the investigation of the Praxis over a three-year period, according to RCMP files. We don't know how many officers were assigned to their investigation, but in the late sixties Sergeant S. Schultz complained in a memo about "manpower problems" from having to keep tabs on a multi-purpose research institute. There were various duties for the officers working the new left desk at D Branch, the counter-subversion unit of the Security Service. The establishment of the Key Sectors program in the force represented an attempt to "modernize" surveillance of areas in Canadian society most prone to being targeted by so-called subversives — government, armed forces, media and education, says professor and security expert Steve Hewitt, at the University of Birmingham in the UK (Hewitt 2002: 169).

The investigation of an organization like Praxis required officers for recruiting and maintaining contact with informants inside Praxis, having quiet and unobtrusive conversations with employees in the targeted group and contacting approachable journalists. There was a lot of work going around since Praxis was engaged in a lot of organizing and research projects that ranged from urban issues to workers' control.

Sgt. Schultz had some concerns about the overall organization of the surveillance. "In view of the recent Praxis involvement at McMaster University [a reference to Buchbinder, who was a part-time instructor] Key Sectors could continue to handle [the Praxis file]; however, I feel it is a poor arrangement to have the various files divided amongst three different sections." The result was that the Security Service force did not have a coherent picture of the scope of Praxis activity and its two main figures, Buchbinder and Hunnius, he wrote (Schultz 1970).

One of those contacted was Ian Burton, one of the lesser known names at Praxis and a self-described left-wing Liberal, politically in sync with Stephen Clarkson. He was teaching geography at the University of Toronto in the late sixties or early seventies when he received a telephone call from a member of the Security Service. Burton's memory is foggy about exact dates and times. "I remembered [the officer] asked questions about Abraham Rotstein and Mel Watkins ... Are they communists, were they trying to overthrow the government? I said, you have got to be joking," Burton recalled. He said the conversation was civil but hard to take seriously. "If he had asked questions that I might have been uncomfortable with, it might have been a big deal. It was my reading at the time as I remember." Then the officer was gone, never to be heard from again. Burton says he did not discuss the visit with his colleagues at Praxis. "It was a short conversation and I kept it to myself" (Burton 2011).

Unknown to Burton and Praxis there was a higher-level conversation about the research institute taking place among federal cabinet ministers, members of the security panel secretariat inside the Privy Council Office (a federal body that advises the Prime Minister's Office) and the RCMP Security Service. Investigators of Praxis at the RCMP documented these discussions in memos among themselves. Theories, conspiracies, insinuations and guilt by association were discussed to explain the motivations of the people in charge of Praxis. Names were tantalizingly mentioned and then dropped. A professor connected to the institute was labelled "a communist" for teaching at a university in Moscow, but no other evidence was provided. Someone's parents had been orthodox communists, and the assumption was that that person shared similar beliefs and the party line of another generation.

Howard Buchbinder's name appeared frequently in memos, coming to the attention for instance of federal External Affairs Minister Mitchell Sharp, according to John Starnes, the director general of the Security Service, in a memo to a colleague. Sharp was most interested in the Praxis poverty director's involvement in the American anti-war movement. "It appears that Mr. Sharp had received some representations from persons in Toronto about Mr. Buchbinder and he wished to know anything that I could tell him about his bona fides. I indicated to Mr. Sharp that the file showed clearly that Mr. Buchbinder, who had immigrated to Canada and had been granted landed immigrant status in August 1969, appeared to have a long record of involvement with civil liberties, anti-Vietnam war demonstrations and the like" (Starnes 1970).

Sometimes unintentional humour showed up in the memos. One Security Service operative heard at a Praxis conference that there was a plan to expand the use of mixed media in a presentation. "As pointed out in the past this facet of the teach-in is designed to boggle the minds of the participants and therefore make them more receptive to the education which follows" (RCMP Security Service 1970a).

A *Toronto Telegram* series by columnist Peter Worthington (more later on that) resulted in upsetting some readers, who wrote to their MPs about what they had read about Praxis. It did not sound good for the country. Solicitor General George McIlraith provided his own assurance on December 18, 1970, to a fellow MP inside the ruling Liberal government. "The concern of your constituent in relation to organizations such as PRAXIS [name deliberately in caps] is appreciated and I am relatively certain this same area is of concern to many loyal Canadians. I can only assure you that Government policy in respect to this particular matter is under active review and I am sure that any policy adjustments that appear necessary will be made" (McIllraith 1970).

The women's movement was a difficult target for the macho RCMP Security Service in the late sixties and early seventies. One subject of interest by an informant for the Mounties was an internal debate regarding the merits of militancy (not defined) among members of the Women's Liberation Group, which shared an office with Praxis. "An unidentified woman," described in a memo as "37–57 years of age, brassy, blond hair, and coarse features," supported the proposal on the grounds it would draw in more women of "liberal attitudes." The investigator then suggested that the Women's Liberation Group was the equivalent of a hockey farm team but on the left. The WLG was a "jumping off organization" for those Marxists wishing to penetrate and form other left oriented pressure groups. These were early days for feminism and so its possibilities were not readily apparent to the memo writer (RCMP Security Service 1970b).

The best way to decipher Praxis's alleged international connections was described by one Mountie in the following way: "Praxis has good connections with Europe, Cuba and some not too good with China.

Large portion of their propaganda material is printed in Europe on the European standard size paper" (RCMP Security Service 1970c). The same memo also discussed Gerry Hunnius, a Canadian citizen who was born in Estonia when it was part of the Soviet Union and who arrived in Canada at the age of 23, after World War II. He was described in a snide fashion by the Security Service: "[He] has made good adjustments to our way of life although quite a number of our adequacies visibly annoy him." The memo writer also claimed: "Hunnius is obviously the real leader, although the front man is held to be Buchbinder. It is suspected that Buchbinder is the titular leader of the movement, perhaps for reasons no other than he is from [New York City]." This was totally erroneous as the two men functioned largely equally within the Praxis organization. Such was not the first instance of the Security Service having difficulty understanding what they were observing at Praxis.

Also closely watched was Doris Power of the Just Society Movement, although none of the accessed RCMP Praxis files indicated that her name came up in conversations about Praxis and the EPO among cabinet ministers in the Trudeau government and senior security officers. Power was described in the Security Service document *The Changing Nature of the Threat from the New Left* as having "cursed" Senator David Croll's 1971 Special Senate Committee on Poverty for its "alleged ineffectiveness." The authors continued: "These and other activities [on the part of Power] were staged for a specific purpose, to gain public recognition of the Just Society by showing contempt for the established welfare structures and thus the Government" (High and Green 1971: 15).

A Columnist Goes After Praxis

Peter Worthington wrote a series of scathing articles on Praxis in 1970. He was not the only columnist/reporter taking a swipe at the new research institute, but he expended considerably more energy than the others in investigating what he called a new political phenomenon in Canada. Worthington conducted a number of interviews with the board members of Praxis but never personally spoke to Gerry Hunnius, whom he called the controlling figure behind the organization's activities. Included in what Worthington provided to Library and Archives Canada as part of his reporting oeuvre are typed notes from short interviews he pursued with the following people associated with Praxis: Howard Buchbinder,

Abraham Rotstein and Charles Hanly. But there is no indication of any similar conversation with Hunnius (Worthington, personal papers).

Hunnius, now retired and living with his wife Valerie in Bancroft, Ontario, confirmed that Worthington never talked to him for the Praxis stories. "One of the first things that a reporter would do, it seems to me, is to interview the person he is zeroing in on. In this case, me. He never did that. He certainly had ample opportunity, since we lived in the same city" (Hunnius 2011).

The first of Worthington's articles appeared in late November 1970 under the headline, "Praxis: The Sound and Fury Signify an Enigma." "The basic method of Praxis is to mix with poor people and those with legitimate grievances and to exploit feelings of alienation. They raise the level of social consciousness, so to speak" (Worthington 1970a). "There is a lot of talk," he wrote (i.e., presumably among his sources inside the RCMP Security Service,), about the "microbe"-like invasion of Praxis, "getting inside the 'establishment' structure and nibbling and agitating away to weaken or change it." Typically, microbes are living single cell microorganisms, viewable only with a microscope and appearing in different shapes and characteristics and encompassing various categories including bacteria and viruses. Worthington and the Mounties (the latter had invented the metaphor) perceived Praxis as an invasive species expanding uncontrollably if not checked inside the federal government via subterfuge. "For the most part, however, Praxis Corp and its directors prefer to stay out of the limelight and employ the microbe concept," stated High and Green in the Mountie document *Changing the Nature of the Threat of the New Left* (1971: 14).

In the same article Worthington cited an earlier piece from his colleague, reporter Maggie Siggins, who also visited the Praxis house on Huron Street and revealed it was "a little like a pre-World War I meeting place for European revolutionaries, where nights were spent discussing political philosophy and the overthrow of capitalism." Notwithstanding the romantic image, what Worthington failed to show in his first article was that Praxis operated in modest circumstances with a small staff at 373 Huron. It is apparent from his notes that he himself never set foot inside the semi-attached dwelling.

The staunch Cold War warrior was convinced that advocates for nuclear disarmament, like Praxis co-director Gerry Hunnius during the 1960s, were "dupes" of the Soviet Union, even if they were opposed to the armament policies of both superpowers. To show that Praxis was pro-Soviet, the journalist only had to suggest that Hunnius was the real force behind Praxis. "But Mr. Buchbinder is not necessarily the motivating force behind Praxis," wrote Worthington in this same first article. "In fact, he isn't. That honour seems to belong to Estonia-born Gerry Hunnius, who could be described as an activist for all seasons." Worthington wondered in the second article in the series what made Hunnius go from the more exciting work in the international peace movement "to become embroiled" in local fights about the Social Planning Council and what was happening with the workers at Dunlop Rubber: "To some it might seem a step-down to switch" (Worthington 1970b). This is a second example of the columnist serving as the stenographer for the Security Service. High and Green wrote that Hunnius had taken charge of Praxis and his co-director Howard Buchbinder was a mere "associate" (9).

When I interviewed Hunnius in 2011, he blamed what he calls Worthington's misleading stories in the *Telegram* for encouraging harassing and threatening telephone calls from unknown people, possibly other more conservative and right-wing Estonian immigrants, which he and his wife experienced leading up to a burglary of the Praxis office in the following month. "He didn't like what Praxis did [and] he pulled out all of the stops that he could, to put us down [with] innuendos. Why [Worthington] zeroed in on me I don't know. I don't think he personally felt threatened. Did he really believe that our aim was that we had some [plan] to destroy the capitalist system in Canada and replace it with people like us? I don't think anybody in Praxis even thought about that."

The series in the *Telegram* helped to nurture tensions between Buchbinder and Hunnius within the Praxis operation, in a classic strategy of divide-and-conquer, according to Hunnius's wife, Valerie. It was possible that Buchbinder saw himself as accomplishing more at Praxis in his anti-poverty work (V. Hunnius 2018–19).

The image offered by Worthington and the RCMP of Gerry Hunnius as the controlling and domineering person does not jibe with his behaviour at conferences on workers' control, which tended to be conciliatory and low key according to those who were there. The Security Service conceded in the *Changing Threat* document that this Praxis director was in fact not getting very far in his promotion of workers' control and industrial

democracy at the Canadian Labour Congress (CLC), the body representing the majority of Canadian unions at the time (High and Green 1971:
21–23). "It also appears that while attending a recent Reform Caucus
meeting, Hunnius was talent spotting delegates with a view to having
them become members of the workers' control task force and at the same
time help consolidate his strength in the CLC," the authors High and
Green wrote. Later in the same document, they added that "it remains to
be seen to what extent those in the Reform Caucus who are receptive to
Praxis's definition of workers' control will succeed in swaying others in
the CLC to this position, or endeavour to implement it in their own areas
of influence [i.e., the workplaces they represent]."

Where did Worthington's accusations in the *Telegram* of Hunnius
come from? It appears that that the political activities of Hunnius came
to the attention of the Security Service as early as 1957, while he attended
Montreal's Sir George Williams University (before the name was changed
to Concordia). Hunnius discovered this after becoming involved with
the Canadian Committee for the Control of Radiation Hazards, where
he served as a part-time executive secretary from 1961 to 1962. The issue
for the peace movement was to pressure both the United States and the
Soviet Union to stop nuclear testing. It became a serious matter with the
discovery of strontium 90 in the baby teeth of children near the testing
sites. Hunnius was closely acquainted with the Hon. Joseph Thorson, an
older man who happened to be both a board member at the CCRH and
a powerful judge at the Exchequer Court of Canada (a precursor to the
Federal Court of Canada). The two engaged in spirited conversations and
even collided on sensitive subjects. An immigrant from Iceland, Thorson
had an irrational dislike for French Canadians, which created tension, but
the judge and Hunnius saw eye-to-eye on the dangers of nuclear weapons
(Hunnius 2011).

One day Thorson told Hunnius that he had come across the younger
man's RCMP file. "Thorsen said to me 'I have your file and I should not tell
you any of this because I am not supposed to know you have a file, and
I am not supposed to read your file but I have. And it is a terrible file.'"
Hunnius found out that his activity as president of the Asian Studies Group
(ASG) at Sir George Williams was being closely monitored. It arose out of
his campus group's efforts to invite a variety of speakers, ranging from left
to right, capitalists to communists. In October 1958 it was reported in the

student newspaper, the *Georgian* that R. Krassilinikov, the third secretary at the Soviet Embassy, had abruptly cancelled a planned lecture. Hunnius, a spokesperson for the Asian Studies Group, stated that the Soviet official was alleging that the decision originated at the federal Department of External Affairs. If true Hunnius promised that a letter of protest would be mailed to the federal government. The student newspaper added that this was the second Soviet official who had withdrawn after agreeing to speak on campus. The ASG was attempting to raise awareness of international events amidst tensions in the Cold War.

One of the Soviet Embassy's officials tried without success to recruit Hunnius, says Valerie. She maintains that her husband never supported the authoritarian and Soviet style communism or even joined a political party, although he voted for the NDP on a regular basis. Nevertheless, the ASG invitations did have consequences that continued to haunt him. "It became clear to Gerry years later (after he saw part of his highly redacted file), that this incident may have been the initial event that drew the interest of the RCMP to his activities, and resulted in covert observation and documentation for years," says Valerie.

It is possible that Worthington managed to gain access to some details in Hunnius's "terrible" RCMP file. What made the Mounties suspicious was Hunnius's participation in a trip to Russia organized by the Communist Party in 1960. But there was no ideological basis for that decision; Hunnius only went, he told me, because he hoped to do a detour into his home country of Estonia, which he had not visited in many years. Unfortunately, the location turned out to be "out of bounds" (Hunnius 2018-19).

For a number of years during the 1960s Hunnius served as executive secretary of the Canadian Campaign for Nuclear Disarmament and later held a top position until 1968 at the International Confederation for Disarmament and Peace (ICDP), based in London. The ICDP was an umbrella group that had representation from member organizations across North America and Western Europe and was established as the non-communist alternative or counterweight to the Soviet-oriented World Council of Peace. All of this was incriminating evidence for Worthington, who had a history of writing red-baiting articles on the peace movement. He could not conceive of any independent peace movement resisting both of the planet's two power blocs. In early 1968 Worthington warned in the *Telegram* against the domestic upsurge of students and professors of the anti-war persuasion: "There are those who expect this militancy to erupt into violence, to exceed the bounds of law and order, to become civil disobedience," he continued, blurring all of these dissimilar violent and non-violent protest concepts together (Worthington 1968a).

Worthington maintained in his conversation with me that for his November 1969 *Telegram* series on Praxis he did not have to interview all of its main players. "My research [was mostly] on Praxis's rhetoric itself" (Worthington 2011–12). Catch phrases on the broad left like "critical analysis" or "peace and mankind" came across as *ipso facto* samples of Soviet jargon for Worthington with his narrow Cold War outlook. In retrospect, his warnings about peace groups vaguely resembled later warnings about Praxis in the *Toronto Telegram*.

Chapter Seven

An Unsolved Crime, a Journalist's Secrets and the Suspected Burglars

The three-storey house on Huron Street that Praxis and other organizations were renting from the University of Toronto was buzzing with activity, recalls Lynn Kaye, who went by her married name, Lynn Lang, in the late sixties/early seventies. The folks fighting to stop the Spadina expressway were ensconced in two large rooms on the ground floor at the front of the house. At the back, also on the ground floor, were another room and stairs leading to the basement. Upstairs on the second floor was the Praxis operation, where Howard Buchbinder worked in the front office while another room was dedicated to the planning of the upcoming January 1971 Poor People's Conference. There were also stairs leading to the third floor, where Gerry Hunnius hovered over his assignments. The Just Society Movement members usually gathered to plan and talk in the back room on the ground floor, where the kitchen was also located. There was typically rotation in the space used internally by Praxis to accommodate the needs of specific projects (Kaye 2018). Buchbinder, for instance, allowed his office to be used by others. There was fluidity in how the interior of 373 Huron became the hub of activist activity in the city.

The Break-In

All of this would come to an abrupt end on the December 18, 1970, when wet snow was already covering the ground. The RCMP Security Service, in a December 22 internal memo a few days later, reported from a number of sources that at approximately 9:30 pm a fire was set by unknown individuals in the basement, just below the kitchen. The possibility that the cause was "an incendiary device" was raised by the Toronto Fire Chief, who requested an investigation by the Fire Marshall's office. Apparently, registration file cards pertaining to the Poor People's Conference were missing. "Other reports of damage to Praxis files range from a total loss to limited damage." Also noted in the December 22 memo was that Bell, in disconnecting the telephone inside the damaged house, had uncovered a wire tap. "Responsibility for the suspected arson has been directed against someone who is reacting to Praxis because of the recent *Toronto Telegram* articles by Peter Worthington." Furthermore, University of Toronto campus security personnel were guarding the premises, and "Praxis has filed a theft report with the Metro [Toronto] city police of $40 and 300 card files," the memo added (RCMP Security Service 1970d).

Before the break-in, the entire day at Praxis on December 18 was taken up with a huge mailing to delegates from participating organizations for the planned Toronto conference, scheduled for January 7–19, 1971. By the end of the day, files were spread on a table on the second floor alongside the windows overlooking the street, says Lang. Normally, the conference registration material would have been inside a Samsonite briefcase, which she carried around with her all the time. This day would be the exception, with unfortunate results.

"I was in the middle of my task when I had to go home to pick something up. I asked people in the office to assure me they would be there until I got back. Unexpectedly, a friend who had been travelling in Europe for a couple of years showed up on my doorstep as I arrived at home. It took me longer than I expected to get back to the office [which was locked by that time] … On returning, I followed a fire truck as it turned up Huron and was devastated to discover it had stopped at Praxis, which was all ablaze. It was devastating to realize that all the delegate information and registration applications were in the burning building and horribly ironic to think that I'd been carrying them around everywhere [until that night]" (Kaye 2018).

On December 22, the same day the Security Service issued its internal report on the fire and theft, Praxis representatives held a press conference. It was Abraham Rotstein (according to Meyer Brownstone) who wrote the press release, which revealed that office staff in the days preceding the burglary had received harassing telephone calls following the publication of Worthington's series of articles on Praxis. "We do not know who took the files or the money. We do not know how the fire started. We do not know if they are connected. We do know that these events occur in a sequence which is closely related in time to a series of irresponsible newspaper articles" (Buchbinder n.d.). Stephen Clarkson told reporter Eric Mills for the *Varsity*, the University of Toronto student newspaper, in an article in an early January, that Worthington had created the atmosphere that would have inspired an extreme right group to torch Praxis. He did not name the Edmund Burke Society but that is whom he meant. "One can be responsible for a crime without actually committing it," Clarkson stated (Mills 1971).

Just days after the Praxis press conference, Worthington shot back in the *Telegram* with a warning: "Only the fact that Praxis feels itself rather unpleasantly wounded with the truth would spur its executive to sanction invective and venom that patently endangers them to a libel suit" (1970c).

Clarkson has never strayed from his perception that Worthington's writing and the break-in, fire and theft were not entirely coincidental: "The link to the *Telegram* to me was pretty clear because when I got to the fire, the only reporter there was from the *Telegram*; it is as if they had some advance notice about this" (Clarkson 2010). Praxis itself had considered suing the journalist for what it viewed as slanderous insinuations in his series in the *Telegram*. But the staff realized too late that the deadline for filing a claim had been missed. In turn, Worthington never pursued his threatened legal action.

The Praxis story continued to have more twists than a pretzel. A few weeks following the break-in, Worthington received a mysterious telephone call that some of the stolen research institute documents were being delivered to him at the newspaper, and they weighed between twenty and thirty pounds. Fearing a set-up, he immediately mentioned what was about to happen to his editor at the *Telegram*. "All I wanted was a witness on receiving the boxes and the Tely's manager editor seemed sufficient." He says he never discovered the identities of the two or three men in heavy coats who "unceremoniously" shoved the files into his arms." One of the visitors had a Ukrainian accent. "They drove onto the parking area on the Tely roof [and came to] the back door and did not enter the building ... The meeting was just a delivery — no discussion" (Worthington 2011–12).

Afterward, the journalist embarked upon reading the delivered material, which related to Praxis, the Just Society Movement, Stop Spadina,

Metro Tenants and the Poor People's conference. More than file cards had been taken. He made note of the internal documents and position papers, finding material relating to how to handle the media, schools targeted for "radical politics" and priorities for political action, as well as workers' control papers and lists of people with specific assignments. The content was disappointing from a reporter's perspective. "The material was interesting but unusable; it did not strike a chord." Worthington remarked that the "easiest to understand" was the material pertaining to the Stop Spadina organization, the other targeted group, which included references to meetings in private homes, notes on the backs of envelopes and a mimeographed list for a conference of the Waffle Movement (the left wing faction of the NDP in the early 1970s). Plus, there was a list of potential left-wing donors whom Praxis could hit up for money (Worthington 1979).

I managed to obtain a copy of the list of the specific items, including Praxis documents delivered to Worthington, via my access-to-information requests through Library and Archives Canada and CSIS. The journalist had indeed come into possession of a bundle of internal and confidential correspondence pertaining to a range of potential contracts inside and outside government and even outside the country — in the US — that would be typical fare in any organization that relies on research for its financial survival. Names galore on various lists of activists, supporters and potential clients were also in the package.

Eventually, Worthington telephoned the Metro Toronto Police, who directed him to the RCMP. "I turned everything over to them and that was the last I heard of it" (Worthington 2011–12). He did not reveal publicly in his columns that he had received the files or what happened to them until 1977, when the MacDonald Commission was called to investigate the RCMP Security Service. What the *Telegram* columnist did not realize at the time was that a second batch of stolen Praxis documents was delivered around the same time or later to the Mounties' headquarters in Toronto by an informant for the Security Service inside the Edmund Burke Society, an extreme right-wing and anti-communist organization. The plot was just starting to thicken.

After the burglary the local Toronto media quickly lost interest in the Praxis story, but *Varsity* reporter Eric Mills decided to pursue Stephen Clarkson's contention that members of the extreme right, inspired by

Worthington's writing, had done the break-in and arson at Praxis. He contacted Paul Fromm, a U of T student and co-founder of the ultra conservative Edmund Burke Society (EBS). The organization was named after a nineteenth-century conservative political thinker who abhorred the French Revolution but would probably not have subscribed to the extreme views of this Toronto body a century later.

Fromm, who had a media profile in the late 1960s, was in a boastful mood, declaring to Mills that the EBS publication *Straight Talk* had undertaken "an intensive investigation into Praxis," which represented "one of the major thrusts of radicalism in the city." He suggested, without providing evidence that an effort was being made to frame the *Toronto Telegram* columnist, who "didn't write anything we didn't already know." The young man also claimed that the Edmund Burke Society was in contact with police agencies in the US in an investigation of Howard Buchbinder. But this was only the beginning, he continued, ominously. "We're willing to go a lot further than Worthington did" (Mills 1971). However, Fromm denied suggestions that the EBS had anything to do with the burglary and fire at Praxis.

A few years ago, I met up with an older and more rumpled Fromm, the godfather of a new generation of white nationalists and white supremacists and an admirer of Ernst Zundel, the Germany-born publisher convicted of publishing anti-Semitic hate material denying the Holocaust — whom he strangely kept quoting in our interview in a crowded donut joint as a font of political wisdom. This seemed designed to make me, a Jew who lost family to the Nazi genocide during World War II, especially uncomfortable. The older Fromm was more subdued on what happened decades ago at Praxis, not recalling the statements he made to Eric Mills of any relationship with police agencies, which is one of unresolved aspects of this story (Fromm 2012).

Meanwhile, in the weeks following the Praxis break-in, the University of Toronto, which owned both 373 Huron and the adjoining semi-detached house at 371 (a rooming house renting space for students), arranged to have both properties torn down. A spokesperson for the campus administration explained in an interview with *Varsity* that the decision was made "in view of the extensive damage and costs of repairing" (Mills 1971). Support for the demolishment also came from the president of the local residents' group, the Huron-Sussex Association.

"I hope that our insurance settlement will be sufficient for demolition, sodding and fencing," wrote K.S Gregory, an administrative assistant in the U of T's physical plant department in a December 30 memo, which can be found in the university's archives (Gregory 1970). The facilities manager was worried about the presence up the street on Bloor of Rochdale College, the alternative youth counter-culture centre. It seemed to factor in the decision to demolish. "I am concerned about the possibility of Rochdale-hippie moves to take over the vacant land [where the burned property stood]."

But these assertions that the property where Praxis was based was so damaged that it had to be torn down were disputed by Peter Holland, a graduate student in placement at the time at Praxis and for many years afterward involved in housing for the Department of National Defence. He speculates that the burglars probably entered the house through the door at the back from the laneway to avoid being heard or seen by neighbours on this leafy residential street (Holland 2012).

Grant Reid, another social work graduate student at Praxis suggests that the decision to demolish the two adjoined houses was purely a practical consideration by the U of T, which had development plans in the works for a whole slew of similar dwellings it owned on Huron Street. In the end the development project was nixed because of opposition from local residents. "[373 Huron] could have been salvaged, but the house was owned by the University of Toronto and there was planning in the long run to tear down those houses in any case. So, there was no motivation on their part to fix it" (Reid 2010).

A unique perspective comes from Peter Russell, a retired U of T political science professor who was an early Praxis board member and the principal of Innis College during part of the 1970s. He denies that the top U of T administrators had any role in the demolishing of 373 and 371 Huron and suggests instead that middle-level facilitates management with more conservative right-wing attitudes had no compunction about eliminating any reminder that Praxis and its house ever existed. Furthermore, 373 Huron was previously owned by the Anglican Church and happened to be the residence of his brother, Campbell, who served as a chaplain on campus. Once Campbell left for another job in 1969, the house became available for the new Praxis research institute. At some point the address was sold to the University of Toronto. Russell agrees that 373 Huron, despite the fire, was in reasonable shape and could have been restored and used again by the university (Russell 2019).

Fortunately, on the night of the fire no one was home in the attached house, number 371, which was largely inhabited by students living in separate rooms and paying their rent money directly to the university. One of them, Bill Allison, a zoology student, was making his way home from a Christmas party later that evening when he encountered blue-uniformed U of T security, who were blocking tenants from returning to retrieve whatever was left of their belongings inside the charred remains of their dwelling. Among the items destroyed or wrecked were Allison's class notes and a field book. He says that before that night he had paid little attention to the goings on of the research institute next door. "It was clear the fire originated on the Praxis side in the basement, burned through the wall and the basement wall into my place. I didn't have a chance to inspect the Praxis side, but peering through the hole the damage on that side seemed worse than on my side" (Allison 2011.)

Finally, in February 2011, I contacted the Toronto Police (no longer the Metro Toronto Police) for any records they might have kept on the unsolved Praxis burglary and fire. I knew that the chances were small because of the immense number of break-ins that occur in this major city. A spokesperson wrote back saying that nothing could be found on the matter. "Please be advised that the record may have been purged under the Toronto Police Service Record Retention Schedule," wrote K. Watts, co-ordinator of the access and privacy section for the force (Watts 2011).

The Poor People's Conference

After the burglary of the Praxis offices, staff member Lynn Lang was scrambling to reassemble the list of delegates for the upcoming conference from scratch. Praxis was now deprived of an office, files or desks and had to set up shop elsewhere. This was before the invention of the Internet, smart phones and other electronic devices that would have helped them communicate with far flung delegates across the country. Leonard Shifrin at the National Council of Welfare, which had been responsible for conceiving the event in the first place, gave Praxis access to free government phones to make arrangements for the conference (Kaye 2018). The unsolved crime and initial media coverage emboldened more people than had been expected to decide to cross the country and show up for the conference. The funding to cover their transportation costs came courtesy of several federal government departments. The largest donor was Health and Welfare, which contributed $68,000 towards the travelling and billeting costs of the approximately five hundred delegates from about two hundred organizations, identified as active low-income groups (Walker 1971: 15).

The Poor People's Conference was held on January 7–10, 1971, at the Lord Simcoe Hotel in downtown Toronto. The national conference had been planned by a committee involving representatives of poor peoples' organizations and Praxis, without the direct involvement of Ottawa. It was a golden opportunity for representatives of marginalized portions of the Canadian population from different parts of the country to meet and share experiences. Media coverage was intense. After a great deal of debate the conference delegates agreed, in a close vote, to allow reporters to cover the general discussion, but they were kept out of the individual workshops. The argument was made that this would allow delegates to speak freely without the presence of TV cameras. "It supplied the delegates with an opportunity to discuss and experience the very real problems related to the power of the media," wrote Bob Smith, a reporter for the Vancouver-based *Georgia Straight*. He said that as he was writing for the alternative media he was given less of a hassle about his presence (Smith 1971). He also noted that delegates upset with some of the news coverage got a thrill out of their decision to poke a stick at the reporters on hand. The list of conference workshops reveals that some provided basic information to delegates who were to new community organizing, such as handling the media, conducting demonstrations and resolving the invariable splits over issues in community organizations.

The reporting was not necessarily all unfavourable, but there were some hiccups along the way. An old stereotype bubbled to the surface in a headline on the first edition of the *Globe and Mail* article: "Bar Business Brisk as 450 Poor Check into Lord Simcoe Hotel for Convention" (Smith 1971; Walker 1971: 35). This headline was quickly changed in the second edition. (In those pre-digital times, newspapers published several editions throughout the day). *Telegram* reporter Pat Johnson broke the delegates into categories by the emotions they individually displayed, which included despair, hope, determination, anger, fear and militancy. Doris Power, a member of the conference planning committee, was cited as displaying the greatest amount of anger during the proceedings. This was ironic, Johnson wrote, because Power was selected to head the press committee to publicize problems of the poor. "Yet, hers was one of the more bitter, angry voices trying to keep the press out" (Johnson 1971). Not mentioned was the possibility that this may have arisen from how Praxis and her organization, the Just Society Movement, were being treated by Peter Worthington in Johnson's newspaper.

A wide range of resolutions were passed that pointed sharply at the state of poverty in Canada in 1971 that sound familiar to our ears today. They included insufficient housing, the high rate of economic inequality, the tax advantages provided to the wealthy and the lack of meaningful work. A raft of motions expressed outrage at the treatment of all poor people, including Indigenous Peoples, people of colour and other minorities, at the hands of the law, police and prisons. One resolution spoke of the police entrapping citizens to commit a crime and then arresting them for doing it. Another requested assistance for those released from a penal institution, and a third asked for less use of solitary confinement. Unfortunately, no specific examples or cases were mentioned in the handbook of resolutions but they seem to reflect discontent in the early seventies with the Canadian justice system. Also taken to task were the provinces and the federal government for not living up to their respective legal obligations in the provision of social assistance under the Canada Assistance Plan (Buchbinder n.d.).

What generated the greatest attention in the press and some political fireworks involved telegrams sent by delegates to governments in Ottawa and Quebec, condemning the "repressive legislation" in the War Measures Act and calling for the restoration of civil liberties to Canadian citizens in Quebec. The War Measures Act was passed by Parliament on October 16, 1970, at the urging of Pierre Trudeau's government during the October Crisis. Only the small federal NDP caucus led by Tommy Douglas stood opposed to the bill.

A state of "apprehended insurrection" was officially declared to exist in Quebec following two kidnappings by separate cells of the underground Front de libération du Québec (FLQ). Kidnapped were British trade commissioner James Cross and Quebec labour minister Pierre Laporte. The Trudeau government turned down the FLQ's ransom demands, which included the release of jailed members of the group, half a million dollars and the broadcast of the FLQ manifesto. Laporte's body was discovered on October 17. Police detained 497 people under the powers of the new federal emergency legislation, the majority of whom were eventually released. Sixty-two remained facing charges.

One of the dramatic elements of the October Crisis was the sight of the Canadian military patrolling the streets and buildings in Montreal. Emotions were still raw in Canada a few months later among those who had supported the actions of the Trudeau government and others who were appalled (including many Poor People's Conference attendees) by the jailing of innocent activists and artists.

Following the Poor People's Conference, there were demonstrations by some of the participants across Canada in a National Day of Action on January 26. Looking back, Laurell Ritchie, a JSM member who had assisted in the organizing of the national conference, says the event was remarkable in that it managed to get off the ground during the winter despite the disappearance of the initial registration forms. "I can't even remember what we went through to get people there. Because again it's not like you could book people electronically or track things. You had to get all these people there who were for the most part poor. These were not people who travelled by train or car, never mind planes. This is not what people have money for. Nor did they know how to go about booking and trusting there was a hotel waiting for them at the other end and working out getting taxis" (Ritchie 2012).

Wilson Head gave Howard Buchbinder high marks for reconciling the sometimes acrimonious discussions of the planning committee to reach an agreement on how the Poor People's Conference would proceed. The former Social Planning Council executive provided some background in his autobiography, *A Life on the Edge: Experiences in Black and White in North America* (1995). Head was sympathetic to the analysis of poverty and welfare and the sheer anger and frustration expressed on the floor. In his book, looking back twenty-four years, he was judgemental and maybe harsh in his general assessment of the ambition and range of resolutions at the Poor Peoples' Conference. "From my perspective, their anger and discontent made it very difficult for them to think rationally. There was no possibility that many of their demands would be met."

There was something missing in terms of concrete plans to move forward after the conference. Fellow delegates shouted him down at one point. Head retrospectively questioned the lack of an ongoing strategy to pressure politicians, who would otherwise ignore them because they had neither the power nor the finances to lobby for change. "My Quaker philosophy was of immense value as we went through some difficult sessions. Over a period of several meetings the negative attitude of poor members began to subside and more constructive dialogue became possible." He felt a chasm as a middle-class professional who had worked for social justice in Canada and the US with those assembled.

The conference was mostly about representatives of isolated poor peoples' groups meeting each other for the first time, Head wrote. But the excitement of that would soon wear off. He felt what was missing here were plans to mobilize poor people for political action, which involved joining political parties and getting out their vote at election time (Head 1995: 281–84). Many in the anti-poverty movement wanted poor people to directly participate in the delivery of social programs, but Head was sceptical, drawing attention to the co-opting of poor people into staff positions in the US in the War on Poverty, where he believed they started to sound and act like the professionals they were opposing.

Leonard Shifrin was more favourable about how the conference had progressed. He also expressed the thought that poor people cannot achieve any gains on their own because of the social, political and institutional barriers they face (Shifrin 2011–13).

Meanwhile, there was no official comment from Ottawa on the resolutions coming out of the Poor People's Conference. The first mention of the conference came on March 16 on Parliament Hill in a lively exchange between a low-profile Liberal backbencher and the RCMP Commissioner W.L. Higgitt during a review of the estimates for the federal Department of the Solicitor General. Harold Stafford, the Member of Parliament for Elgin in Ontario, asked Higgitt if he was "at all concerned" about the Poor People's Conference and the resolution sympathizing with the jailed members of the Front de libération du Québec. "Of course, I'm concerned. I am as concerned as is every Canadian," replied Higgitt. Stafford also questioned the top Mountie about the role of conference organizer Praxis, "which seems more interested in promoting dissatisfaction and agitation towards changes in the system we live under than it is in helping the poor." (The MP was making the assumption that the two motives were incompatible.) (*Hansard* 1971; Walker 1971: 39–40). The RCMP commissioner was non-committal during the parliamentary session with Stafford, claiming he had never heard of Praxis or of its two principal directors, Gerry Hunnius and Howard Buchbinder. Indeed, Higgitt did not want to disclose publicly that for national security reasons the RCMP Security Service was monitoring the research institute and secretly in possession of the stolen Praxis documents, including the missing registration forms for the Poor People's Conference.

In retrospect Leonard Shifrin gave the national Poor People's Conference credit for the event happening at all, given the challenges facing those who had to organize it and the difficulties many people had in making their way to the conference. He described the role of Praxis as positive and crucial since it was a trusted organization by the most militant of activists within the anti-poverty movement, which gave the conference the credibility it required. "We had no doubt whatsoever about the kinds of resolutions that the Poor People's Conference was going to generate, and we hoped that would increase pressure on the government to do the things that we were trying to get them to do." It is very likely that Shifrin wanted the conference to publicize the issue of poverty as the Trudeau government was shifting in a different direction (Shifrin 2011–13).

Another assessment of the conference comes from David Walker, author of a 1971 PhD thesis, "The Poor People's Conference: A Study of the Relationship Between the Federal Government and Low-Income Interest Groups in Canada," and later elected as a Liberal MP in Manitoba. He says the Trudeau government in its first term (1968–1972) invested funds to help poor people's organizations get off the ground across Canada. In 1970 the amount reached an estimated $7.5 million. John Munro's department, Health and Welfare, starting in 1969 had its own welfare grants program, which distributed $2.5 million annually for community action and research for low-income neighbourhoods. Similar programs were set up at Secretary of State and Central Mortgage and Housing Corporation. Walker says that the first grant given to a community went to Nova Scotia's Black United Front, which received a total of $100,000 annually over a five-year period from Health and Welfare and Secretary of State.

"Many departments in the federal government were reorganized in order to deal not only with the poverty question but also with the wider problem of alienation among citizens. It was felt that the failure of many government projects was taking its toll on the democratic nature of the

Canadian political system. 'Community development,' 'social animation,' 'participation' and 'power to the people' became the words to describe the new techniques and slogans of government," wrote Walker (1971: 5).

In the long term, participatory democracy would prove to be a little intimidating for politicians inside the Trudeau government. In the early summer of 1970, the federal Liberal cabinet set up an interdepartmental committee to investigate the government's support of various voluntary associations. The ambivalence of the government towards the anti-poverty movement could be felt here. "In cabinet meetings during June there were several references to the disquieting effect that low-income groups were having on the urban environment especially in Toronto," Walker wrote (66).

Cabinet minister Robert Stanbury, in a review of government assistance for voluntary associations, stated that a "'splendid" opportunity existed in knowing the nature of activities and people receiving the support ahead of the 1972 federal election, where his government faced stiff opposition from the Conservatives and the NDP. He emphasized the Liberals could benefit politically from these new relationships. (Walker 1971: 67)

Others in the Liberal Party, especially Toronto MPs close to politicians at the civic level, questioned the value of granting funds to community groups to support citizen participation. Toronto's mayor William Dennison, although not a Liberal himself, told a gathering of urban renewal officials about how ancient Greece had collapsed from "too much talk and not enough action." He continued: "The continued erosion of the authority and responsibility of the elected politicians can lead to a balkanization of our society" (quoted in Enright 1970a: 1). Mayors Dennison, Jean Drapeau (Montreal) and Tom Campbell (Vancouver) all called for the cancellation of these grants to local residents' groups in their respective cities. There was so much opposition by municipal politicians that the federal Liberal Party policy convention of 1970 defeated motions favouring direct funding of local citizens' and tenants' associations. Trudeau's federal cabinet ignored this resolution.

Walker, who had good contacts in the Trudeau government, reported that there was concern that helping poor people organize might provide a vehicle for resentment and anger targeting local democratically elected authorities. This argument was given new impetus following the resolutions passed at the 1971 Poor People's Conference. In a proactive measure the RCMP Security Service had planted agents or found informants among the delegates at the national conference. "The purpose of the Conference was to unite the poor into a national force to solve the problems of poverty. Praxis Corporation and the Just Society viewed the Conference as a vehicle through which the delegates could be politicized and by placing their own followers in key positions on the National Committee," wrote High and Green (1971: 17). This was not the experience of Wilson Head, who found delegates at the Poor People's Conference to be fractious and not easily controlled by anybody, including Praxis.

In October 1970, around the time the crisis in Quebec was unfolding, Don Beavis, an official with the Security Panel Secretariat at the Privy Council Office (PCO), contacted the RCMP Security Service. He stated that four senior cabinet ministers — Robert Andras, Robert Stanbury, Donald MacDonald and John Munro — were showing an interest in "any additional information concerning Praxis." The list included Munro, whose department had hired Praxis to organize the national Poor People's Conference but appeared uneasy about the contract. Quietly though, Munro "had requested that a full confidential report on all Praxis people be supplied," wrote F.E. Goudge, an official from the Department of Health and Welfare to the RCMP Security Service on December 30, 1970, just two weeks after the break-in and fire at the institute office. Later, on January 8, 1971, the second day of the Poor People's Conference, Arthur Butroid, a departmental security officer at Manpower and Immigration also requested an assessment of Praxis (Higgins, Summers and Zelmer 1982: 1-2). "May I be provided with an assessment on the Praxis Corp, please? I understand it may be infiltrated by Communists but members not necessarily supporting subversive activity," Butroid told Inspector G. Begalki at the Security Service (Butroid 1971).

By either late 1970 or early 1971, the Privy Council, which advises the Prime Minister's Office, was taking on the role of the "co-ordinating centre for information on Praxis" Unknown to Praxis, its almost charismatic ability to generate research contracts among some federal department managers had aroused suspicions in Ottawa. A letter from the Department of the Secretary of State was addressed to Don Beavis at the PCO just a month after the Poor People's Conference. "Dear Don. Howard Buchbinder of Praxis Corp. has been suggested as the man to do a study on an aspect of the relations of voluntary associations with government under the auspices of the Voluntary Action Committee of the Canadian Association for Adult Education. The Citizenship Branch will be called upon to finance the work. Is there any particular reason why we should not proceed with this?" (Secretary of State 1971).

One side story is that on January 18, 1971, an internal RCMP memo was circulating with news that the Poor People's Conference was "in the hole." Howard Buchbinder was at one point asking for additional $400–$500 and later in the document is quoted wanting another $1,250. The tone suggests a desire inside the RCMP Security Service to compromise or punish Leonard Shifrin, head of the National Council of Welfare, for his role in making the conference happen. "Considering the amounts of money already allocated to the conference and the suggestion 'Sheffrin' has 'outfoxed' the Treasury Board and would be in trouble if he was found out, the government might well be advised to look into this matter, at this particular time," the investigator wrote. Shifrin's name was misspelled throughout this short memo (RCMP Security Service 1971h). The gambit did not work. Nothing came of a move to discredit the NCW head. Shifrin continued to run the National Council of Welfare until 1975 and then later wrote on social policy for newspapers.

CMHC and the Challenges of Staying Afloat

Praxis had developed a strong interest in housing for low-income people, and this expertise was sought by what was then known as the Central Mortgage and Housing Corporation (CMHC) (since renamed the Canada Mortgage and Housing Corporation). The federal Crown agency had shifted away in 1971 from subsidizing controversial urban renewal projects across Canada but its move into the direction of social housing did not occur until after the 1972 federal election, when the newly elected Liberals found themselves in a minority government supported by the NDP.

In this transition period Praxis was awarded one research contract by CMHC valued at $68,000 to examine "the relationship of organizational forms and structures of primarily low-income citizens groups concerned with social change," and it was anticipating more work to come. A number of memos in the RCMP Praxis files show that the Security Service had informants inside Praxis attending meetings and taking notes of internal conversations about negotiations with clients and funders. In one communication dated June 11, 1970, Inspector Eric Madill wrote to another inspector, G. Begalki, about Praxis's failure to get a new $90,000 research grant with CMHC (RCMP Security Service 1970e). This job was turned down because the project contained a social action component involving organizing, which was strongly opposed. Furthermore, a CMHC official met with Howard Buchbinder and Gerry Hunnius about possibly redoing their submission so it focused entirely on pure research and cost only $26,000, which was sufficient to pay a portion of the salaries of Gerry Hunnius and Howard Buchbinder. Both men were also doing part-time teaching. Typically, this memo, like others in the batch of RCMP files, reflected an understanding of the precarious situation of Praxis, as well as a suspicion that any community organizing would invariably contribute to social unrest. (This was another sample of the hyperbole surrounding Praxis in Security Service communications.)

The Security Service seemed to be in the dark about federal civil servants inside CMHC making decisions to provide Praxis with contracts, beyond knowing their names and responsibilities. Many of the details about them are redacted. In a December 11, 1970, memo Constable R.G. Hurst discussed with Sgt. S. Schultz the challenge of understanding the inner workings of the crown corporation. "Through the activities of various groups, it had become evident that CMHC has in its employ several individuals in whom we hold an interest. Individually, they would appear of little significance from a penetration point of view but collectively they may pose a threat of some magnitude in relation to the objective working of the department." Constable Hurst then admitted that, "to date a lack of information is crippling a thorough assessment of their activities," beyond knowing that university graduates and former campus activists were moving into government jobs (Hirst 1970).

Meanwhile, an unsigned August 9, 1971, Security Service memo reported on the events surrounding an existing Praxis contract with CMHC. "The principals involved with Praxis have recently expressed concern that the grant they have been receiving from Central Mortgage and Housing would be terminated." Furthermore, "pressure has been put on Praxis to supply CMHC with more detailed information in relation to the names of the organizations they are studying, how many visits have been made to each organization; how many people have been interviewed; what positions or roles do they represent and what documents they have examined." (RCMP Security Service 1971i). In the same communication by the Security Service it was noted that Meyer Brownstone was paying a visit to the president and vice president of CMHC to see if the grant could be maintained. But Gerry Hunnius was described as pessimistic and purportedly urging Praxis to stall proceedings for another month so they could still collect a $4,000 cheque from CMHC. "There is evidence of a time element here and Hunnius feels that if they (Praxis) are able to force CMHC to hold another meeting regarding their grant, it would provide the necessary time lapse for Praxis to receive the cheque" (RCMP Security Service 1971i). At the same time Howard Buchbinder was reassured by one CMHC official that things were not as dire as they appeared to be. This same person was going to recommend that Praxis continue to receive the grant until the expiry date; a commitment had been made and the Crown agency was keen not to renege. Nonetheless, the answers to these detailed questions about the grant (which seem designed to end the whole thing) were absolutely necessary. Buchbinder was advised by the CMHC official to "play it cool."

Closer to the demise of Praxis, Security Service director general John Starnes informed Solicitor General Goyer in a September 23, 1971, letter that he was waiting to confirm the institute's status. "Although we have not received definite word that Praxis Corporation will in fact become defunct, it is suggested that this could occur should the grant [from CMHC] be terminated. For operational planning purposes, it would certainly be beneficial if we could determine what decision CMHC has reached in this particular case," continued Starnes. "As indicated Praxis Corporation appears to be totally dependent on its CMHC grant and until the required intelligence is received, we cannot accurately forecast the future of this organization" (Starnes 1971). In 1973, Security Service inspector Ron Yaworski reported to John Starnes that "the problem at CMHC has diminished considerably over the past year," since the money stopped going to Praxis (Yaworski 1973).

Chapter Eight

The Dirty Tricks Scandal

Howard Buchbinder, Gerry Hunnius and others working at Praxis might never have known about the circumstances surrounding the missing files following the unsolved burglary and fire had it not been for an opposition MP making a startling assertion during Question Period on February 3, 1977. Frank Oberle, an Alberta-based Progressive Conservative, stood up in House of Commons and accused the Mounties of having participated in and benefited from an illegal entry at the office of an unnamed Toronto organization (i.e., Praxis) in December 1970 and having used the information to create a secret list of twenty-one potentially disloyal civil servants (King 1977). What was not reported at the time was that although the people on the secret list did not suffer any consequences (one of them even became the president of the CBC), their names were shared with foreign intelligence agencies (Dare n.d.). The list was also circulated confidentially to fellow federal cabinet ministers by then solicitor general Jean Pierre Goyer. This was done to warn the Trudeau government that Praxis was mounting a new left–based extra parliamentary opposition.

The Mounties were not happy with the accusation that they had been responsible for the break-in and fire at Praxis, and they contacted Peter Worthington to set the record straight. Worthington, who was by then editor-in-chief at the *Toronto Sun*, was obliging, but he had probably assumed that his role in the sordid affair would never come to light. On the next day, Worthington wrote a *Sun* article carrying the blazing headline: "I gave RCMP Praxis files." He relayed again how he came into possession of the stolen material, but then made a surprising new charge about the identity of the burglars, with no evidence to back it up. "From my viewpoint, I'd be inclined to think it was an inside job from the Just Society or one of the disillusioned radical satellite elements" (Worthington 1977: 3).

McDonald Inquiry Concerning Certain Activities of the RCMP

Worthington was trying to absolve the RCMP and perhaps the extreme right of any responsibility for what happened at Praxis, but the Security Service was still facing a major crisis from revelations in the press of a host of "dirty tricks," or acts of law-breaking. Quebec was ground zero for most of this activity, which was carried out by the Security Service to counter the separatist movement following the October Crisis and the passage of the War Measures Act. The dirty tricks included break-ins, kidnappings of separatist supporters, phony FLQ memos, burning a barn to prevent a purported meeting between the FLQ and the US-based Black Panthers, stealing the Parti Québécois' membership list and tampering with the public mail.

This was happening even as the FLQ was in decline and disrepute as many supporters of the province's independence were turning to the peaceful path of a new credible political party, the Parti Québécois. The transition to a peaceful road to Quebec independence by its advocates was not fully appreciated at the Security Service, which had been given its marching orders by Ottawa to disrupt and undermine pro-independence organizations in Quebec, including law-abiding groups. The Mounties promptly extended some of the dirty tricks into English-speaking Canada against the political left, of which Praxis was the prominent if not the only example. "They were encouraging [the Security Service] to launch these disruptive operations rather than do passive surveillance, act to disrupt groups and mess with them in a number of ways including illegal methods and [Praxis] might have been part of that," said security expert Steve Hewitt, an historian at the University of Birmingham in Britain, in a 2012 interview. "Once the RCMP made this decision to take this aggressive approach things kind of spiralled out of control. Once you unleash that, it is not so easy to control and all kinds of people are caught up in these efforts." Also John Starnes, as the director general of the Security Service, would not have acted on his own. The Mounties' security and intelligence was not a rogue operation: "I've met Starnes a couple of times. He is a team player. Someone who follows orders," the academic added.

Globe and Mail journalist Jeff Sallot covered much of what happened in Quebec and Ottawa in his book *Nobody Said No: The Real Story about How the Mounties Always Get Their Man*. The title came from his surprise that nobody in any of these police operations questioned the propriety and legality of their early seventies operations. He wrote that the Security Service quietly instructed its officers that its legal branch had determined that they would not be charged for any bending of the laws in the course of their duties. RCMP commissioner W.L. Higgitt issued a memo that read as follows: "Members know — or ought to that whatever misadventure happens to them our Force will stand by them so long as there is some [underlined to stress a point] justification for doing so" (Sallot 1979: 186–89).

As mentioned previously in this book, in his role as assistant commissioner the man had been in touch with External Affairs about Praxis in February 1969. He was later questioned, in 1971, before a Commons committee about what he knew about Praxis. He told MPs he was not familiar with the name. More significantly, the top Mountie had figured prominently during the height of the Security Service dirty tricks in the early seventies, wrote Jeff Sallot. This is what the *Globe and Mail* journalist said about William Leonard "Len" Higgitt: "A trim man even in his fifties, he looked every inch the policeman who had risen to the top because of intelligence, dedication and honest hard work. His sharp facial features betrayed no hint that he knew about skeletons in the closet. But in thirty-six years with the force he had learned a lot, especially about how to keep secrets" (Sallot 1979: 17–18).

In essence, Higgitt was really providing political cover for these officers since the Trudeau government was reluctant to press charges against the RCMP officers who were up to their eye balls in the dirty tricks operations, says historian Reg Whitaker, co-author of *Secret Service: Political Policing in Canada from the Fenians to Fortress America* (2112). Whitaker suggests that these internal memos by Higgitt to officers had no serious legal weight but that did not matter at the time. "[Higgitt] might have been confident *politically* that he could deflect charges, which would say something about relations in the 1970s between the police and the government that was supposed to answer for police conduct, which might explain the lack of criminal charges filed [in the dirty tricks affair]. But that is different from some ironclad guarantee of immunity, which I don't think he had any legal basis for offering" (Whitaker 2014).

In July 1977 the Trudeau government mandated a royal commission headed by Judge David McDonald to examine "certain activities" of the RCMP. The aim was to clean up what was turning into a public relations nightmare for a prime minister whose civil libertarian reputation had already been tarnished by the suspension of the liberties of Canadians in October 1970. The McDonald Commission's director of research, Peter Russell, told me in an interview that the inquiry was focused more on reforming the Mounties than providing a full picture of credible reports of law-breaking by the Security Service. Russell's research staff, sitting at one end of an L-shaped space, had little professional contact outside of a few personal occasions, such as playing recreational sports for fun, with the commissioners at the other end and thus had little sway in how the conclusions were drawn in the inquiry's final report. "We really didn't meet at all. We had no conversation about their side of things including are we going to recommend criminal charges [for the Security Service officers]." Furthermore, the mandate of the commission was focused on the "more positive aspects" of "how to recontract the security service," than getting to the bottom of what happened in the early seventies (Russell 2019).

A decade earlier, Russell had participated in early Praxis meetings and served on its board. Before his formal appointment several years later as research director of the McDonald Commission, which involved the examination of sensitive documents, he found himself during a security check the object of suspicion from the Mounties. A large file had been kept on him, presumably on his robust sixties and seventies activism, including protesting the US war in Vietnam. Judge McDonald and his commissioners dismissed all of this and agreed to hire Russell, saying in passing they were potentially as subversive in supporting political causes as their colleague, according to the Russell.

Russell explains that the Security Service had three targets during the Cold War — terrorism, espionage by the Soviet Union and subversion — the latter vaguely aimed at anybody like him engaging in political protest. One positive result of the commission's work was a recommendation to eliminate subversion as a target by Canada's security and intelligence service. That was followed in the writing of the mandate for the new security and intelligence service, CSIS, which replaced the Security Service and was established as a separate agency from the RCMP in 1984 (Russell 2019).

The whole experience of the McDonald Commission was entirely disappointing for Praxis lawyer Paul Copeland, whose request to appear before the inquiry to discuss what had happened to his client was turned down (Copeland 2012). Unknown to him there was an intense debate behind the scenes among McDonald Commission lawyers as to whether Corporals G.K. Grant and Ron Pankew, the RCMP officers responsible for accepting a second batch of Praxis documents in early 1971 (in addition to what Worthington had given the force one month earlier), should be charged for their actions. Ontario's attorney general Roy McMurtry made the decision in May 1978 not to charge any of the officers in the Praxis affair. He issued a press statement quoting his comments in the Ontario legislature defending the decision: "The documents were not retained by [the RCMP Security Service] for criminal purposes and there was no intention on their part to obstruct us in our investigations ... The RCMP had co-operated fully with us ... As a result of the investigation, the Metropolitan Toronto Police are satisfied that no member of the RCMP or any agent of theirs was involved in the offence [the criminal acts at Praxis in December 1970] (McMurtry 1978).

There were also no legal consequences for the late 1974 destruction of records by the Security Service in operations Oddball, Tent Peg and Checkmate, which might have provided the commissioners with further insights into the surveillance of the Canadian new left by the force in general. The Mounties wanted to avoid what had happened in the US — where a disturbing picture of the FBI's counter-intelligence program (COINTELPRO) of illegal break-ins of the offices of anti-war and African American activists (dubbed "black bag jobs") had come out in Congress. One name that comes up among the RCMP Security Service officers who participated in the decision to eliminate these sensitive documents is none other Ron Yaworski, the author of various internal memos quoted in this book about Praxis, CMHC and curbing restless young activist youth in Canada.

The dirty tricks scandal during the late 1970s represented a dramatic climb down for members of the RCMP Security Service, who had regarded themselves as untouchable earlier in the decade, says award-winning investigative journalist James Dubro, who started reporting on police activity and organized crime around 1974 (Dubro 2012). Doug Grant, another journalist who followed the Mounties, in the late seventies for CBC News, refers to "a culture of deniability" within the RCMP: "A lot of officers in the RCMP Secret Service did things they never told anybody about ... They would do something and the RCMP brass claimed they didn't know what was going on" (2012).

Superintendent John Venner, who in the late seventies was responsible for overseeing the southwestern Ontario branch of the Security Service, which included Toronto, is quoted in an internal June 1977 memo by Corporal G.K. Grant (in the my accessed RCMP Praxis files) as informing a meeting of officers that the future of the Security Service was at stake and "could very well be destroyed over this issue, the Praxis affair" (Grant 1977).

"There was ferocious non-cooperation from the Mounties, which is very evident in the transcripts of the in-camera hearings with Mountie witnesses," says Reg Whitaker. "Even on the printed page the contempt and hostility of some of the Mounties is palpable. In the face of this, there was only so far the commission could delve," the professor continued. Clearly, RCMP officers personally responsible for the dirty tricks were scared of being hung out to dry for decisions made by their political masters in the Trudeau government, who admitted during the hearings to giving out the general orders, but not specific ones, regarding the illegal acts reported in the press. Whitaker argues that the MacDonald Commission failed to go after the Trudeau government on the matter of ministerial responsibility. "The worst example of this is the study done for the commission by its legal staff on ministerial responsibility that the commissioners buried, even denying it had ever been commissioned or completed. I have read this document, which did survive in the commission records, and it does implicate ministers in some degree of knowledge of illegal activities" (Whitaker 2014).

Questions were raised about the Liberal Party affiliation of some of the people running the McDonald Commission and how that might compromise their work. More charitably, Whitaker suggests that the commission made the calculation that its major priority was to split the policing and intelligence functions of the RCMP (hence the creation of the separate agency, CSIS, in 1984). The proposal had been discussed earlier but this time there was a better chance of success if the culpability of ministers or the Prime Minister himself in the scandal was not explored.

Parallels with a Quebec Break-In

What had precipitated the McDonald Commission was another burglary, this one in 1972, where the involvement of police officers was indisputable. Praxis lawyer Paul Copeland says the parallels with the Praxis case are fascinating but we will get to that shortly. The circumstances surrounding the break-in at the Agence presse libre du Québec (APLQ) were revealed by RCMP officer Robert Samson while on the stand in March 1976 at a fire commissioner's inquiry in Montreal. He was answering questions about the injuries he suffered from an incendiary device exploding in his hands one night in front of the home of a supermarket executive. Worse things than planting a bomb had happened, Samson told the hearing.

Jeff Sallot in his book provides a good account of what happened. The APLQ was a small left-wing news agency operating out of what he described as a "drab, grey stone building" in east end Montreal. It published a magazine, the *Bulletin*, and shared spaced with the Movement for the Defence of Political Prisoners of Quebec, which was working to reimburse the legal bills of jailed FLQ members. A report that one of the APLQ members had been in touch with a one of the FLQ kidnappers of James Cross living in exile in Cuba caught the attention of the three police forces — the Montreal Police, the Quebec Provincial Police and the RCMP Security Service. The combined police operation carried out the burglary and brought out a load of documents, including back issues of the *Bulletin* in hockey bags. In the end the operation proved to be fruitless since no incriminating evidence of new FLQ-style terrorist plot was discovered (Sallot 1979: 21–37).

Instead, the officers in the APLQ break-in found a long letter from a chastened former FLQ member Jacques Cossette-Trudel. He was contrite about his own role in the kidnapping of James Cross and clearly unhappy living in exile from Quebec. Jeff Sallot reported that the documents stolen in Operation Bricole were eventually destroyed. After the burglary, the APLQ publicly accused the police of staging the burglary and theft in telegrams sent to senior politicians and police officers. This was five years before the revelations of RCMP dirty tricks and so the news media did not take these claims seriously. Also, nobody in an official capacity in Quebec City or Ottawa owned up to what had occurred. It seems that the three major men overseeing national security in Canada when the break-in happened in September 1972 — RCMP commissioner W.L. Higgitt, Solicitor General Jean Goyer; and Security Service Director General John Starnes — were all familiar with what had happened at the APLQ after the event if not before and participated in the cover-up afterward, the *Globe* journalist wrote (Sallot 1979: 21–37).

Starnes was personally disappointed that he was not told ahead of time about the planning of Operation Bricole, which was supposed to deter another planned terrorist act, supposedly in the works after the October Crisis (Sallot 1979: 21–37). What is interesting here for Praxis watchers is how the police reacted to the revelations about the APLQ break-in after Robert Samson revealed it, says Paul Copeland. The Montreal police made sure the officers involved in Operation Bricole from the three forces were charged, but not for breaking-and-entering and theft at the APLQ — the offence they had committed. Instead they faced what Copeland calls "a made-up offence" of entering the premises without first obtaining a search warrant in a national security operation (Copeland 2012). All three senior officers received an absolute discharge when they pleaded guilty. Sessions Judge Roger Vincent ruled that to convict the police officers involved would "tarnish" their careers for what were "noble motives, and disinterest" in their investigation to root out potential terrorism. The decision was denounced by the *Globe and Mail* in an editorial headlined, "A crime goes unpunished" (*Globe and Mail* 1977: 6).

But there was no similar fuss over what happened at Praxis. After Worthington admitted in early February 1977 receiving the stolen Praxis documents and handing them over to the RCMP Security Service, the journalist should have been questioned by the Metro Toronto Police, according to Paul Copeland. "It is clear that the Toronto Police Service and its predecessor the Metropolitan Toronto Police Service never had any interest in investigating the break-in, theft, and arson that occurred at the Praxis office on Huron Street in Toronto in 1970" (Copeland 2012).

Worthington and Praxis lawyer Paul Copeland clashed frequently in duelling letters to the editor about the role that the journalist might have played in the Praxis affair. The lawyer wrote in one letter to the *Globe and Mail* that what happened at Praxis represented "an RCMP dirty tricks operation" and Worthington was used by the Mounties to destroy the reputation of the research institute (Copeland 1989: A6).

Copeland and Worthington were polar opposites. Before his recent retirement Copeland wore a black leather jacket and jack boots while driving his motorcycle daily to and from the law firm. He co-wrote a book about the law with fellow lefty lawyer Clayton Ruby during the 1960s, represented American draft evaders and novelist and journalist Ian Adams, and in later years took up the cause of Muslims accused of terrorism.

Worthington, who had served in Korean War and was the son of a military man, looked the part of the warrior. "Chiselled facial features, military haircut, steel gaze and probably a temper" is how one person described him. Then writing for the *Telegram* he would come to my journalism class in the mid-1970s at Western University in London, Ontario, for the occasional lecture. His wife Yvonne, who also taught there, would diplomatically end the session if her husband started on one of his anticommunism rants.

Worthington was open to an interview a few years ago, before he passed away. We communicated by email, probably because he was not well. I asked him why he did not immediately hand back the files to their rightful owner after the Praxis burglary and fire and put the matter behind him. His answer was that this was a rather an awkward situation since he was the subject of a suspicion on the left. "You got to be kidding," he exclaimed. "I was driving from Ottawa to Toronto when CBC carried news of the Praxis break-in and the Praxis people were accusing me and the *Telegram* of orchestrating the break-in and theft. Later, when boxes were delivered to me at the Tely, my immediate concern was that it was a setup and maybe Praxis intended to plant the stuff on me" (Worthington 2011–12).

Worthington vehemently denied Copeland's description of him as being more than an observer in the Praxis case. Yet, he seemed to have an insight into the thinking of the different levels of the police at the time. "I don't think the police — local or RCMP — were in the least interested in catching the burglars. I didn't know [the culprits in the criminal acts at Praxis] and was mainly anxious to distance myself from whoever did it. Just didn't want to know and the cops never questioned me — just were happy to accept the documents, which, as I remember didn't amount to much," he emailed. "My recollection is that the cops had no use for the Edmund Burke people, John Birchers or any of that ilk."

The journalist's close relationship with the Mounties is confirmed by a December 21, 1977, report written by G.H.R. Cooper, director of criminal investigation at the Ontario Provincial Police into the Praxis affair for the Ontario Attorney General's department following the revelations of the RCMP dirty tricks. The report confirmed that Worthington was in regular contact with an unidentified sergeant (possibly Schultz) heading the Security Service's Key Sectors program. This officer was responsible for targeting "subversive front organizations," served as a "liaison with the news media" and "through this aspect he came to know Peter Worthington, a staff reporter on the now defunct *Toronto Telegram*" (Cooper 1977: 16). It is a curious document since it repeats the insinuations made about Praxis in the early seventies by the Security Service and Worthington himself in the *Telegram* even though by the late seventies these allegations were being dismissed as having little merit by RCMP Superintendent John Venner in private conversations and statements. He had been asked by his superiors in the RCMP Security Service to investigate the Mountie role in the Praxis affair.

Panic at the Security Service

Security Service Superintendent John Venner, in a spring 1988 interview with the *Globe and Mail*'s reporter Peter Moon, discussed how a second batch of stolen Praxis documents, in addition to what Worthington had retrieved, arrived into the hands of the force. The two officers (Corporals G.K. Grant and Ron Pankew) who did the pickup understood that the documents were "hot" but did not realize at the time that they had been stolen. There was an apparent reluctance on the part of the Mounties to say they had come into possession of stolen goods, which was a criminal act. Venner did admit to the reporter that keeping the documents was a mistake on the part of the Security Service (Moon 1988: 1).

In other internal Security Service communications, the superintendent vehemently maintained that the RCMP had nothing to do with either the planning or execution of the break-in, theft and fire by the suspected Edmund Burke Society. More recently and living in retirement, Venner declined a request for an interview for this book, citing restrictions placed on current or former members of the RCMP and CSIS on speaking to journalists. However, I was able to obtain Venner's internal memos as part of the RCMP Praxis files that I received under the access-to-information legislation.

Meyer Brownstone recalls Venner telling him in 1977 that he would never have investigated Praxis if he had been around Toronto in the early 1970s, Venner told the former member of Praxis that he was working in Washington as the RCMP's liaison to the CIA during the 1970s and was not around at the height of the dirty tricks operations in Canada.

Venner's reputation was challenged by the two officers responsible for receiving the Praxis documents. Reg Whitaker read the June 13, 1977, memo from RCMP Corporal G.K. Grant (who has since died) and says he is not sure whom to believe in the he said–he said content (Whitaker 2014). What is without dispute is that Corporals Grant and Pankew had consulted superior officers, including Assistant Commissioner H.P. Tadeson, about dealing with an informant inside the Edmund Burke Society who seemed to be stuck with the bags of stolen Praxis documents and was anxious to unload them as soon as possible. Later revealed as Steve Drodz, this man was in such a panic that he apparently hid the material inside a church basement at one point. An anonymous RCMP source revealed to me that Cpl. Pankew, the officer responsible for developing "a trap line" of intelligence sources and informants in Toronto, had treated Drodz to a Crown Royal whiskey and dinner at a Chinese restaurant while discussing arrangements for the Security Service's pickup of the "hot" Praxis stuff. (Pankew turned down repeated requested to be interviewed.)

Grant wrote in his memo that he and Pankew accepted the claim of innocence from Drozd (referred to simply as "Informant") in terms of what transpired at Praxis in December 1970. They also had no idea that another batch of stolen Praxis documents happened to be in the hands of the Security Service and D Section, courtesy of Peter Worthington. "Informant did mention that one other party had been given access to the Praxis papers but prolonged questions failed to force him to disclose the identity of that person(s)" (Grant 1977).

After permission was given by Tadeson, Corporals Grant and Pankew and a third officer retrieved the two or three bags containing index cards and handwritten and typed pages of correspondence left by Drodz on the sidewalk on Jarvis Street in front of the Toronto RCMP office. "I was totally unfamiliar as to the nature and content of the Praxis Corp," wrote Grant, who like Pankew also dealt with finding new sources on the street. Neither was attached to D Section, which was conducting the surveillance of suspected groups like Praxis.

Corporal Grant's memo describes awkward meetings in 1977, after obtaining the stolen documents, with Superintendent Venner and other senior officers regarding the strategy to deal with the fallout of the Praxis affair as part of the greater scandal surrounding the Security Service. In Grant's version of the events, Venner wanted to put Grant and Pankew through a rehearsal of what either might say if called to testify before the

McDonald Commission. Grant and Pankew were asked to undergo a "tailored," half hour Q/A process. "[We] would be supplied with questions and the corresponding answers. This was what the Force [blank space] wanted to hear," said Grant. But he was not comfortable with this process. "Our primary concern was that we were being counselled ... to participate in what we considered to be a scheme to obstruct justice," Grant said.

Grant's memo also reveals that a plan was in the works to block the civil court action that had been started by former Praxis staffer Howard Buchbinder against the RCMP Security Service for keeping the stolen documents, which could have resulted in jail time for the officers. Someone at this internal Security Service meeting noted that the "judicial system would place barriers in the way, making it impossible for Buchbinder to lay charges." One officer stated "it was sort of sad that the system could do this" and participate in a "bureaucratic containment."

Cpl. Grant's memo was given short shrift by Superintendent Venner in a counter-statement, where the latter expressed surprise and consternation for how his 1977 meeting with Grant and Pankew was depicted. He disputed the allegation of any scheme to fix the judicial process. Grant and Pankew wrongly assumed, Venner stated, that "I was somehow trying to shift all the blame to them and thereby spare others, senior to them, from any criticism." Furthermore, the two officers "had nothing to fear" (Venner 1977).

There was something else intriguing in Corporal Grant's memo which Venner did not contradict. Grant had masqueraded as a member of an extreme right group from New York State in order, with Steve Drodz's assistance, to meet with an alleged participant in the break-in, theft and fire at Praxis. This was a "street-wise, young, political thug," Grant wrote. "[The suspect] was obviously very politically naïve, capable of only mouthing the standard diatribe, but at the same time deeply committed to the revolutionary concepts and polemics of the radical right." Grant continued: "I came away from this interview with the distinct impression that the boy was in all probability at least partly responsible for the B.E. (break and enter) and theft and possibl[y] arson. Also, "he was most definitely capable of any act injurious to anything he viewed as being in opposition to his simplistic political leanings." Grant commented that the revelation of Steve Drodz's identity as a Security Service informant to the Metro Toronto Police Department "would place him in extreme jeopardy at the hands of the boy and his confederates [inside the Edmund Burke Society]." How an exchange of information with the local police to assist in any criminal investigation of the perpetrators of the crimes at Praxis might get leaked to the Edmund Burke Society was not fully explained by Grant. No further course of action was undertaken in the case and "Cpl. Pankew and I were to consider the matter closed," Grant concluded.

Parallel conversations also occurred among McDonald Commission lawyers as to whether the two officers, Grant and Pankew, should be charged with accepting the stolen Praxis property, according to a January 25, 1980, internal memo made available through access-to-information as part of the RCMP Praxis files. Yvon Tarte, a commission lawyer was implicitly acknowledging to the three men overseeing the inquiry (Judge David McDonald, D.S. Rickerd and Guy Gilbert) that the Praxis lawyer Paul Copeland had a point (without including him in the conversation). "Under what authority can the RCMP receive and retain documents which have been received without the permission of the owner or by criminal means?" he asked. It turns out that another lawyer on staff at the commission, Margaret Hodgson, had written her own legal opinion, concluding that by holding onto stolen documents for six years, the RCMP could be charged with a criminal offence under section 312 of the Criminal Code, which deals with "possession of property obtained by a crime" (Tarte 1980a).

Nonetheless, Tarte took into account the bigger political picture, saying that Hodgson's opinion, which he shared, did not "concern itself with the niceties of ministerial discretion nor with the considerations which a judge might study for sentencing purposes after a conviction has been registered." A third lawyer on the commission, Brian Crane, countered that the documents were received and retained for national security reasons and therefore "a court would not convict." That was the position that Tarte ultimately accepted, recommending to Judge McDonald and others heading the commission that the Praxis file "be closed without conducting any further investigation." He added: "I have taken the liberty of drafting a letter which I suggest should be forwarded to Messers Buchbinder and Copeland."

Informed about these internal proceedings many decades later, the former commission research director, Peter Russell, expressed surprise that nobody from among the in-house counsel, such as Tarte, revealed any of this to him. He also regrets that none of the participating officers in the Security Service's stint of law-breaking activity, including the surreptitious opening of public mail (a serious offence), ever faced legal consequences for their actions. "As for Praxis I am sure that the Commission did not get to the bottom of the story. That can be said for a number of other cases in which the RCMP harassed and inflicted damage on what they called 'the extra-parliamentary opposition' I don't think that Commission counsel took those cases seriously enough" (Russell 2019).

Freelance Operation?

Historian Reg Whitaker argues that what happened at Praxis in December 1970 was likely a "freelance" operation, conducted by the thuggish types inside the Edmund Burke Society. Furthermore, he suggests that the stolen documents landed fortuitously in the Mounties' institutional laps in two batches, and they just ran with it. "Once [the RCMP] got the stuff, they were certainty going to use it. They had a dedicated section in the counter-subversion branch for the new left; this would have been fodder for them." Yet, he also concurs that the relationship between the Mounties and the extreme right group was especially murky and never fully explained. "The Mounties knew they had a problem, receiving and retaining stolen documents, not to speak of potential connections, via their undercover sources, with arson. Covering their asses in the face of several investigations was their prime directive" (Whitaker 2014).

As the journalist closest to the Praxis story, Worthington maintained he was never tempted or sufficiently curious to pursue the real story about the Praxis burglary, although he had written reams of copy on the politics of the institute. Worthington may have been tired of the Praxis story and wanted to move on or had other irons in the fire in terms of subjects to write about. The problem is that he was not always completely candid. He revealed in an April 11, 1979, statement, which was found in the RCMP Praxis files, that he had more than one encounter with the circle of people in the extreme right in the time period following the burglary. This was contrary to what he had originally written in his column in the *Toronto Sun*, when he admitted to having accepted stolen documents from a one-time session with them. "I remember being at some garage or place that was more like a junk yard at the back or behind a house in the Bathurst Street area. It was not like a service station that pumps gasoline. I don't recall the names of any persons at this garage but you could label them as right wing or anti-communists," says Worthington. He recalls spending half an hour or so removing some of the documents in the garage and copying them for his own use but stresses he would not have given them to the RCMP "because that's not my way of operating." He is also not certain this material had anything to do with Praxis. "What sticks in my mind is that it was mainly old newspaper clippings dating back to the 1940s and pertaining to Jewish things and the old peace movement." This was probably the auto body repair shop that Steve Drodz ran. It is also likely that Worthington found anti-Semitic material, which was the staple of anti-communist and extreme right groups in the post-World War II period.

Worthington was a little exasperated with me at this point in our email conversation about long forgotten people. I was posing a lot of questions and he was straining to remember an event a long time ago. He also downplayed his role in the Praxis affair. "You're asking a lot of stuff I simply do not remember. Praxis was just another assignment in those days — 40 years ago — and I doubt if any reporter ever has much influence, though some might like to think so."

James Dubro has his own unique perspective on the Praxis affair: "It is more likely that the [RCMP] 'actually had a role' in the burglary and arson. The Edmund Burke was a very small group; I don't think they would have had the resources or the clout" (2012). In the early seventies, Dubro was a younger journalist researching for the CBC's *The Fifth Estate*. He saw a direct parallel between the Praxis incident and the 1972 bombing of the Cuban trade mission in Montreal by an anti-Fidel Castro outfit, the Young Cuba. The aim was to get their hands on internal documents. When the local Montreal police arrived after the bombing and climbed the stairs to the twelfth floor, they were confronted by six employees in the Cuban trade mission, three of whom were armed with submachine guns while others in the group were burning sensitive papers. One of their comrades, Sergio Perez, had been killed in the explosion that had been set by the anti-Castro intruders. Eventually, the Canadian government apologized to the Castro government in Cuba for the actions of the local cops, and none of the armed Cuban mission employees faced charges. Nobody was charged in the death of Perez (Macadam and Dubro 1974).

"It was swept under the rug by the intelligence people and the Trudeau government. For some reason even Castro was happy to not make too much of an issue of the incident, I suspect not wanting to bring more attention to Cuba's own spying and influence ops," says Dubro (Dubro 2019). The incident in 1972 at the Cuban trade mission was part of an operation that had the support of the US Central Intelligence Agency and was assisted by the Montreal police, and RCMP," says Dubro, who covered this story about the CIA operating in Canada with another journalist, Bill Macadam, in an article entitled "How the CIA Was Spooked," for *Maclean's Magazine* in July 1974. They wrote that the Mounties would "run" a CIA agent's clandestine activities in Canada as a partial payment for a supposed treasure trove of intelligence data from Washington that turned out to be "largely useless." Dubro draws parallels to what happened in Toronto in December 1970. "It does remind me of the Praxis thing; it was a time when police had omnipotent power. Compared to now. You couldn't get away with now what they did in the 1970s," he continues. "The Toronto Police would have helped [the RCMP] in the Praxis situation. Just like the Montreal Police helped whoever was behind the operation in Montreal at the Cuban trade mission. Certainly, they would have helped, that is the way it was, in the seventies" (Dubro 2012).

Also taking the position that the RCMP Security Service did not accidently come into contact with the stolen Praxis documents were Howard Buchbinder and journalist Ian Adams, the latter having gravitated since the early 1970s to writing about the Mounties in both fact and fiction. Published in *This Magazine* in March 1978, their article "The Praxis Affair: How Stolen Goods Became a Cabinet Document" argued that the burglary arose out of a "classic political intelligence operation," which involved the "penetration" and "manipulation of members of the Edmund Burke Society" (Adams and Buchbinder 1978).

Two other journalists come to mind in this saga. CBC radio reporters in the late seventies, Ted Fairhurst and Doug Grant, did a lot of legwork to nail down the Praxis break-in but ended up stuck (Grant 2012). They did discover other unsolved and similar burglaries in Toronto. The most complete story of theirs involved a break-in in November 1971 by unknown people at the office of the exiled Greek Socialist Party (PASOK) on Gerrard St in Toronto. The difference is that PASOK did contact the Metro Toronto Police but sought to keep the matter quiet because of suspicions that the RCMP Security Service was the recipient of their missing files and passed that information on to the members of complementary intelligence agency in Greece working for that country's military dictatorship. This was no ordinary burglary but the CBC reporters were unable to prove any direct RCMP connection or if names in the office ended up going outside the country.

PASOK activist Spyros (Stan) Draenos told the CBC reporters that both the locks to the doors and the partition wall for their rented upper office area were broken. It was clear that membership lists containing about 250 names of exiles and their addresses and phone numbers and telexes were missing. "These were names of people who had taken a stand [in Greece] against the military dictatorship." The consequences for dissent were serious, he stated. "It ran the whole range of aggressive mechanisms from torture to simply trying to intimidate people and this list could be used to make it difficult for relatives in Greece or for people here [in Canada] who needed the services of the [official Greek government] consulate [in Canada] for whatever purposes" (Fairhurst and Grant 1978).

Draenos explained that a "hostile climate" existed for the Greek exiles in Canada in the early 1970s because of this country's relationship with Greece, both of which were NATO members. Andreas Papandreou, a PASOK leader living in Canada who taught at York University and later became prime minister of his country following the end of military rule, tried during his exile to talk to Prime Minister Trudeau but was given "the cold shoulder," Draenos told the CBC. He added that "it was clear that Trudeau didn't want anything to do with Papandreou or to disturb relationships with valuable NATO partner Greece."

No direction connected was ever made between the Praxis and PASOK break-ins. But Draenos told the CBC reporters that he did sense that there was surveillance of exiled opponents of the Greek military regime living inside the Greek community in Canada. He did call for an investigation by the McDonald Commission of any possible RCMP Security Service connection, which he agreed was speculative on his part.

Role of the Edmund Burke Society
Several years ago I met up with Jeff Goodall, a now retired Toronto City Hall employee and a member of the Edmund Burke Society in his youth, in downtown Oshawa in an almost deserted Chinese restaurant (no fancy whiskey this time). Initially, he had nothing to say about the EBS role in

the Praxis break-in, arson and theft on December 1970, maintaining he played no part. But in 2019, my source, in his seventies and mobile with a walker, appears freer personally to point to Aarne Polli as the "15-year-old ring leader" in the criminal acts. Polli was also accompanied by a second EBS member and someone outside the organization, Goodhall continued. All this was "common knowledge" inside the Burkers. "Aarne was bragging about how he was able to give the stuff to important people but I don't remember the details," says Goodall, who also heard (and this is third hand) that the back door at Praxis was accidently open, which made the break-in a much easier task. (This is new information and I cannot confirm from other sources if this was indeed true.) Furthermore, Polli was only 13 when he joined the Burkers in 1968 or 1969, to the chagrin of his Estonian-born mother, who tried unsuccessfully to take him home. Whether this is the boy that Cpl. G.K. Grant met while going underground in the far right, Goodall would not speculate, except to say that Polli looked older than his tender age and was "entirely capable of carrying out the burglary" (Goodall 2012–19). Goodall, like some other aging ex-Burkers, adheres to what we now call white nationalism. He also reveals that as an EBS member he was a big fan of segregationist governor and US presidential candidate George Wallace. But he denies that the EBS founders were originally motivated by race.

Founded in the later 1960s by Paul Fromm, Don Andrews and Lee Smith, the Edmund Burke Society started off as an officially clean-cut (i.e., anti-hippie), conservative and anti-communist alternative to the new left. They were politically aligned with US Republican politicians like Barry Goldwater and positioned themselves as defenders of Western Civilization and as militant free enterprisers. Pretty soon they expanded with a panoply of extreme positions in opposing immigration, welfare, abortion, homosexuality and especially Pierre Trudeau, writes Stanley Barrett in his authoritative book *Is God a Racist? The Right Wing in Canada* (Barrett 1989: 56–65), which relied on extensive and indepth interviews of participants. Also known as the Burkers, the society gained attention in the later sixties for their aggressive posture compared to other more diplomatic expressions of right-wing thought at the time. They had a small but annoying presence (to some) on campus at the University of Toronto, where Paul Fromm, a major spokesperson for the EBS, won a seat on student council.

Goodall confirms the research institute was certainly regarded "as the enemy" by the EBS. "Praxis Exposed! Your Money ... Their Revolution," was the front-page story in the January/February 1971 issue of *Straight Talk*, the official publication of the Edmund Burke Society. Paul Fromm was listed as the editor and Goodall as the associate editor. There was also a short profile by Fromm of the newly founded Hamilton Welfare Rights Organization and its ominous "counselling table" inside the steel city's local welfare office. The HWRO was accused of harassing welfare officials, and organizer Bill Freeman was given a special mention as a "political people planner" seeking to "insight [i.e., incite] the rabble to further despoil the working backbone of this country" (Buchbinder papers, York)

The Burkers portrayed themselves originally as upstanding conservative warriors opposing anti-Vietnam War activists and their possible influence on children and young people in the classroom. "The rightists who check up on our schools," read a headline from one *Toronto Daily Star* article by reporter Frank Jones (1968: 4). (Don Andrews, EBS co-founder and leader later of the more neo-Nazi leaning Western Guard, stares impassively in a photo adjoining the piece.) The primary function of the Burkers was to harass opponents of the American intervention in Vietnam at various street rallies and protests. "We didn't see it as a 'free speech' issue. We saw it as people supporting our enemies with whom our allies (America, Australia) were at war. More precisely, we saw them as traitors who should have been locked up, not allowed to parade around Toronto waving the enemy's flag," states Goodall, who was an immigrant from England (Goodall 2012–13). He served in the British military as a teenager and immigrated after viewing a television show about junior forest rangers in Canada. For a time he worked as a debt collector for a popular furniture store.

Intimidating the anti-war left at demonstrations and other events was a challenge for the Burkers since they were tiny in numbers compared to the many hundreds coming out against the war at protests in Toronto. "We were always outnumbered and quite frankly we relied on the police as part of our strategy to stay alive. Our job was to disrupt the protesters and take publicity away from them," Goodall recalls.

In a typical Burker counter-rally, a gaggle of its members would arrive at the US Consulate on University Ave. and then encircle the building as if to protect this symbol of America before the arrival of anti-war protesters. The Metro Toronto Police in turn would create their own cordon around the EBS members to create a distance from the anti-Vietnam War protesters.

A firsthand account of the encounter with the EBS comes from Karl Furr, who had just immigrated to Canada from the US and was attending his one and only protest in Toronto against President Richard Nixon's controversial May 1970 invasion of Cambodia during the height of the Vietnam War. The military move sparked large protests across North America. Ten to twelve Burkers, some holding signs and others ominously carrying sticks with nails, states Furr, were being protected by the Metro Toronto police at the same time that a much larger group of the anti-Vietnam War protesters were being cornered by other Toronto police officers on horseback and with nowhere to move. When Furr lodged a complaint at a Metro Toronto police station, he faced hostility from two officers, one of whom he identified as possibly one of the uniformed cops doing little to counter the threat of the Burkers at the US Consulate. Furr believes the police afterward started to investigate him. In the end, a friendlier officer did shortly telephone him and agree that his uniformed colleagues had acted inappropriately. Around this time Furr was active in the Toronto Anti-Draft Program as a volunteer assisting young Americans who had left their country after receiving a draft notice to serve in the military. After the May protests against the US invasion of Cambodia, Furr was invited to appear on local television, where he found himself surprisingly pitted in a debate with a "calm and collected" Paul Fromm. Furr recalls being ill prepared while other members of the Burkers milled outside the studio. Ultimately, the experience of what happened in May 1970 was so "intimidating" that he has stayed away from public protests ever since (Furr 2011).

From 1968 to 1970 Goodall was the official communications spokesperson for the EBS, which mostly involved contacting possibly sympathetic journalists like Worthington about upcoming events. But he was not allowed to speak for the organization and was a little put out by this exclusion by the higher ups in the organization, such as Paul Fromm and Don Andrews. Yet, Goodall told me he has no personal regrets about the time spent as a young man in far-right politics. It was a high point in his life.

In the late sixties the spectrum of the far right was quite small in Canada, ranging from Peter Worthington, an established newspaper reporter and columnist, to the more fringe Edmund Burke Society. Both shared sympathy for the white supremacist regimes in South Africa and Rhodesia as bulwarks against communism. But the difference was that Worthington was more of a straight arrow anti-communist obsessed with the spread and reach of the KGB, real or imagined (as in the case of Praxis). He kept these beliefs intact like a museum relic long after the Cold War ended. But the writer for the *Toronto Telegram* and *Toronto Sun* could surprise you. He did not fall in the trap of post-9/11 Islamaphobic paranoia that exists on portions of the right. In later years, Worthington wrote sympathetically and humanely, for instance, about the plight of former child solder Omar Khadr at the hands of Ottawa and Washington, which probably shocked some of his fellow Conservative Party supporters who were outraged that the young man was allowed back into Canada to live a normal civilian life (Worthington, 2012).

The Burkers, as time went on in their short existence, turned inward and became obsessed with race, immigration and the presence of Jews, and this exploded more openly when there was a split and the more violent Western Guard faction under Don Andrews emerged in 1972. (Both Fromm and Goodall declined to join the new group.)

Earlier, before this shift, the EBS had attempted publicly to maintain the image as an ultra conservative group focused mostly on its ideological opposition to communism. It supported Israel as a bastion against potential Soviet influence in the Middle East. Yet, anti-Semitism festered below its surface, according to Goodall. He recalls the EBS did have a Jewish member, whose name was Celia Airst. She joined for a period of time because of specific concerns about the plight of Jews living in the Soviet Union and drawn to the anti-communist rhetoric of the Burkers. She stood out as a new woman member, but there was also general distrust among some members toward Airst and her husband, who tagged along to meetings, sometimes with their child, and attempted to get to know everyone, which may have added to the general suspicion. Don Andrews said nothing, but he was convinced the couple were spies for the local anti-fascist Jewish organization N3, says Goodall. The woman and her husband were murdered years later, at the end of 1970s, long after the Burkers had disbanded. The crime was never solved but there has not been any suggestion that it was somehow connected to the Airsts' politics.

Goodall says he was grateful to Steve Drodz (unknown to him a secret

RCMP informant) for assisting in a move away from the dangerous tenants inside a rooming house owned by Don Andrews. As a new member and immigrant Goodall found himself threatened with a knife and also managed to avoid the ricochet of a bullet that blew up a pillow. This was somewhat emblematic of the unstable nature of the Burkers and associates living there and paying rent to Andrews. Drodz, albeit discreet by nature, seemed relatively sane in comparison.

When the revelations about the RCMP role in the Praxis affair came out in 1977, Solicitor General Francis Fox and the Mounties were keen on protecting Drodz's identity as the intermediary in the handover of the second batch of documents from the Burkers to the RCMP Security Service in early January 1971. Reporters and Praxis lawyer Paul Copeland eventually discovered the name despite the efforts to keep it confidential. Like many of the Eastern Europeans in the EBS, the secret RCMP informant managed to avoid any confrontation with the anti-war left on the street, says Goodall. "I don't remember him ever being injured for example" (Goodall 2012–19).

Drodz and Goodall were friendly as comrades in the Burkers but the relationship never went beyond that. "Steve never invited me into his house," says Goodall. Nor did he ever meet Drodz's wife. (She did exist, turning me down flat for an interview some years after her husband died. I had managed to track down the telephone number of the Drodz family residence in St. Petersburg, Florida.)

Journalists Doug Grant and Ted Fairhurst tried without success to interview Drodz in the later 1970s at his home in west end Toronto to clarify what happened at Praxis. "He lived on Delaware just west of Ossington and Bloor. We went to his house once and hounded him on the phone. And he went to Florida for part of the year. He owned a motel or something in Florida. And he basically wouldn't talk to us." But there was fallout for these efforts. At one point Grant was invited to lunch in downtown Toronto by a senior RCMP officer, who admitted that Drodz was one of their agents in the Eastern European community in Toronto and that their man should be left alone. "Drodz is an RCMP informant. He's one of the informants we have in the Eastern European Community in Toronto. And he keeps an eye on things. He listens. You know, if there's something we're interested in. And he tells us. He gives us information," the journalist was told (Grant 2012). This Mountie also emphasized that

Drozd had no involvement in the Praxis burglary and arson. "[Drozd] got these documents from somebody, he didn't steal them," the unidentified RCMP officer stated. "He acted as some kind of intermediary. And that's the end of the story. You guys know the story; there's no more story; Drodz has nothing more to tell you. So please stop bugging him."

Apparently, it was the desire to protect Drodz's identity that became the major rationale for Ontario Attorney General Roy McMurtry in May 1998 to decide not to lay charges against RCMP Security Service officers Grant and Pankew (Copeland 2012). "The RCMP's concern for the safety of their informant was based on fear of potential retaliation from either Praxis members or the persons responsible for the original break-in," stated Ontario Crown Attorney J.P. Rickaby in a letter to Paul Copeland (Rickaby 1977). As an aside, John Venner did pay a visit to Steve Drodz in Florida (RCMP Security Service Anonymous) as part of a late seventies investigation of the Security Service's role in the Praxis affair following the revelations in Parliament. There is some suggestion that the Ukraine-born Drodz was a U.S. citizen (Adams and Buchbinder 1978). I have also learned that the Security Service apparently approached Drodz in the summer of 1969 to become an active member of the EBS and report to them on the society's potentially violent activities (RCMP Anonymous). He may have moved south for protection from the extreme right.

Another player in the EBS and its more violent offshoot, the Western Guard (which was also more openly anti-Semitic and racist), Aarne Polli, claimed to reporters and others that he had the inside story on what transpired at Praxis in December 1970 but demanded money in exchange for details. Paul Copeland refused to pay Polli for whatever supposedly vital secrets were held in his possession. Drawing similar conclusions was Yvon Tarte, a McDonald Commission lawyer. "Mr. Polli is not inclined even in the best of circumstances, to give an accurate account of what he knows" (Tarte 1980b). A few years ago, I managed to track down Polli near Owen Sound in Ontario but he slammed the phone on me, angry that I had gotten his number from his mother, from whom he was estranged. Goodall says that Polli lived by his wits and the largess of friends and family and never had a real job during his entire life. Polli and a companion subsequently died in a house fire outside the town in 2015.

For all their pain and legwork there was little or no interest in the Praxis-related stories at CBC radio in the late seventies, says Doug Grant.

He is also convinced that Polli, "a stocky and overweight man of medium height," had some involvement in the Praxis burglary and did indeed hand over the stolen documents to Steve Drodz but was never charged for the crime for unknown reasons. "It was my first experience with investigative journalism. And I have seldom done it again because we had no support from the CBC. We're two young guys; we didn't really know what we were doing. We didn't get any guidance support. The *National News* never ran any of our stories." The one exception was when it was revealed in 1977 that the solicitor general had passed around a list of new left sympathizers to fellow federal cabinet members inside the Trudeau government. Grant recalls Fairhurst was more tenacious about the stories while he himself lost interest. "Ted was a detail guy, probably better at it than I was ... But I just thought it was all a career limiting exercise" (Grant 2012).

The one aspect of the Polli story that still fascinates Grant is the strange discovery of the former Burker working sometime later on a Conservative candidate's federal election campaign in a wealthy Toronto riding and even obnoxiously booing the Liberal opponent at a rally. The journalist seems to regret that he did not pursue this intriguing side note in the Praxis story.

As stated before, a split occurred in 1972 in the Edmund Burke Society, and a more violent Western Guard faction, displaying blunter racism and anti-Semitism, took charge. Both Goodall and Paul Fromm stayed away from the new organization as their colleague Don Andrews headed the new group joined by Aarne Polli. Andrews was subsequently convicted and jailed for two years in an arson plot involving an Olympic event in Toronto and an Israeli soccer team. There were signs before the Western Guard formed that the Burkers were heading in an even more dangerous direction. Some of the members, including Jeff Goodall, had their homes raided by the Mounties, who found a frightful arsenal of weapons, including rifles, revolvers, pistols, hunting knives, ammunition, mace and bayonets. "Many of us owned firearms. In those days it was legal to own military weapons which became [sport weapons] to only fire one bullet each time the trigger was pulled. If you held the trigger down, you still only got one shot" says Goodall. He recounts that the Burkers' favourite weapons included the British FN (.308 NATO), the American AR15 version of the M16 (.223) and the German G3 (.308 NATO) and the AR180, which was a folding stock version of the AR15. Apparently, the Burkers regularly headed off into the woods outside of Kaladar (northeast of Toronto) to do target practice. These weapons were all "legally owned and returned to us after the raids. Mine certainly were," Goodall stated. Meanwhile, Stanley Barrett, author of *Is God a Racist*, writes that two EBS members were arrested for possession of restricted weapons (1989: 60).

In October 1971 in Ottawa, one man associated with the Burkers, Geza Matra, jumped on the back of the visiting Soviet Premier Alexei Kosygin shouting "free Hungary." The man was quickly pulled off and later charged and convicted; the visiting foreign dignitary was not hurt.

From internal memos and conversations with Meyer Brownstone, Superintendent John Venner stood out as the sceptic inside the RCMP Security Service when it came to the suspicions of alleged subversion about Praxis by his colleagues. He directed his strongest language against members of the Edmund Burke Society. "During the 1970–1971 period there were numerous instances of violence in Toronto involving members of the political extreme right," he wrote. He also defended the protection of the informant, Steve Drodz: "It was of considerable importance for the Security Service to keep abreast of this activity and the penetration of such groups by human sources was the Security Service's most effective means of accomplishing this task" (Venner n.d.).

To Sue or Not to Sue

Praxis became better known publicly in 1977 with the revelations about the Mounties' role in the affair. It still had corporate status but was not operating as a functioning organization.

After reading the 1971 Worthington piece admitting to receiving the stolen Praxis files and handing them over to the RCMP, former Praxis board member Meyer Brownstone contacted Assistant Commissioner H.P. Tadeson about retrieving the files. The senior officer was cautious, displaying no sign of knowing anything about Praxis or admitting a role in the Security Service's acceptance of the second batch of stolen documents in early January 1971. Now six years later Tadeson told Brownstone he saw no difficulty in their return to the rightful owner. That is when Meyer Brownstone came into contact with John Venner, who arranged for the handover of the missing Praxis property. Brownstone retrieved some of the Praxis related files, while other files remained missing; the RCMP reported they had been destroyed. "They had proceeded to destroy our corporate property without of course letting us know," he wrote to his former boss, NDP leader Tommy Douglas, who was now a federal NDP MP and the party's justice critics in the House of Commons (Brownstone 1977a and b). Brownstone expressed misgivings in the correspondence about Howard Buchbinder's desire to sue the RCMP for its role in the Praxis affair although he acknowledged that Praxis was still a corporation in good standing with a board of directors. So the lawsuit was able to proceed legally. Embarrassing the government is one thing but Brownstone needed to be persuaded that something useful could come out of a lawsuit "in terms of curbing arbitrary power." Douglas wrote back telling Brownstone that having it "thrashed out" before the Standing Committee on Justice and Legal Affairs in Ottawa would be the best course of action. "The one point on which we all agreed is that this matter should not be left in abeyance, but should be given a thorough airing, if not in the courts, then certainly in the committee and, if necessary, in the House of Commons itself" (Douglas 1977).

Howard Buchbinder got his wish through two separate court actions and the results were rather illuminating even if ultimately frustrating for those keen on getting to the bottom of the matter. The first one involved the launch of a private prosecution against identified RCMP Security Service officers, including Corporals Grant and Pankew, for accepting the stolen documents and not returning them to the original owners. Ontario Attorney General Roy McMurtry had refused to take action against the possessors of stolen Praxis property and so Buchbinder, with the help of Paul Copeland, appeared before a justice of the peace to lay their complaint. They were joined by a lawyer acting for another activist, Ross Dowson, whose organization, the League for Socialist Action (a Trotskyite group), erupted into turmoil following a disruption campaign by the Mounties to sow division with phony letters from purported members. One letter included details about a certain person's emotional state and his ability to lead the LSA, which had been surreptitiously gleaned from confidential Ontario health records (Whitaker, Kealey and Parnaby 2012: 337–338). This communication was leaked to the targeted person and his wife as well as other members without consideration for the mental health consequences of the action.

Here, I rely on the reporting by Michael Valpy, a *Globe and Mail* columnist who closely followed the Buchbinder-Dowson private prosecution (Valpy 1983). The charges against the Security Service officers included possession of stolen documents, forgery and conveying false messages. Ontario Attorney General McMurtry stayed or halted the proceedings before the justice of the peace was able to hear the details of the private complaints. Subsequently, both the Ontario Supreme Court and the province's Court of Appeal ruled that there was nothing illegal about McMurtry's actions. But to the surprise of everyone, the Supreme Court of Canada on October 23, 1983, sided with Buchbinder and Dowson in ordering that the two men be free to lay their complaints in front of a justice of the peace without interference from the Ontario attorney general.

For Valpy it was one of those rare occurrences where the repressive state apparatus had been beaten: "The court decision is one to be happy about — not simply because it may lead to some future judicial ruling that policemen are not beyond the law. It is a happy decision because it also upholds the right of private prosecutions as a citizen's critical safeguard against an executive contemptuous of liberty" (Valpy 1983: 6).

But the celebration for the civil libertarians was short-lived. Paul Copeland says the federal government quietly amended the Criminal Code to allow a provincial attorney general to stay a private prosecution before it was heard by a justice of the peace. "I am not aware of any debate in Parliament about the amendment. So far as I recall it came into effect very shortly after the Supreme Court of Canada decision "It showed how much of a cover-up there was [with regards to the RCMP dirty tricks]," Copeland stated (2019)

The second court action by Buchbinder and Praxis involved directly suing the RCMP Security Service in the courts. Paul Copeland believed he had a strong case against the Mounties if he could gain access to 115 internal government documents which would have provided a clear indication of the involvement of the Privy Council Office and at least five federal Liberal cabinet ministers "in the examination of security matters relating to the Praxis Corporation" (Copeland 1977–88). This evidence would have offered further insights into how the Mounties lobbied federal government ministers to stop hiring Praxis for research contracts and thereby kill its business. One such contract was potentially valued at $250,000. Copeland was also hoping for more incriminating information on how Peter Worthington relied on sources inside the Security Service "to smear Professor Buchbinder and Professor Hunnius."

However, Deputy Solicitor General Frederick Gibson successfully argued in a certificate filed under the Canada Evidence Act in the Federal Court of Canada that the Praxis request for the internal government documents would jeopardize national security and therefore could not be released. Once the Federal Court made this decision and with the Praxis court costs mounting, Copeland and his clients agreed to accept a settlement. Although no admission of liability was made by the government and the RCMP, the Mounties' decision to hand over an undisclosed amount of money represented an implicit admission of culpability in the Security Service's acceptance and the keeping of stolen Praxis property. "The amount of money [in the settlement] is a significant amount of money ... It's not huge, but it's significant enough to embarrass [the government]," Copeland told the *Globe and Mail*'s Peter Moon on May 4, 1988 (Moon 1988).

In one unusual communication, the lawyer for the Crown, John Laskin, on June 19, 1988, instructed Paul Copeland and his Praxis clients that the pre-trail examination of discovery testimony of Superintendent John Venner had to be kept confidential for perpetuity. "It is appropriate to remind you of the implied undertaking to which both you and your client are subject, not to use the documents produced or evidence given on discovery for any purpose other than the prosecution of this case" (Copeland 1977–88). Paul Copeland had initially warned me decades later that this ruling was still in force and so I as a journalist was obliged to respect it. However, the lawyer later had a change of mind, now maintaining that this restriction on reporting the details of Venner's testimony in the discovery process only applied to Buchbinder (now passed away) and Copeland himself. The lawyer explained that I was in the clear in reading and reporting on the testimony since I obtained it many years later from another source, one of Howard Buchbinder's sons, before it was delivered to the York University archives along with a voluminous stack of his father's personal papers.

I have now read the discovery evidence (which any visitor to the York University Clara Thomas Archives can freely peruse) and it is rather underwhelming. The Crown lawyer, John Laskin, during the discovery prevented Paul Copeland from asking specific questions about the scale of the Mountie surveillance of Praxis and the new left because they were considered outside the scope of the Praxis lawsuit against the RCMP. What is clear from internal 1984 RCMP memos is that there was a deliberate effort to thwart Copeland's line of inquiry by the Crown. "A high degree of coordination will be required to ensure that testimony provided by Supt. Venner ... does not exceed the limits of public knowledge," wrote J.B. Giroux, the director general of the Security Service. He added that the Security Service "legally came into possession of Praxis documents in 1971" (Giroux 1984).

After the announcement of the government's settlement with Praxis, Peter Worthington on May 19, 1988, wrote his last column on Praxis, for the *Financial Post*. "Praxis papers would embarrass," read the headline, but Worthington never explained what he meant. "I guess the Praxis case really is closed — 18 years after the organization was robbed, burned and neutralized" (Worthington 1988). That word "neutralized" appears to sum up what exactly happened to a promising new organization like Praxis that ran afoul of the powers that be in Ottawa because of its advocacy and research for the poor.

Chapter Nine

The Clashing Poverty Reports

Much has changed since the passionate days in the sixties, but despite the distance in time many anti-poverty themes still persist — just packaged in a different wrapper. Guaranteed annual income (GAI), as it was called in the 1960s, is making a comeback, renamed as "basic income" around the world, but not for the right reasons, writes Tom Walkom, *Toronto Daily Star* columnist and economist (Walkom 2017). It was proposed as a solution to eradicate poverty when it was first recommended by Senator David Croll's Special Senate Committee on Poverty in 1971. Nowadays, basic income is being pitched as an income supplement for the gig economy to address the growing numbers of people struggling to survive on precarious, unpredictable and inadequately paying temporary contracts. It is also being proposed to address potential job loss in the future due to unbridled automation.

These challenges were the primary reasons for the implementation of a pilot "basic income" experiment involving 4,000 people in four cities, undertaken by the Ontario Liberal government of Kathleen Wynn in 2018. Individuals were randomly selected to receive to receive an income supplement of up to $16,989 a year, while couples got up to $24,027, less 50 percent of any earned income. In order to qualify, singles had to make less than $34,000 a year and couples less than $48,000. Walkom argued that this was lower than the amount people would be getting if they were still on either of the province's two welfare programs: Ontario Works or the Ontario Disability Support Program. At least they would still be getting the free drug and dental care, he said.

Since Walkom wrote the piece, the province has experienced a sharp turn to the right with the June 2018 election of a Progressive Conservative government under Doug Ford, who appears to be mirroring the initiatives of the Trump presidency in the US. Ford's focus is on cutting government programs in the name of "efficiency." His administration called a halt to the basic income pilot before the results had been analyzed. Less compassionate Victorian attitudes about the poor have bubbled to the surface and threaten to turn back the clock on the progress that was made to social programs over fifty years ago.

Indeed, the several thousand Ontarians participating in the experiment saw their lives and personal commitments cruelly upended by the surprise move. They thought they had a clearer path out of poverty through further education and jobs. This was far better than remaining on welfare, where one is only allowed to keep a small portion of earnings to supplement the meagre benefits provided each month. If there is a positive side to this, it is that the recipients of basic income have organized and are fighting back.

Back in the sixties anti-poverty groups like the Just Society Movement and activists such as Howard Buchbinder viewed the guaranteed annual income as another form of welfare, minus the social worker bureaucracy, which would pay a minimal and inadequate rate. It had been devised by Chicago-based economist Milton Friedman and was championed by a few conservative-minded people. A more generous version was endorsed by Stephen Lewis, leader of the Ontario NDP, in 1966 because of his disillusionment with the Canada Assistance Plan (CAP), the federal/provincial social welfare program passed that year (Struthers 1994: 238). The Poor People's Conference called for the more generous version of a guaranteed annual income to be adopted by the country in January 1971.

Report of the Special Senate Committee on Poverty

Senator David Croll's 1971 *Report of the Special Senate Committee on Poverty* described the welfare system as broken (an admission that had gotten Wilson Head into trouble a few years earlier). The report agreed that a guaranteed annual income on its own was not a magic bullet to solving poverty but called for the scheme to be part of a comprehensive package of social reforms, which also included expanded daycare, community health centres, expanded access to unionization, equal pay for equal work, improved minimum wages and a negotiated federal/ provincial workers' compensation plan. Croll proposed that the GAI be widely available, with the exception of single and unattached people under 40 and immigrants who were not yet Canadian citizens. Instead, they would be eligible for social assistance under the Canada Assistance Plan. But there was a problem here. The GAI was supposed to replace welfare as a way to save money, not become an add-on to existing social services (Croll 1971: 5–9).

It is not surprising that Prime Minister Trudeau and his Liberal government ignored the Croll report while the NDP endorsed it because the recommendations appeared to come out of the social democratic playlist. A further insight into the federal Liberals' discomfort with the poverty issue can be gleaned from its reaction to the acrimonious split that broke out within the Special Senate Committee. Two reports were in fact delivered, the official *Poverty in Canada* report from Senator Croll, and a second document, *The Real Poverty Report,* by Ian Adams and three other researchers and writers, which was published and sold in bookstores. Senator Croll argued that Adams and his colleagues, his four former writers, should be criminally charged, because their actions were "tantamount to thievery" (*Toronto Daily Star* 1971). Nothing came of that.

David Tough has gone over the official and dissenting reports from the Croll Special Senate Committee on Poverty and finds little difference in the recommendations. He says what split Adams and Croll was both personal and generational (Tough 2017). The Senator was an older man who had served as a cabinet minister during the 1930s in the Ontario government of Mitch Hepburn, while Adams had grown up after World War II in the baby boom generation and was in his thirties when the kerfuffle on the Special Senate Committee happened in the early seventies.

William Langford says he found recommendations in the dissenting book, *The Real Poverty Report,* rather "conventional." "It called, for example, for a guaranteed annual income at the relative poverty line which is something to keep people out of poverty without eliminating the incentive to work," Langford said (2018–19). But in an interview, Ian Adams provided an entirely different take on the matter. I will get back to that. Cynics might suggest that the Croll report was perhaps an example of a government spending millions to hear from 801 witnesses, receive 109 briefs and compile all of this data into a report, but not proceed with the crucial step of following through on the recommendations to tackle the thorny issue of poverty directly.

Vancouver-based Michael Clague remembers well the tension which built up in the Special Senate Committee. He had worked with the Company of Young Canadians and was later seconded from the Department of Secretary of State to work for Senator Croll when he was mandated to conduct the Special Senate Committee hearings in late 1968. Clague fondly recalls Croll's record as a social reformer when he was mayor of Windsor and later, as provincial minister of labour in an anti-union Hepburn government, when he quit his post out sympathy for the striking workers at the General Motors plant in Oshawa. But in overseeing the Special Senate Committee, Croll was aloof and not especially communicative with the research staff. "With due respect, Senator Croll was a one-man band. And so, he was not interested in building a staff. He wanted a group of people that were capable of doing what he wanted," Clague says. There was not a lot of discussion between Senator Croll and the researchers about what the committee was planning to achieve. "We were never quite sure where Croll [was]" (Clague 2012, 2019).

From the beginning the expected outcome from the Senator's perspective was to recommend a guaranteed annual income. At one point Senator Croll played a little mind game. He asked each person working for him what they thought the outcome should be, but this could not be shared with fellow staffers. "I don't just think you do good work that way. He very much wanted control," said Clague. In the fall of 1970 Clague's employment with Senator Croll and Special Senate Committee ended as planned and before things got out of hand. He recalls unease among the staff about how "substantive" the final report was going to be.

The Real Poverty Report

Ian Adams was asked, as the author of *The Poverty Wall*, to work for the Special Senate Committee after his best-selling book came out in 1970. He was interviewed briefly by Senator Croll for the position. It sounded like the two men took an immediate dislike of each other. Adams says the session was "bizarre," with the Senator putting down economists. "You are the new boy on the block, so be careful," Senator David Croll said to Adams in the lounge of the palatial office overseeing the Rideau Canal, according to the journalist and author (Adams 2018).

In his new position, Adams hired fellow journalist Bill Cameron to do the writing. He also worked with economists Peter Penz and Brian Hill. Adams and his crew were responsible for digesting the accumulated information from cross-Canada hearings over a two-year period, which involved listening to ordinary people such as fishers and miners in small communities and residents of large communities, as well as organizations like unions and business. Other reports were also submitted in the special jargon of economists and sociologists. Having written a book on this subject, it was fascinating for Adams to come into contact with all of this new information about poverty. Strangely, the federal government's internal information on poverty was not at first accessible to researchers. It was all declared confidential, says Adams. "Data on poverty, data on statistics of levels of poverty and stuff like that in various places. I mean how stupid can it get. Was that a question of national security to talk about the level of poverty in the country?" Fortunately, Senator Croll took steps to have this secrecy provision removed.

What might have set off the rift between the two men was that Adams and his group shared Senator Croll's enthusiasm for a guaranteed annual income but they also wanted the committee to tackle the large systemic issues of poverty within capitalism in Canada. As a Liberal, Senator Croll was not prepared to go this far. Notwithstanding the Senator's autocratic style, he took a "pragmatic" approach to guaranteed annual income and did not want to mess up any progress towards attaining it, argues Clague (2012, 2019). Senator Croll's goal at the time was to complete the progress of the Canadian welfare state, following the success of the Canada Pension Plan and Medicare. He supported reformist Tom Kent's wing of the party, which was keen on building and expanding Canada's social safety net. Sometime after Clague left the team, the dissenting researchers and writers on the Special Senate Committee decided in the spring of 1971 they had had enough. These men had concerns that Croll, in the face of difficult re-election prospects for the Liberals in 1972, was willing to compromise on the recommendations of the final report. "Croll was trying to present Trudeau with a political election sound bite, for their re-election. A guaranteed annual income for everybody and the nation could afford it. But it was going to be status quo, welfare by another name," Adams explained (2018).

Adams had written on the working poor in *The Poverty Wall* as a component of the poor who were getting short shrift in the discussions that focused on welfare recipients during the 1960s. He wanted national standards for minimum wages to be established at the federal, provincial and municipal levels to help get working people out of their difficult circumstances. He and Bill Cameron laid out how this would work in a 100,000-word draft with the sanction of the research director and research staff on the committee. The Senator wanted none of this, demanding that Adams and Cameron rewrite the report. "He wanted all of the realistic proposals, economic and financial, taken out of it," according to Adams. In retrospect it is hardly likely that a Liberal government, which was loath to enforce the provisions of the Canada Assistance Plan, would impose new requirements on the provinces. Adams seems to concede that point during our interview. "The Conservatives and the Liberals, who were basically conservatives, were terrified of tinkering with the minimum wage anywhere in the country."

Adams remembers that it was at this point that he decided to resign, saying he had taken the job "in good conscience" to write a report based on the research and testimony gathered from the committee hearings across Canada. The dissenters at the Senate Special Committee on poverty decided it was important to get vital information on the issue of poverty out to the general public. McClelland & Stewart was initially approached by Adams since it had published his previous book, *The Poverty Wall*. But M&S said no, so *The Real Poverty Report* ended up going to Mel Hurtig's Edmonton-based publishing company.

One side story is the successful effort by Adams to have an excerpt of *The Real Poverty Report* take up an entire issue of *Last Post*, a left-wing national monthly which had a small circulation but featured young enterprising journalists, such as Mark Starowicz, who would later became a top producer at the CBC for shows like *As It Happens*. "Telling the chairman of the Senate Committee on Poverty, David Croll to get stuffed was not only an incidental but necessary act," read the headline on the front cover of the summer 1971 issue of *Last Post*.

Before that issue appeared on newsstands across Canada, Adams met with the board of *Last Post* in June 1971. What was unknown to this gathering is that their conversations were being secretly recorded by the RCMP Security Service at a time when it was undertaking its dirty tricks operations. What transpired can be found in pages of notes that are part of a larger report, *Penetration of Canada,* which was included in the RCMP Security Service files I obtained. At the bottom of one of the pages states the following: "No action is to be taken which might jeopardize our source" (RCMP Security Service 1971b). A discussion about the upcoming issue devoted to *The Real Poverty Report* took place about the logistics of publishing the report. Marc Starowicz, a *Last Post* board member, was clearly excited by the publicity of putting out 30,000 copies of the *Last Post* issue containing this controversial document from Ian Adams and company (Starowicz 2012). Drummond Burgess, the publisher, was quoted by the Security Service as saying that it would cost about $3,500 to put out this special issue. *Last Post* was willing put up most of the money but somewhere in the range of $250 to $500 had to be taken up by somebody else. "This amount of money would be put up ... to allow for the distribution of free copies of the report to poverty organizations [not named in the memo]," wrote one note taker for the Security Service (RCMP Security Service 1971f).

Years later, Robert Chodos, who was a writer at *Last Post* and is now a freelance editor, expressed bewilderment that his magazine was under surveillance for three years. The notion of a police agent mixing among a group of *Last Post* journalists, who were and are friends today, remains disturbing to him (Chodos 2012). What primarily held the Mounties' interest was that *Last Post* was one of the few media outlets in Canada willing to publish critical reporting following the federal government's imposition of the War Measures Act during the October 1970 crisis. The RCMP files also reveal that the Security Service was concerned about the embarrassment that Ian Adams and the dissidents of the Senate Special Committee were bringing to the federal government. "If this is published by the *Last Post* to be distributed free to poverty organizations, it likely will receive a lot of attention and give poverty groups further cause to take issue with the government," an unnamed investigator wrote in a memo (RCMP Security Service 1971g).

Meanwhile, Leonard Shifrin did not take a position on the contending Croll versus Adams reports coming out of the Special Senate Committee on Poverty except to say the conflict was largely academic in the end since its report and recommendations were totally disregarded. Senator Croll's cautionary approach was ultimately pointless, he emailed me: "As it turned out, in this case Croll need not have bothered being strategically clever, and could have been a hero by calling for the moon, because the Trudeau government had no intention of doing anything on the subject" (Shifrin 2011–13).

Chapter Ten

The Poverty File Today

"I am 75 and I work with a lot of young people and they don't even understand that there used to be a time when there was hardly any homeless, and when there was a lot more equality. They cannot even comprehend it." Jean Swanson is talking about the sixties, which was fabled for its music, fashion, recreational drugs, political commitment, low unemployment and an economic boom that people thought would last forever. The veteran advocate for the poor and newly elected Vancouver city councillor says with some reservations that this was also probably the best time to be poor in Canada, before things started going downhill politically. "The attitudes of society [in the sixties] were not great; it was patronizing," she says flatly over the telephone. "But at least [the poor] were treated like human beings [compared to the nineties], when they were [considered to be] drug users and cheaters" (Swanson 2018).

Swanson is an extremely busy person these days as a councillor who has promised to unleash a proactive agenda among her politically diverse colleagues. Her big issue is the lack of affordable housing in the priciest city in Canada. The first resolution on her plate involved putting a stop to evictions of tenants by private landlords through unnecessary renovations. I managed to contact the outspoken woman on the telephone, ahead of her election, about her 2001 book *Poor-Bashing: The Politics of Exclusion.*

Swanson did not personally experience the high expectations and idealism of the anti-poverty movement in Canada of the late sixties and early seventies. Indeed, Swanson's involvement with the anti-poverty cause did not begin until 1974, when she was still serving beer at the Patricia Hotel on East Hastings in Vancouver to support her small children. The Downtown Eastside Residents Association and specifically Bruce Eriksen (also a future city councillor) lured her into a better and more exciting job involving community organizing in the city's skid row district. Among the organizations she has been a member of and headed are the National Anti-Poverty Organization and End Legislated Poverty.

Her 2001 book, *Poor Bashing* is one of a number of books that have covered the incremental shift in the seventies, eighties and nineties in Canada towards a deregulated market, accompanied by austerity policies in a corporate-driven, globalized free trade environment — what we have come to know as neoliberalism. For all of the talk about Liberals straying away from the issue of poverty in its first term, internal documents, such as the 1970 white paper *Income Security for Canadians and the Guaranteed Income,* show a more respectful attitude towards the poor, says Jean Swanson. There was an emphasis in the text "on an adequate income on which to live" and an acknowledgement of "humiliating procedures and policies" in the social welfare system as it existed then. This was when John Munro was the Minister of Health and Welfare (Swanson 2001: 67–70).

Swanson contrasted this with the absence of the poor's perspective in the business-friendly 1994 green paper *Improving Social Security in Canada,* produced by the Chrétien government. This time there was no consultation with the people affected by the new exercise. The goal in the 1994 discussion document was to apply drastic surgery to Canada's social safety net to reduce the deficit. The priority was to make people competitive in the Darwinian sense in the new economy, which meant withdrawing federal support for provincial welfare programs, shutting down the social housing programs and replacing unemployment insurance with a less generous employment insurance program This tsunami of austerity reached its crescendo in the 1990s with media stories about welfare fraud and immigrants that had racist overtones (Swanson 2001: 90–105). There were echoes of earlier moralistic Victorian and culture of poverty attitudes about low income people lacking initiative and generous social programs creating dependency. New thinkers across the border in the US such as George Gilder sprung up to provide an intellectual gloss to what was old-fashioned poor bashing. All major parties in Canada at the federal and provincial levels indulged in the practice and passed legislation passed that introduced tough rules and reduced benefits. New Democratic Party BC Premier Mike Harcourt proved to be the biggest disappointment for Swanson because his party was previously a major defender of the poor (Swanson 2001: 106–29). Harcourt called welfare recipients "varmints" and even fired a cabinet minister in charge of social services for modest improvements in welfare in BC and stating that welfare fraud was no more prevalent than fraud in other areas of society, she recalls (Swanson 2001: 100–01).

Laying the groundwork were the drastic measures applied to a major piece in the Canada's safety net, the Canada Assistance Plan. It was essentially dismantled by the federal Liberal government of Jean Chrétien. Federal money for provincial welfare plans was reduced and a looser arrangement, the Canada Health and Social Transfer (CHST) was established. The provinces had more leeway to reduce welfare rates and even impose work for welfare schemes that had been disallowed under Lester Pearson's Canada Assistance Plan. "The thing was, with the feds paying half of welfare [under CAP], provinces could keep the welfare rates up a little higher. When the feds quit paying half of welfare, then provinces started slashing, or letting inflation slash welfare," Swanson explains (Swanson 2018).

In the second decade of the twenty-first century, Swanson bears the political scars of past battles against two powerful and influential corporate lobby groups (the Business Council for National Issues and the Fraser Institute), which opened their doors in the seventies (respectively 1974 and 1976) and successfully pushed an agenda of free trade, deregulation and reduced social supports. Both played a role in shaping society's mindset to not caring about people falling through the cracks, representing a shift towards neglect and a change from the hopes of the 1960s, she says. Canada is still living with the consequences of a diminished welfare state today.

Yet Marc Zwelling, the president of Vector Research, finds no evidence in the polling that there is an anti-poor attitude within the Canadian population, either now or going back to Pierre Trudeau's first term as prime minister. He suggests that the parties in Ottawa have been expert at convincing Canadians, even those with modest means, to do things that are not exactly in their own economic interest. At the height of cuts undertaken by Jean Chrétien and Paul Martin, Canada's social safety net was spread widely among the population at large. More than half, he estimates, were receiving a benefit for themselves or their family — ranging from family allowance to student financial assistance or employment insurance, to Old Age Security and the Guaranteed Income Supplement, among others. "The Chrétien–Paul Martin reductions in transfers to the provinces for social programs were positioned as financial necessities to sustain the federal government and reduce deficits, not as withdrawing welfare from undeserving people," says Zwelling (2018–19). He says that in Doug Ford's Ontario, the current cuts in programs such as the basic income program come out of a similar ideological fixation about reducing government spending, not poor bashing.

"The PCs' priority is deficit busting; every policy is aimed at that target. That's why people elect them … It's not an anti-poor bias. Look at how Ford constantly asserts he's for the forgotten, little persons (the tax cut for low-income wage earners instead of the higher minimum wage, e.g.). And a buck-a-beer plus lower gasoline prices. Dumb policies, but they give him a good alibi for his other policies that aren't so friendly to low-income people," the pollster continues (Zwelling 2018).

At the same time though, the Ford government has taken such a scatter-gun approach that its measures are starting to affect, for instance, the ability of young people from lower economic strata to further their education or find affordable accommodation. If what Zwelling says about Canadians not being anti-poor is true, there is some hope that progressives can oppose these social cuts, which seem to come in waves every few years by different political parties. The perennial issue is how.

I should add that Jean Swanson in her book respectfully disagrees with Zwelling's assessment of public attitudes towards the poor, especially during the 1990s. She cites an Ekos research study commissioned by the Human Resources Development Canada in Jean Chrétien's government that interviewed focus groups to prepare for the introduction of the Canada Child Tax Benefit. It discovered that among the participants in the study "welfare recipients are seen in unremittingly negative terms by the economically insecure" (Swanson 2001: 111–12). On the other hand, the working poor received more sympathy and support.

Meanwhile, Bill Freeman says that organizing and fighting for the poor remains a difficult task. It was one thing in the early 1970s to fight the local administrative policies of the Hamilton welfare office, which he accomplished in building up the Hamilton Welfare Rights Organization. But it was another to go after social policies at the federal level, where the decision-makers are distant and difficult to access, he continues. Furthermore, income equality not poverty is what people in social policy are talking about today in the twenty-first century in Canada. "In my view this is the correct term for it. Income inequality is really the problem. Welfare is only a small part of the poverty problem. The poor people's movement has never been able to solve that problem" (Freeman 2018). The biggest challenge facing progressives from his point of view is the segmentation or isolation around separate issues. Freeman cites how the people concerned about daycare are in one committee and those are worried about affordable housing are on another committee and thirdly there is the need to deal with precarious work and then there is the division between welfare recipients and the working poor. Poverty, or social inequality now, encompasses a raft of issues that were not considered in the late sixties, such as the health impact of poverty and the divide among racialized lines in Canada's largest cities.

A number of activists who I've interviewed agree that a lack of affordable housing has taken on such importance that it has become the central issue today in Canada. Trent University professor Jonathan Greene covers contemporary protest among the poor. He suggests that much of the activity in Toronto tends to be local and below the radar; for instance, groups are forming all the time around the homeless issue (Greene 2018).

Another example is the proliferation of tenant rent strikes in Toronto, Hamilton and Vancouver to fight legal applications by corporate landlords for extensive renovations to force out low-income residents from older stock apartments and replace them with people who presumably can pay higher rents. This is happening in major cities across Canada as apartments and rental units are becoming less affordable. Like the problem of unemployment in the thirties, politicians are unable or loath to respond coherently or creatively beyond market-oriented bromides to deal with a real estate market out of whack.

Finally, to put things into perspective, the *Bleak House* style of welfare administration that existed in the sixties is at one level more liberal in Ontario now. Social assistance recipients in Ontario can work part-time and have training while receiving benefits. We don't have the "man in the house rule" of an earlier era, where the personal relationships of women on welfare were scrutinized. But Victorian attitudes about the dangers of being too generous towards the poor still persist within social services offices and among politicians, reports Johnny Morris in Hamilton, who still has people come to him for help in appealing decisions made by local officials in the welfare bureaucracy. "I go to the welfare department, I go to the WSIB, anything. I am still doing that. Sometimes, not as much as I used to but I still do it. If somebody comes to me and says, 'well John, I have got a court date; I can't afford a lawyer.' No problem" (Morris 2018).

But politicians left and right are reluctant to raise the rates of social assistance to make it enough to live on in today's economy. One small Ontario-wide group, Put Food in the Budget, has spent ten years fighting to restore social assistance to the level it was before the Mike Harris PC government undertook its high profile 1995 cuts of 21.6 percent. The group's long-term goal of restoration of social assistance to the previous level was never reached even under two separate Liberal premiers and governments (2003–18) despite its lobbying, deputations, rallies and imaginative public campaigns, such as "Do the Math," to demonstrate that current benefits are insufficient to pay for the basic necessities of life, like food. Some promising changes were undertaken under the last Liberal provincial government of Kathleen Wynn, such as small increases in social assistance rates, a $15 minimum wage and the basic income experiment. But even these modest moves are being pulled back by the Doug Ford government, which has made other major cuts in areas affecting the poor, such as the elimination of legal aid for refugees.

The whole purpose of Put Food in the Budget is now being called into question and forcing it to close its doors "sadly and after much soul searching," says a volunteer and retired professor Bob Luker. He taught a course for community workers at George Brown College in Toronto. "We were running low on energy and more importantly with the Ford crew in power, could not see a way forward on the core issue for us."

In essence Mike Harris's cuts were never reversed if one takes into account the cost of living today in Ontario. Here I rely on a widely respected social policy commentator and consultant, John Stapleton, who spent twenty-eight years in a senior position at the Ontario government Ministry of Community and Social Services, working in the area of social assistance. "The correct answer to your question is that none of the 21.6 per cent was restored and that a $75 or 11 per cent increase would be needed just to get rates to the amount that Harris cut in real terms in 1995." In September, one month before Mike Harris's cuts, the social assistance rate for a single person on Ontario Works was $663. Today, if that rate was adjusted for inflation, it would be $1,030 and "therefore a

41 per rate increase would be needed to get back to the amounts in place before the cuts."

Put Food in the Budget had a small but lively membership of two hundred members, mostly women either on Ontario Works or the Ontario Disability Support Program, the two main welfare programs. One of its founders happened to be Marvyn Novick. "We feel pretty good about what we have been able to accomplish with very small numbers of members and limited resources and an organizer (mostly unpaid) who is really wonderful," says Bob Luker,

Upon reflection Luker has difficulty with what he sees as the downgrading of the poverty issue, which he argues has fallen below the radar even among progressives, including unions, on their list of priorities. He does support the current emphasis on issues such as inequality and the growing precariousness in the workforce. But we also need political rhetoric with a "sharper" edge, such as poverty or deprivation, to fully capture a still-existing social reality, according to this activist. Like many current anti-poverty groups, Put Food in the Budget has never had significant stable financial support from either unions or churches (the latter, a diminishing source of revenue for social justice organizing). "Poverty is not upfront for most unions. Anti-poverty work; they are supportive in principle but it is not close to the top of leadership. And the union movement is not immune to the stigmatization of the poor," adds Luker.

For a brief moment poverty returned to the news pages of the major media outlets. In March 2019 there was an announcement by the federal Liberal government of Justin Trudeau that its 22 billion dollars of investment in the middle class and the poor had resulted in a major drop in the official poverty rate from 10.6 percent in 2016 to 9.5 percent in 2017. All of this is attributed to the Canada Child Benefit and a top-up to the Guaranteed Income Supplement, according to the government press release. The result is that there are now 3.4 million Canadians defined now as living in poverty, following the movement of approximately 825,000 Canadians out of this category.

The goal in Ottawa is for poverty in Canada to be cut in half by 2030 but David McDonald, a senior economist at the Canadian Centre for Policy Alternatives, warns that other social measures have to be introduced before this has the remotest chance of succeeding. His organization charted how despite this announcement child poverty remains serious and deeply rooted, for instance in Indigenous communities — where children are over two and a half times more likely to live in poverty than non-Indigenous children. Also, he noted that inequality continues unabated in Canada since the international 2008 financial crisis even as the poverty rate goes down. McDonald disagrees with the advocates who suggest that inequality and poverty are necessarily interchangeable as inequality touches the overwhelming majority of the population while the poor represent a minority (McDonald 2019).

How does Bob Luker at PFIB see all of this? He says that McDonald raises a lot of useful questions about how to connect anti-poverty campaigning with the growing number of people experiencing "oppressive" inequality in many manifestations. A key one for him is how to connect the fight for equality with the fight for the social wage coming out of government programs. "But it is illusionary to think that inequality which generates and maintains poverty can be separated from poverty analytically or their rates will move in opposite directions for very long," he adds.

The Security Angle

The good news is that 1970s style dirty tricks operations used in the Praxis and APLQ cases can no longer occur. Judicial warrants are required if CSIS wishes to conduct the kind of intrusive surveillance measures we saw happen in the late sixties and early seventies, when the Security Service officers did not have to consult anyone outside their operation. Reg Whitaker explains that CSIS, which is not a law enforcement agency (unlike the RCMP) is prevented legally from telling its officers that they have *carte blanche* to break the law for the good of the country (Whitaker 2018–19).

Now here is the bad news. We in Canada are repeating the mistakes of the past in allowing our security and intelligence agency to return to the days of disrupting the activities of lawful dissenters (today, they are more liable to be Muslims, Indigenous Peoples or anti-energy pipeline activists) and jeopardize their Charter Rights (which didn't exist in the early seventies) with a judge's okay (not difficult to get) in the interests of national security. (Nobody talks about subversion anymore.) This trend started in the post-9/11 period under Stephen Harper and has continued under Justin Trudeau's Liberals, albeit less tough than what the Conservatives contemplated. Some judges are reportedly willing to ask CSIS to provide a report following a granting of a warrant, but there is nothing in the new national security law in Bill C-59 that makes such a practice mandatory, says Tim McSorley, national co-ordinator of the Ottawa-based International Civil Liberties Monitoring Group (McSorley 2019). One positive development is the appointment of two knowledge-able people in the area of national security, Murray Rankin (chair) and Craig Forcese to the National Security and Intelligence Review Agency, which now has greater accountability and oversight capability. It can keep tabs on all federal government departments engaged in security and intelligence, not just CSIS. But a wrinkle exists. McSorley's main concern is that the CSIS agents with their new disruptive capability can still do a lot of damage to those targeted before the review committee is able to come along and examine the matter. He anticipates that legal challenges may clarify matters.

The other disturbing aspect is that in the new digital age, security and intelligence operations are more sophisticated and expansive, involving a greater number of federal government departments outside CSIS and the RCMP and working in tandem with the private sector in the monitoring of Indigenous and environmental groups opposing fossil fuel extraction and transmission. From a CSIS threat-assessment perspective, these groups are regarded as the most dangerous, says Jeffrey Monaghan, a Carleton University professor and co-author of *Policing Indigenous Movements: Dissent and the Security States* (also a Fernwood book). There is less attention paid to the far right, even if they pose a larger threat (Monaghan 2017). Meanwhile, the political left and labour can rest easy in that they are no longer perceived as threats under CSIS's assessment process, according to Monaghan. I don't know if that is a good thing since posing a potential threat demonstrates that you are a serious movement, which helps to pressure governments to act or respond. That explains why poverty mattered in the late sixties and early seventies. Governments were worried then about a violent alternative if they did not set out a policy.

Recalling the Praxis Legacy

In retirement Peter Russell enjoys talking to journalists who telephone him and ask questions about the Canadian constitution. But he had time for me on the subject of Praxis. He says ruefully he wishes that Praxis had been successful in agitating the poor to mount a revolution, which some members of the Security Service and of the Trudeau government had accused the organization of doing. "It was not the Mounties who pulled us down. We ran out of steam and did not have any money [to continue]" (Russell 2019).

What remains of Praxis lies in the memory of the few participants who are still alive and in their work, which resides in dusty volumes of completed studies sitting on a shelf in a university library somewhere or in draft form in the York University archives, where Howard Buchbinder's papers are stored. *Citizen Participation: A Research Framework and Annotated Bibliography* is one such work of over 300 pages in a large format and co-written and researched by Buchbinder, Gerry Hunnius and Ellen Stevens (the latter was one of the staff people at Praxis). It was published in 1974 by the federal Ministry of Urban Affairs, two years after the money started to run out for the research institute and the Security Service were conducting their death watch from afar (Buchbinder, Hunnius, and Stevens 1974). Praxis limped along as long as it could in the early seventies, getting its paid assignments done and trying to stay afloat before finally shutting down, forcing the staff to scramble for other jobs.

Citizen participation, the subject of the 1974 report for Urban Affairs, has gone out of political fashion, as have the other political themes that were central to the philosophical direction of Praxis, such as community control and workers' control. There are always a lot of "what ifs" when it comes to history, and one of them is whether Praxis could have evolved into providing a competitive left-wing intellectual alterative to business-oriented think-tanks taking root in the 1970s. Unions did not come in to save Praxis with a pot of money. Years later labour finally understood the necessity of having well-researched progressive studies of the economy and society, and so today, we have the labour-backed Canadian Centre for Policy Alternatives and the Broadbent Institute carrying on what Howard Buchbinder and Gerry Hunnius were just getting off the ground decades earlier.

At York University Howard Buchbinder branched off into local faculty union politics on campus and co-wrote a book with Professor Janice Newson, *The University Means Business: Universities, Corporations, and Academic Work*. I met Buchbinder in the early 1980s and tried without success to interview him about Praxis. This had been a central item in his life and so wanted to be its major chronicler. He sought to recapture what happened at Praxis in a partial draft but was unable to find an interested publisher. Maybe the rejection happened because the story of a sixties research institute was considered old news at the time. "It is difficult to resurrect the atmosphere of the late 1960s and early 1970s from the present vantage of no growth, austerity and remarkably passive acceptance of worsening conditions," wrote Buchbinder and Paul Copeland in an August 1980 article for *Canadian Forum*. Living in a period neoliberalism, they were lamenting the decline in the kind of radicalism and movements for social change that had emerged "paradoxically" in the late 1960s, during a period of growth and prosperity.

But Buchbinder and Copeland were wrong to say that activism was never again going to be what it was in the sixties. As I write this in 2019, there is a new generation of young people fighting for a serious political response from leaders to the climate change crisis. One might say that the rallies and demonstrations are larger now and involve a greater range of people than the ones that occurred about fifty years ago. On the other hand, the political left in Canada appears hesitant to engage in the kind of sixties-inspired radicalism that is required to tackle the multiple issues today. It is true that we cannot repeat the exact kind of passion that was redolent of the late sixties and early seventies. Buchbinder described it as the soil that allowed Praxis "to germinate and grow." But at least we can try, with better insight from the past to guide us.

Afterword

Picking Up the Pieces

After their Praxis work ended, both Howard Buchbinder and Gerry Hunnius managed to get teaching positions at York University, thanks to Meyer Brownstone. "I contacted my old Winnipeg friend Harry Crowe, the principal of Atkinson College and he made the appointments once I had told him about the Praxis stuff, and the Mounties and the qualifications of Howard and Gerry. Any pulling of strings had to do with budget and openings for positions. In fact, they were unusually fit because Atkinson was the right kind of school for mature and working students" (Brownstone 2018).

Doris Power
In the spring of 2019 Doris Power was one of two recipients of the Frances Lankin Community Services Award for lifetime achievement for her work in social justice, given by Social Planning Toronto. During our conversation in a coffee shop on the Danforth, an older and white-haired Power (minus the pony tail) wore a light-coloured top festooned with political buttons past and present — including a late eighties classic containing the single word "eh," to symbolize a defiant, and sadly futile, Canadian opposition to free trade with the Americans.

Power still shows up at activist meetings, such as the ones held by the Ontario Coalition on Poverty, which organizes protests, generates publicity and advises people caught up in the social services bureaucracy. There are some echoes of the old Just Society Movement here except that OCAP, founded in 1989, has lasted longer because of a more stable structure. Long-time leader John Clarke was paid full-time, albeit at a modest amount, before his retirement. Of late the organization has been coming out with reports on homelessness and the state of the shelter system in Toronto. It remains a vital and important organization today.

When we spoke, Power was boycotting OCAP. The veteran activist from the sixties draws a line at OCAP's tactic of staging pickets and carrying signs in front of the homes of powerful people in normally quiet residential areas. It was not something that the Just Society Movement would have done back in its day, even with its militant anti-corporate stance, Power says (2018).

A mother of six children, she has lived for years in the same social housing unit in the old east end of Toronto. Retirement is out of the question. "I am the full-time caregiver to my disabled son, who is six years old in a 32-year-old body … and I have to be very active in disability and housing issues with what little energy I have left." The activist puts out three newsletters "in spite of chemo-affected eyesight and slow two finger typing." In the past she turned down separate requests from political allies Howard Buchbinder and Wilson Head to co-author books. Journalists tracking her down were also rebuffed. But CBC dramatist Len Peterson did succeed in convincing Power that he needed to interview her for material for his radio play.

"I had no idea who [Peterson] was when I spent a day with him which resulted in a play. I'm told he was asked who were the most interesting people he met when doing research for his plays and mentioned us and I am pictured in that documentary. He told me his interpretation of the Lilith myth, which he felt related to the rise in female power at that time … and opined people were threatened by the new women but couldn't help being attracted to them at the same time. Result was I included Lilith in the names of one of my daughters," Power explains.

She is bitter about the old RCMP Security Service, accusing its officers of preventing her from pursuing a career in the corrections field after she worked for a time at the Don Jail. Power said that John Mooney, another former Just Society Movement activist, experienced similar treatment for his political past, but she had few details to provide and no idea of where this friend is today. She alludes to "some of the unbelievable things the Security Service and the RCMP have done to me … and how their actions black-balled me from employment and have caused my files to get flagged in many government departments." I cannot verify the stories about Power and Mooney. Powers never tried to access her RCMP file, if it exists, which can be an arduous process.

Power also told me that the Security Service tried without success to recruit her ex-husband to spy on her as an informant. He was a member of the Seafarers International Union, which attempted at one time to drive out the boats from another union. Yet, he did support Power's political activities and was the one who suggested naming her new organization the Just Society Movement. "After I ripped two applications for marriage licence that he brought me, I finally agreed and filled it out and married him ... I had two children by him. Then when he came ashore one time, the youngest did not recognize him. [My husband] quit the boats and stayed in Toronto. We divorced shortly after."

Laurell Ritchie
Laurell Ritchie remembers the tensions between radical graduate students in social work at Praxis and the less-educated women and men on welfare in the Just Society Movement. Ritchie found herself caught between the two sides. She did not make much money at Praxis (nobody did at the institute), but it was here where she developed close friendships and decided to join a housing co-op. "I mean I was poor but I wasn't a poverty activist living in a project. I was asked to kind of shift into the associate category and work with Praxis" (Ritchie 2012).

The Just Society Movement activists would sometimes get frustrated or felt restricted by Praxis. For example, if they were planning a protest activity after someone had their benefits cut, the Praxis members might counsel caution or propose an alternative course of action. "It might have been a very good argument. I mean, I certainly recalled some of these tactics if they were questioned in any way or timing. The suspicion was immediately held that 'social workers' were trying to stop us from doing what we needed to do," Ritchie said. "Social worker" was a broad accusatory word thrown in these circumstances at anybody, not just social workers, who had never been on social assistance. And yet, Ritchie conceded, it was important for poor people to know that defenders in the middle class were available to write the newspaper op-eds and communicate with the authorities in power in a way that was effective.

The other challenge was that community organizing, which had been at the centre of sixties activism especially in the anti-poverty movement, was fundamentally flawed, from Ritchie's perspective. "I had various involvements with community organizing. And it seemed to me always so precarious. And it was inevitably short-lived. And I wanted to be involved with organizing that had potential for being longer term."

The instability of groups representing welfare recipients and the poor often came up in my interview with Ritchie. It was not uncommon for people to stick around until their problem with social services was solved or, like Susan Abela, they obtained post-secondary school education and a job. This explains why the labour movement proved to be the more durable option for Ritchie. She says there was one idea from the *Our Generation* anarchist crowd which appealed to her and that was the extra parliamentary opposition. In her mind it was another way of talking about coalitions of like-minded people and groups representing women, the poor, people living with a disability, etc. and unions working at the grassroots in communities outside Parliament and regular political channels.

Ritchie considered that broad coalitions not tied to a political party represented greater possibilities in terms of drawing a bigger tent of supporters. During the 1980s this strategy was viewed by union leaders as "competition for the NDP," but that did not have to be the case, she says. The Canadian Auto Workers (since renamed UNIFOR following a merger with the Communications, Energy and Paperworkers Union) did embark for a short time on a path of social or movement unionism to build alliances with these coalitions.

Ritchie recalls fondly the high quality of the debate and discussions she witnessed as a young woman inside the Praxis house. "It was like being in a big kitchen except some people were on chairs and lots of us were seated on the floor. And some people were standing around. These were large meetings. They were unlike conventions in a lot of mainstream organizations where you go to the microphone and take your turn. This has its place. But this [at Praxis] was more of a committee of the whole. And it meant people butted in and people tried to keep some semblance of order. But there were incredible debates that happened in that place."

Ritchie is nonchalant about organizations, like the Just Society or Praxis, coming to an end. She views it as a natural and seamless progression to broader involvements, such as the National Action Committee and the women's movement, where organizations also come and go. "I certainly feel very privileged having grown up and experiencing all this and having participated in some of that. People were stretching the normal boundaries that existed. You know the fact that things don't go on forever doesn't mean that they have not generated some other things that will in turn generate other things and/or become more long-term organizing."

Johnny Morris

Today Johnny Morris, who used to work at the Hamilton Welfare Rights Organization, and his wife Francis live quietly in the Strathcona neighbourhood in Hamilton. He is a bit of a political recluse, not having anything to do with any existing anti-poverty organizations. For a number of years and he and Frances ran a moving company. Sometime in the early 1980s, he says the police invaded his home and beat up his entire family. Officers arrived at the door, guns drawn and proceeded to yell racial epithets and kick and punch him and his wife as well as their teenage son and daughter. All of them as well as a cousin who came to visit were taken down to the police station and charged with obstruction of justice and assaulting police, says Morris. Another cousin of his and another musician to boot, Joe Rhodes, was the first person to relay to me what had happened to Johnny and confirms some of the details. Morris was hospitalized for his injuries to his ribs and eyes, blaming himself for being rude to the cops during the violent encounter. "I should have not said this, 'but my wife hits me harder than that' [he told the officers]. My God then I had a beating" (Morris 2018).

Lawyer Ray Harris, who worked with the Hamilton Welfare Rights Organization while going to law school, ended up representing the Morris family. "You picked the wrong man; Morris is my brother," Harris told the police, according to Morris. The charges were dropped and there was a settlement. But nailing down any details of the case is hard since Harris, who later became a judge, passed away after suffering serious dementia at the end of his life. And Johnny Morris seems to want to forget the whole thing. Local police will not comment, except to suggest that I pursue a time consuming freedom-of-information application. And Harris's former legal partner, Scott Henderson, referred all inquiries to Morris. Doing a database search at the *Hamilton Spectator* on the story is impossible because the event happened before 1990. Morris says the beating probably happened in the 1980s, long after his public work with the Hamilton Welfare Rights Organization had ended and his profile diminished. He could not say if his former political activity had any bearing on this case.

References

Abela, Susan. 2018. Interviews and series of emails. Feb. 9, March 9.

Adams, Ian. 1967. "The Lonely Death of Charlie Wenjack." *Maclean's*, February.

___. 1970. *The Poverty Wall*. Toronto: McClelland and Stewart.

___. 2011. Interview. Nov.

___. 2018. Interview. March 8.

Adams, Ian, and Howard Buchbinder. 1978. "The Praxis Affair: How Stolen Goods Became a Stolen Document." *This Magazine*, March.

Adams, Ian, William Cameron, Brian Hill and Peter Penz. 1971. *The Real Poverty Report*. Edmonton: M.G. Hurtig.

Adelman, Howard. 2011. Interview. Oct. 7.

Aivalis, Christo. 2018a. Interview. July 3.

___. 2018b. *The Constant Liberal: Pierre Trudeau, Organized Labour and the Canadian Social Democratic Left*. Vancouver: UBC Press.

___. 2018–19. Series of emails.

Allen, David. 1969a. "Metro's poor form their own union." *Toronto Daily Star*, July 5.

___. 1969b. "Project gives poor a hope of escape." *Toronto Daily Star*, Oct. 18.

___. 1970a. "Guaranteed Income no cure-all, Munro Says." *Toronto Daily Star*, June 19.

___. 1970b. "National meeting of poor set in Metro." *Toronto Daily Star*, Sept. 16.

___. 1970c. "Seething discontent of Montreal's poor fuels political unrest." *Toronto Daily Star* Oct. 30.

Allison, Bill, 2011. Interview. July.

Baetz, Rueben. 1969. "We Must Work Within Our System." *Toronto Daily Star,* Sept. 15.

Bagnell, Kenneth. 1970. "Blasting Holes Through the Wall Complacency Built." *Globe and Mail*, March, 7.

Barrett, Stanley. 1989. *Is God a Racist? The Right Wing in Canada*. Toronto: University of Toronto Press.

Battle, Ken. 2017. Remarks at the memorial for Leonard Shifrin. February.

Broadbent, Ed. 2019. Interview. July 15.

Browne, Norman. 1969. "I'm Poor by Choice – It's More Fun, Says a Man Who Lives on $25 a week." *Toronto Daily Star*, June 11.

Brownstone, Meyer. 1977a. Letter to Assistant Commissioner, H.P. Tadeson. Commanding Officer, O Division, RCMP. Feb. 7.

___. 1977b. Letter to NDP leader T.C. Douglas.

___. 2018. Interviews. Jan. 29, July 25. Series of email 2018–19.

Bruner, Arnold. 1976. "Lawyer Urges Training of Citizen Advocates to Help Welfare

Recipients Secure Legal Rights. *Globe and Mail*, April 7.

Brushett, Kevin. 2003. "Reaching Out and Biting Back: Grassroots Activism and Toronto's Social Service Community, 1960–1975." Paper presented to the Canadian Historical Association, Halifax, May 29.

___. 2014. "Guerrilla Bureaucrats: New Social Movements and the New Ottawa, 1960–1980." Unpublished paper presented at the Canadian Historical Association Annual Meetings, St. Catharines, May.

Buchbinder, David. 2011. Interview. March 1.

Buchbinder, Howard. 1969. "Welfare Council Can't Cure Poverty, Critic Claims." *Toronto Daily Star*, Sept. 15.

___. 1970. "Participation, Control and the EPO: A Combination of Strategies." *Our Generation* (double issue), 7, 4; 8, 1.

___. 1972. "Social Planning or Social Control: An Account of a Confrontation with the Social Welfare Establishment." In Allan Powell (ed.), *The City: Attacking Modern Myths*. Toronto: McClelland & Stewart.

___. 1979. "The Just Society." In Brian Wharf (ede.), *Community Work in Canada*. Toronto: McClelland and Stewart.

___. 2000. Draft material for book. Dec. 1.

___. n.d. Personal papers, material related to Praxis, Poor People's Conference, Just Society, legal action against the RCMP and McDonald Inquiry, F0455- Howard Buchbinder fonds. Clara Thomas Archives. York University.

Buchbinder, Howard, and Paul Copeland. 1980. "Rights and Wrongs: Tent Peg, Oddball and the Praxis Coverup." *Canadian Forum*, August.

Buchbinder, Howard, Gerry Hunnius and Grant Reid. 1972. "Theory and Practice of Representative Democracy." Chapter One. *Citizen Action in Urban Canada: A Comparison of Structures, Goals and Action Styles in Five Low Income Groups*. Praxis Research Institute for Social Change, March.

Buchbinder, H., G. Hunnius and E. Stevens. 1974. *Citizen Participation: A Research Framework and Annotated Bibliography*. Ottawa: Ministry of State for Urban Affairs.

Burton, Ian. 2011. Interview. July 20.

Butroid. A. 1971. Letter to RCMP Security Service. Department of Manpower and Immigration. January 8.

Carota, Mario. 1969. *The Citizen Group Movement Among the Low-Income Citizens of Urban Canada*. Ottawa: Department of Health and Welfare.

Chodos, Bob. 2012. Interview.

Clague, Michael. 2012. Interview. Emails. Jan. 2019.

Clarkson, Stephen (ed.). 1968. Conclusion for *An Independent Foreign Policy for Canada?* for the University League for Social Reform. Toronto: McClelland & Stewart.

___. 1969. Minutes of Praxis meetings.

___. 2010. Interview. Aug. 19. Emails. 2010–12.

Cohen, Dian. 1970. "Dismal Job Prospects Darken Quebec Scene." *Toronto Daily Star*, Oct. 30.

Cooper, G.H. 1977. Memorandum to the Assistant Commissioner, Special Services

Division, Ontario Provincial Police, Dec. 21.

Cooper, Nancy. 1975. "A $200,000 PR Firm for Poor." *Globe and Mail*, May 22.

Copeland, Paul. 1977–1988. Correspondence with regards to Praxis in the form of letters between him and lawyers representing the Ontario Attorney General's office, the Crown at the federal level, the McDonald Commission, the RCMP Security Service, journalists and his own clients.

___. 1989. "The Praxis Incident." Letter to the editor. *Globe and Mail*, Oct. 23: A6.

___. 2012. Interview.

___.2019. Emails.

Croll, David. 1971. The Honourable David A., Chairman. *Poverty in Canada: A Report of the Special Senate Committee on Poverty*. Ottawa: Information Canada.

Daly, Margaret. 1971. "A New Kind of Community Newspaper Tackles Downtown Issues." *Toronto Daily Star*, June 19.

Dare, Michael. Director General. n.d. RCMP Security Service.

Dickens, Charles. 1853. *Bleak House*. London: Bradbury & Evans.

Donaghy, Greg. 2018. Interview. March.

Donaghy, Greg, John Hilliker, and Mary Halloran. 2017. *Canada's Department of External Affairs, Volume 3, Innovation and Adaptation, 1968-1984*. Toronto. University of Toronto Press.

Douglas, T.C. 1977. Letter addressed to Meyer Brownstone. April 6.

Dubro, James. 2012. Interview. n.d. and 2019 July.

ECC (Economic Council of Canada). 1968. *Fifth Annual Review*. Ottawa.

Ehrenreich, Barbara. 2012. "Michael Harrington and the Culture of Poverty." New York: *The Nation Magazine*, March 14.

Enright, Michael. 1969a. "No Party Split." *Globe and Mail*, Sept. 25: 5.

___. 1969b. "The Stylish Professor on a Crusade." *Globe and Mail*, Nov. 27: 7.

___. 1970a. "The Establishment Fears a New Political Faddist — The Professional Citizen." *Globe and Mail*, March 14.

___. 1970b. "The Split in the Social Planning Council on its Function." *Globe and Mail*, April 7.

Fairhurst, Ted. 2012. Interview. Nov.

Fairhurst, Ted, and Doug Grant. 1978. Co-writers and reporters for CBC Radio script on the break-in at the PASOK office. Interview with Spyros (Stan) Dreanos. July 4.

Freeman, Bill. 1979. "Selling Out: The Story of the Victoria Park Community Association." In Bill Freeman and Marsha Hewitt (eds.), *Their Town: The Mafia, The Media and the Party Machine*. Toronto: Lorimer.

___. 2018. Interview and series of emails. April 5.

Fromm, Paul. 2012. Interview. April 5.

Furr, Karl. 2011. Interview. n.d.

Georgian, The. 1958. Oct. 28.

Giroux, J.B. 1984. Director general RCMP Security Service. No title: internal memo. June or July.

Globe and Mail. 1968. "Douglas Says Trudeau Echoes R.B. Bennett on Fiscal Priorities." May 23.

___. 1969. "Poverty Body Not in Plans, Trudeau Says. April 24.

References

___. 1970a "Croll Shocked as Woman Wastes No Words." Mar. 13.

___. 1970b "Ottawa Won't Drop Action Groups." July 10.

___. 1970c. "No Grant for Group, Munro Letter Says." Aug. 28.

___. 1971a. "Welfare Staff Ask for Protection." Feb. 3.

___. 1971b. "What Are the True Costs?" Editorial. Nov. 12.

___. 1971c. "Hamilton Group Asks Law to Bar Job, Bias Against Welfare Case." Nov. 16.

___. 1971d. "Low-Income Grants to Continue: Munro." Dec. 10.

___. 1976. "Students Say Review Unfair." July 6.

___. 1977. "A Crime Goes Unpunished." Editorial. June 17: 6.

Goldblatt, Murray. 1969a. "Low Priority for Poverty Fight Criticized." *Globe and Mail*, April 23: 4.

___. 1969b. "US-Style Violence Likely if Poverty Tackled, McQueen Warns." *Globe and Mail*, April 25.

___. 1970. "Liberal Conference Backs Guaranteed Annual Income." *Globe and Mail*, Nov. 23.

___. 1971. "Welfare Council Brief Criticizes the White Paper on Income Security, Urges Annual Income." *Globe and Mail*, April 28.

Goodall, Jeff. n.d. Interview.

___. 2012–19. Series of emails and phone call.

Graham, Peter. 2018–19. Interview and a series of emails.

Graham, Peter, and Ian McKay. 2019. *Radical Ambition: A Portrait of the Toronto New Left*. Toronto: Between the Lines.

Grant, Doug. 2012. Interview. Nov. 3.

Grant, G.K. Cpl. 1977. Internal memorandum, RCMP Security Service. June 13.

Gray, Malcolm. 1971. "John Would Be Poorer Working." *Hamilton Spectator*. Jan. 26.

Green, K.D. 1971. Internal Memo. RCMP Security Service, April 14.

Greene, Jonathan. 2018. Interview. Dec. 17.

Gregory, K.S. 1970. No title: Internal memo to F.J. Hustle, director of physical plant, University of Toronto. Collection of internal memos following December 1970 fire at 393 Huron St. Dec. 30.

Hamilton Spectator. 1971a. "Poor Plan to Burn Income White Paper." January 16.

___ . 1971b. Photo. Jan. 26.

___ . 1971c. "Welfare Table Request Opposed. Feb. 8.

___ . 1971d. "Warning Issued to Welfare Group." March 9.

___ . 1971e. "No Need for Welfare Crisis." Feb. 11.

___ .1971f. "Taxes that Buy Trouble." July 31.

___ . 1971g. "MPs Warn the 'Poor'." Feb. 3.

___ . 1971h. "Welfare Staff Ask Protection." Feb. 3.

___ . 1971i. "City Feels Snubbed Over Welfare Aid." Feb. 2.

___ . 1971j. "Mother of Eight Turns Crusader to Help Others." March 13.

___ . 1971k. "Welfare Sabotage Charge — HWRO." Oct. 27.

___ . 1971l. "Munro Blames Militant Tactics for Grant Cut." Dec. 10.

___ . 1971m. "HWRO Was Exploited, Says Munro." Dec. 13.

Hansard. 1971. "Parliamentary Committee Review of the Estimates for the Federal Department of the Solicitor General." Ottawa. March 17.

Harrington, Michael. 1962. *The Other America: Poverty in the United States*. New York: Macmillan Publishers.

Head, Wilson. 1968. "Some Comments on New Directions for the Social Planning Council (for staff discussion only)." City of Toronto archives. Collection on the Social Planning Council of Metropolitan Toronto.

___. 1995. *A Life on the Edge: Experiences in Black and White in North America*. Toronto: University of Toronto Press.

Hewitt, Steve. 2002. "Reforming the Canadian Security State: The Royal Canadian Mounted Police Security Service and the 'Key Sectors' Program." *Intelligence and National Security Magazine*, Winter: 165–184.

___. 2012. Interview.

Higgins, J. Summers, J. Zelmer D. 1982. An account of internal communications within the Canadian government with regards to Praxis in court case by the research institute against the Crown. "Prosecutions and Civil Actions Against Members of the Force—Praxis. Aug. 24.

Higgitt, W.L. 1969. Internal Memo. Assistant Commissioner, Director, Security and Intelligence Branch, RCMP.

High, B. Col., and K.D. Green. 1971. *The Changing Nature of the Threat from the New Left—Extra Parliamentary Opposition, Penetration of Government*. May. RCMP Security Service.

Hirst, R.G. 1970. Internal memo. Re: CMHC. RCMP Security Service. Dec. 11.

Holland, Peter. 2012. Interview.

Hunnius, Gerry (FC). 1968. *Student Revolts: The New Left in West Germany*. London: War Resisters' International.

___. 2011. Interview. Nov. 25.

Hunnius, Gerry, David Garson, and John Case. 1973. *"Workers' Control: A Reader on Labor and Social Change*. New York: Random House.

Hunnius, Valerie. 2018–19. Series of emails.

Jacek, Henry. 1979. "John Munro and the Hamilton East Liberals: Anatomy of a Modern Political Machine." In Bill Freeman and Marsha Hewitt (eds.), *Their Town: The Mafia, the Media and the Party Machine*. Toronto: Lorimer.

Jacobs, Jane. 1961. *Death and Life of Great American Cities*. New York: Random House.

Johnson, Pat. 1971. "The Poor's Hope, Anger, Despair and Determination." *Toronto Telegram*, Jan. 8.

Jones, Frank. 1968. "The Rightists Who Check Up on Our Schools." *Toronto Star*, Jan. 27.

Katadotis, Peter. 2011. Interview. Dec. 12.

Kaye, Lynn (formerly Lynn Lang). 2018. Interview. Aug. 28. Series of emails. 2018–19.

Kent, Tom. 1965. "Canada Opportunity Plan: A Proposal." Queens University Archives, 26 January 1965, 1, 1300, Box 4, File 4 – Correspondence – Jan. 26.

King, John. 1977. "RCMP Stole Files to Compile Secret List, MP Hints." *Globe and Mail*, Feb. 3: 1.

Kirkland, Jack. 2011. Interview.

Kirkwood, Leone. 1969. "Leader Denies Communist Links: Group Called Just Society Encourages Poor to Direct Action to Obtaining Rights." *Globe and Mail*, Oct. 16.

References

Lang, John. 2018. Interview.

Langford, William. 2017. "Introduction: 'Helping People Help Themselves,' Democracy, Development and the Global Politics of Poverty in Canada, 1964–1979." Ph.D., History, Queens University. <Langford_William_R_201708_PHD. pdf>.

___. 2018/19. Interview. Jan. 13, 2019. Series of emails.

Lee, Lou. 1969. "New Breed of Poor." *Globe and Mail*, July 10.

Levin, Martin. 2018. "Jack Ludwig, 95, Was an Author Best Known for His Sports Journalism." Obituary. *Globe and Mail*, March 14.

Lewis, Oscar. 1959. *Five Families: Mexican Case Studies in the Culture of Poverty*. New York: Basic Books.

Lind, Loren. 1969a. "Welfare Recipient Wins Seat on Planning Body. *Globe and Mail*, March 27.

___. 1969b. "Council in Agonizing Review: Wanted: Greater Impact on Social Ills." *Globe and Mail*, April 15.

___. 1969c. "Chained to Agencies, Social Planning Council Wants More Ties with People." *Globe and Mail*, April 16.

Little, Margaret. 2007. "Militant Mothers Fight Poverty: The Just Society Movement. 1968–1971." Edmonton: *Labour-Le Travail*, Spring.

Macadam, Bill and James Dubro. 1974. "How the CIA Was Spooked." *Maclean's*, July.

McSorley, Tim. 2019. Interview. National Co-ordinator. International Civil Liberties Monitoring Group. Ottawa. July.11.

McDonald David. 2019. Senior Economist, Canadian Centre for Policy Alternatives.

MacFarlane, George. 1968. "Douglas Says PM a 1930s Tory with 'That Balanced Budget Stuff." *Globe and Mail*, May 25.

Mann, Paul. 1970/1971. "The Black Knight." *Hamilton Spectator*. n.d.

McGrath, Susan. 1998. "The Politics of Truth: A Case Study of Knowledge Construction by the Social Planning Council of Metropolitan Toronto." PhD thesis, Faculty of Social Work, University of Toronto.

McIllraith, George. Solicitor General of Canada. 1970. letter to Norm Cafik MP, Dec. 18.

McMurtry Roy. 1978. "Statement by the Hon. Roy McMurtry, Attorney General for Ontario re: Praxis Corp." May 23.

Milligan, Ian. 2014. *Rebel Youth: 1960's Labour Unrest, Young Workers and New Leftists in English Canada*. Vancouver: UBC Press.

___. 2018. Interview. May 28.

Milloy, John. 2017. *A National Crime: The Canadian Government and the Residential School System, 1879 to 1986*. Winnipeg: University of Manitoba Press.

Mills, Eric. 1971. "About Worthington and Praxis." *Varsity* (University of Toronto student newspaper). January 13.

Monaghan, Jeffrey. 2017. Interview. June 16.

Moon, Peter. 1988. "Praxis, Ottawa Make a Deal in Suit." *Globe and Mail*, May 4: 1.

Mooney, John. 1970. "A Former Member of the Just Society Wants to See Full-Time; Paid Organizers Come from the Ranks of the Poor." Letter to the editor. *Toronto Daily Star*, June 2.

Morris, Barry. 1971. *The Just Society Movement, Summer of 1968 to Spring of 1971.* Toronto: United Church of Canada. (Available in Howard Buchbinder's personal papers or fonds at York University. Call number 2013-005/002. York University Archives.)

____. 2018. Series of emails.

Morris, Johnny. 2018. Interview. Oct. 23. Follow-up telephone calls.

NCW (National Council of Welfare). 1973. *The Press and the Poor: A Report by the National Council of Welfare on How Canada's Newspapers Cover Poverty.* Ottawa.

Novick, Marvyn. 2013. Interview. Aug 15.

Our Generation. 1969. "Towards an Extra Parliamentary Opposition in Canada." Editorial. Vol. 6, No. 4.

Packard, Vince. 1957. *The Hidden Persuaders.* New York: D. McKay Co.

Parent, L.K. 1972. RCMP Security Service. Memo to Robin Bourne in the Solicitor General's office. Oct. 12.

Pal, Leslie. 1993. *Interests of State: The Politics of Language, Multi-Culturalism and Feminism in Canada.* Montreal: McGill-Queen's University Press.

Palmer, Bryan and Gaétan Héroux. 2018. *Toronto's Poor: A Rebellious History.* Toronto: BTL Books.

Pineault, Monique Kelly. 2011. *Shifting the Balance: Indigenous and Non-Indigenous Activism in the Company of Young Canadians, 1966–1970.* Canadian Studies and Indigenous Studies M.A. Graduate Program, Trent University.

Porter, John. 1965. *The Vertical Mosaic: An Analysis of Social Class and Power in Canada.* Toronto: University of Toronto Press.

Poverty Wall file. McClelland and Stewart Fonds. McMaster University. The William Ready Division of Archives and Research Collections.

Power, Doris. 2018. Interviews, Jan. 31 and June 6. Series of phone calls and emails.

Praxis. 1969. Prospectus and other early internal documents.

Pritchard, Cate. 2012. "Private Fundraising, Expertise and Welfare Rights: Radical Social Workers Confront the United Community Fund of Greater Toronto." Unpublished graduate school paper.

____. n.d. "Citizens Concerned about Charity. Young Social Workers Challenge the United Way of Toronto." Unpublished graduate school paper.

Randall, Stanley. 1970. Letter to Robert Andras, Minister of Urban Affairs, Ottawa. Dec. 1.

RCMP Security Service. Library and Archives Canada.

____. 1970a. Internal memo. International Forum Foundation. May 15.

____. 1970b. Internal memo. (Woman's Liberation Group.) Sept. 24.

____. 1970c. Internal memo. Industrial and Community Democracy Conference held in Toronto. Nov. 26.

____. 1970d. Internal memo. (Praxis Break-in.) "O" Division Security and Intelligence Branch to "D" branch at Headquarters. Dec. 22. (Unnamed).

____. 1970e. Internal memo between Inspector Madill and Inspector G. Belgalki. (CMHC) June 11.

____. 1971a. Internal memo. (Metro Toronto Social Planning Council.) March 25.

____. 1971b. Internal memo. (Metro Toronto Social Planning Council.) March 31.

References

_____. 1971c. Internal memo. Draft of Cabinet Directive 35. Oct. 19.

_____. 1971d. Document on Praxis: Infiltration of Key Sectors. n.d.

_____. 1971e. Document on Praxis: Major Strategy and Tactics.

_____. 1971f. Document on Praxis. March 18. No title.

_____. 1971g. "Re: Government – Penetration of Canada." Draft Reply. Sept. 1.

_____. 1971h. Internal memo regarding the National Conference of the Poor. January.

_____. 1971i. Internal memo. CMHC. Aug. 9.

_____. 1972a. Internal memo addressed to Robin Bourne, Solicitor General. Oct. 12.

_____. 1977–1981. McDonald Commission related material. 1977–1981.

_____. Anonymous (a former Security Service Officer who declined to reveal his name publicly) files (on Praxis), accessed via Library and Archives Canada.

RCMP SIB (Security and Intelligence Branch). 1969a. Internal memo, Oct. 24.

_____. 1969b. Internal memo. Nov. 24. (In 1970 the SIB was renamed the RCMP Security Service.)

Reid, Grant. 2010. Interview. n.d.

Rettie, E.R. 1969. Letter to the RCMP. Under Secretary of State for External Affairs. March 19.

Rickaby, J.P. Ontario Crown Attorney. 1977. Re: Praxis Corp. Letter to Paul Copeland. June 6.

Ritchie, Laurell. 2012. Interview. n.d.

Ross, David. 2015. Entry on "Poverty." *The Canadian Encyclopedia*. Ross is the author of the 1983 book, *Canadian Fact Book on Poverty*.

Rotstein, Abraham. 2010. Interview. Sept. 27.

Roussopoulos, Dimitri. 2018. Interview. Oct. 15.

Rowan, Mary Kate. 1971a. "Poor Vote to Admit Press after Ejection Demanded." *Globe and Mail*, January 8.

_____. 1971b. "How a Band of Reformers Mounted Their Challenge to the Establishment of United Appeal." *Globe and Mail*, Aug. 13.

_____. 1971c. "Hamilton Group Asks Law to Bar Job, Bias Against Welfare Case." *Globe and Mail*, Nov. 16.

Rubin, Lillian. 1969. "Maximum Feasible Participation: The Origins, Implications and Present Status." *The Annals of the American Academy of Political and Social Science*. September.

Russell, Frances. 1969a. "Poor Should Be Paid for Violated Rights, Shifrin Says." *Globe and Mail*, Aug. 12.

_____. 1969b. "Poor Oppressed by Welfare: Just Society." *Globe and Mail*, August 25.

Russell, Peter. 2011. Interview. Dec. 14.

_____. 2019. Email.

Sallot, Jeff. 1979. *Nobody Said No: The Real Story about How the Mounties Always Get Their Man*. Toronto: Lorimer.

Sass, Robert. 1997. "Chapter 9: Self Enforcement of a Rights Based Approach to Workplace Health and Safety." In Eleanor D. Glor (ed.), "Policy Innovation in the Saskatchewan Public Sector, 1971–1982. North York: Captus Press.

_____. 2018. Interview. Dec. 18.

Schultz, S. Sgt. 1970. RCMP Security Service. June 9.

Seale, Louis. 1968a. "Humorous, Challenging in Victory, Trudeau Calls for Just Society in Canada." *Globe and Mail*, April 8: 8.

___. 1968b. "PM Has Small-C Conservative Message for Ontario." *Globe and Mail*, May 27: 8.

___. 1968c. "Economic Council Denounces Degree of Poverty." *Globe and Mail*, Sept. 6.

Secretary of State, Federal Department. 1971. Letter to Don Beavis, Privy Council Office. Ottawa. Feb. 3. Author unknown.

Shifrin, Leonard. 2011–13. Interview. March 1. Series of emails.

Smith, Bob, 1971. "Coverage of the Poor Peoples Conference." *Georgia Strait*, Jan. 22.

Squires, Jessica. 2013. *Building Sanctuary: The Movement to Support Vietnam War Resisters in Canada, 1965–1973*. Vancouver: UBC Press.

Starnes, John. 1970. Memorandum to Inspector G. Begalki. April 24.

___. 1971. Internal memo. Directed to Solicitor General Jean Pierre Goyer. RCMP Security Service. Sept. 23.

___. 1977. Testimony before McDonald Inquiry.

Starowicz, Marc. 2012. Interview. n.d.

Stevens, Geoffrey. 1968a. "Trudeau Promises to Work as PM for a Just Society" *Globe and Mail*, April 8.

___. 1968b. "Trudeau Sounds like Conservative in Quick Swing through Tory Territory. *Globe Mail*, May 22: 8.

Stewart, Don. 1970. "Fights Landlords, City Scrooges." *Hamilton Spectator*.

Straight Talk! 1971. "Praxis Exposed! Your Money… Their Revolution." January–February.

Struthers, James. 1994. *The Limits of Affluence: Welfare in Ontario, 1920–1970*. Toronto: University of Toronto Press.

___. 2018 Interview. March 15. 2018–19. Series of email.

Summers, John, L. Higgins and D. Zelmer. 1982. Internal memo: Prosecutions and Civil Actions Against Members of the Force — Praxis. RCMP Security Service. Aug. 24.

Swanson, Jean. 2001. *Poor-Bashing: The Politics of Exclusion*. Toronto: Between the Lines.

___. 2018. Interview. July 27.

Szende, Andrew. 1969. "Getting His Name Known Clarkson's Big Problem." *Toronto Daily Star*, Nov. 6.

Tarte, Yvon. 1980a. McDonald Commission counsel, Memorandum. Jan. 15.

___. 1980b. McDonald Commission counsel. Memorandum. Feb. 20.

Toronto Daily Star. 1969. "What It's Like to Be Poor in Affluent Toronto." June 28.

___. 1970. "Many Women Made the News in 1970." Dec. 29.

___. 1971. "Senate May Probe 'Breach of Faith' by 4 Staffers." June 22.

___. 1972. "Poor People and Reformers Desert the Social Planning Council." April 7: 8.

Tough, David. 2014. "At Last! The Government's War on Poverty Explained: The Special Planning Secretariat, the Welfare State and the Rhetoric of Poverty in the 1960s." Planning Secretariat. *Journal of the Canadian Historical Association*, 25.

___. 2017. Interview. Nov. 5.

References

___. 2018. *The Terrific Engine: Income Taxation and the Modernization of the Canadian Political Imaginary.* Vancouver: UBC Press.

Townsend, Assistant OIC. 1982. "D Operations," RCMP Security Service. Memorandum made available to the McDonald Commission. Aug. 8.

Trudeau, Pierre. 1968. Recorded remarks at Queen's University. The Trudeau recording (SR34) is available for download at <https://qshare.queensu.ca/xythoswfs/webui/_xy-e7392327_1-t_IrsBaA4S>.

Turkstra Herman. 2018. Interview. Aug. 29.

Valpy, Michael. 1983. "The Righting of Wrongs." *Globe and Mail*, Oct. 14.

Venner, John. Internal memo. RCMP Security Service. N.D.

Wainman, Helen. 1972. "Poor People and Reformers Desert the Social Planning Council." *Toronto Daily Star* April, 7: 8.

Walker, David. 1971. "The Poor People's Conference: A Study of the Relationship Between the Federal Government and the Low-Income Interest Groups in Canada." Ph.D. thesis, Queen's University.

Walkom, Tom. 2017. "Kathleen Wynn's Basic Income Plan Is Bread Without Circuses." *Toronto Star*, April 26.

Walz, Jay. 1968. "Prime Minister Calls for More Involvement in the Just Society." *New York Times*, Nov. 29.

Weinberg, Paul. 2013. "The Last Post Files: Fighting Subversion or Protecting the Government from Embarrassment." Toronto. *J-Source.ca*. March 6.

___. 2014. "Snooping in the Cold War." Toronto: *Peace Magazine*. March.

___. 2015. "The Praxis Affair." Ottawa. *The Monitor* (Canadian Centre for Policy Alternatives).

Weisman, Judith, and Karen Swift. 2011. Interview. Sept. 17. Earlier Interview with Weisman alone. n.d.

Westell, Anthony. 1968a. "Trudeau Blueprints a Three-Point Thrust Against Regional Poverty." *Globe and Mail*, June 1.

___. 1968b. "Consult Premiers in War on Poverty, Economic Council of Canada Urges." *Globe and Mail*, Sept. 6.

Whitaker, Reg. 2014. Interview by email. 2017–19. Series of emails.

Whitaker, Reg, Gregory Kealey and Andrew Parnaby. 2012. *Secret Service: Political Policing in Canada from the Fenians to Fortress America.* Toronto: University of Toronto.

Williamson, Ken. 1969. Memo from academic relations section, information division. Department of External Affairs. Aug. 20.

Winsor, Hugh. 1971a. "Can Ottawa help the People Bring Down City Hall?" *Globe and Mail*, May 27.

___. 1971b. "How Hamilton's Welfare Group Lost Its Federal Grant." *Globe and Mail*, Dec. 29.

Worthington, Peter. 1968a. "What the Anti-War Movement Is All About." *Toronto Telegram*, Jan. 27.

___. 1968b. "Anti-War Groups: Extremist Power: Metro Peace Establishment." *Toronto Telegram*, Jan. 29.

___. 1970a. "Praxis: The Sound and Fury Signify an Enigma," *Toronto Telegram*,

Nov. 25.

___. 1970b. "Presenting Gerry Hunnius, All Around Activist." *Toronto Telegram*, Nov. 26.

___. 1970c. "Praxis's Over Reaction." *Toronto Telegram*, Dec. 24.

___. 1970d. "The Radicalization of an Establishment Organization." *Toronto Telegram*, n.d.

___. 1977. "I Gave RCMP Praxis Files." *Toronto Sun*, Feb. 4.

___. 1979. Statement of Peter Worthington. (Possibly for the McDonald Commission). April 11.

___. 1988. "Praxis papers would embarrass." *Financial Post*, May 12.

___. 2011–12. Interview via email.

___. 2012. "Khadr is not a traitor." *Toronto Sun*. April 27.

___. Personal papers, Peter Worthington Fonds Library and Archives Canada. 4221819 4 22 File Poor People's conference, planning committee documents, agenda, articles. 1970–71. 4221817 4 20 File Praxis Corp, letters, articles, notes 1969–1970.

Yaworski, R. 1973. Background notes for your meeting with the director general. RCMP Security Service. July.

Zwelling, Marc. 2018–19. Interview via email.

Index

Index

Index